How To Farm
$uccessfully
— *By Phone*

Deborah Johnson, Ph.D.
and
Steve Kennedy

Argyle Press, Inc.
Carson City, Nevada 89701

Also Available from Argyle Press, Inc:

2,001 Winning Ads For Real Estate
Real Estate Advertising That Works!
How To Farm $uccessfully — By Mail

This publication is designed to provide accurate and authoritative information in regard to the subject matter covered. It is sold with the understanding that the publisher is not engaged in rendering legal, accounting, or other professional services. If legal advice or other expert assistance is required, the services of a competent professional should be sought.

10 9 8 7 6 5 4 3 2

Book design and illustrations by Joel Friedlander, San Rafael, California.
Cover design by Steve Kennedy & Mary-Ellen Shields, Carson City, Nevada.
Cover Graphics by Diana Elkins, Carson City, Nevada.

Library of Congress Cataloging-in-Publication Data

Johnson, Deborah, 1952-
    How to farm successfully—by phone / by Deborah Johnson
and Steve Kennedy.
        p. cm.
    Includes bibliographical references and index.
    ISBN 1-887145-03-6 (pbk.)
    1. Advertising--Real estate business. 2. Telemarketing
3. Telephone in business. I. Kennedy, Steve. II. Title.
HF6161.R3J64 1995
333.33'068'8--dc20   95-36493
                                                      CIP

Printed in the United States of America.

Introduction

How To Farm $uccessfully — By Phone is a unique contribution to the field of real estate sales. It takes basic, proven telemarketing principles and applies them to one of the most challenging tasks facing any real estate agent. While "prospecting" or "farming" is the key to long-term real estate success, it is difficult. You have to build up an immunity to rejection and at the same time, maintain a high degree of self-confidence and enthusiasm. The challenge is multiplied over the phone, where contacts are person-to-person and rejection can be felt more deeply.

This book is designed to help you reduce the possibility of rejection, as it presents a series of offers that will enhance your professional standing and cultivate the contacts you need for success. Less "sales-oriented" than other materials on the market, *How To Farm $uccessfully — By Phone* is packed with simple, creative ways of approaching prospects. The goal is not to close a sale with every call, but to establish and maintain the relationships that will lead people to contact you when they're ready to sell or buy. When people in your farm think of real estate, you want them to think of you.

A companion to *How To Farm $uccessfully — By Mail*, this book contains many of the same offers packaged for a different media. This provides you with the flexibility of deciding whether to present an offer on the phone, by mail or both. Or you can split your farm in half and test a mail offer against a phone offer. For some offers, the phone may work best. For others, mail will be preferred. The biggest advantage of direct marketing is its immediate, measurable results. You never have to guess if an offer is a success.

How To Farm $uccessfully — By Phone can be an important resource in your marketing mix. After tailoring the scripts in the book to your speech patterns and comfort level, you can stick with them — or you can study the sections on telemarketing principles and then write your own scripts.

Telemarketing can intimidate even long-term farmers. It doesn't have to. When you call prospects, you get to know them in ways that you never can by letter. Your contact is immediate, real, one-on-one. There's an excitement in this kind of contact. And that excitement can push your business to new heights.

You will also find quotes through out the book. These quotes are not an endorsement of this book. They are there to offer you inspiration to attain those greater heights.

Right now, read on to find out how to do it right.

Dedications

To the voice inside that set me free. — D. J.

To D.J., colleague and friend, whose creativity is only surpassed by her perseverance and dedication. — S.K.

Acknowledgements

From Deborah Johnson, Ph.D., a special thanks to

  Bethany and Paul Ramos, for their company as I wrote
  Gary Schwartzenberger, for his encouragement and taking care of
    things while I worked
  Marion Wilson, for big daily doses of love and understanding
  Denise Ramos for support that never flinches

From Steve Kennedy, a special thanks to

  Alyce McCracken, Coldwell Banker-First Western Real Estate,
    Carson City, Nevada for her knowledgeable insights into real
    estate
  Barbara "Poco" Shields, Consultant, Carson City, Nevada for her
    editorial critiques, insights into telemarketing and her unfailing
    support
  M.E.K., for all your help and dedication to this project

Table of Contents

SECTION ONE

How to Choose and Organize Your Farm

CHAPTER 1

Farming—What Is It?

> *The person who moves a mountain*
> *begins by carrying away small stones.*
> *— Confucius*

WHAT IS FARMING?

In real estate, farming means focusing on one particular market segment. This segment is called, not surprisingly, a "listing farm" or simply, a "farm."

In commercial advertising, the concept of farming resembles audience targeting. Advertisers aim their efforts at groups based on shared characteristics such as income, buying patterns or lifestyles. Farming and targeting share one basic premise:

Find out what your prospects want and need, then concentrate on satisfying them.

The top salespeople of our time know that singling out a section of the market and making it the focus of their sales strategy is the secret to success. Farming enables them to turn "hit-or-miss" income into a steady stream of commission checks.

Building and nurturing a continuing relationship with a set number of prospects or clients is what real estate farming is all about. Why is farming so effective?

Ernie Blood and Bernie Torrence give four reasons in *The Pocket Prospecting Guide for Real Estate Professionals:*

1. Farming provides a consistent and reliable source of income in the form of listings.

2. Farming allows you do to mass advertising.

3. Farming gives you the opportunity to become a real estate specialist in a particular area.

4. The value of everything you do multiplies when you specialize in a farm.

Unlike a stockbroker or insurance agent, the real estate salesperson lacks continual contact with his or her clients. When a stockbroker gets a hot tip, he or she has a Rolodex full of prospects to call. And the insurance agent has it even better. Even without any direct contact, he or she gets renewals (and renewal commissions) each year.

Unfortunately, in real estate there are typically no hot tips, no automatic renewals. Worst of all, even your best and most satisfied clients may not be heard from for many, many years. But through farming, you build and maintain communication links that keeps you in the forefront of people's minds when a real estate question or need comes up.

But farming isn't easy. It takes time and patience and the rewards are not immediate.

Joyce Caughman in *Real Estate Prospecting* notes that it takes six months before the average real estate farm begins producing satisfactorily. A farmer should expect to get 20% of the farm's total listings by the end of the second year, 50% in the third year and up to 75% after that.

In this book, we discuss three types of farms: (1) a geographic farm, (2) a social farm and (3) a client farm. Geographic and social farms involve making contacts and building relationships with people who have not used your real estate services. A client farm, on the other hand, means maintaining contacts with people who have previously turned to you for real estate assistance. Because geographic and social farms take more strategizing and work than client farms, we'll concentrate on them. However, you will find sample phone scripts for a client farm in Chapter 15.

GEOGRAPHIC FARMS

According to Michael Abelson, president of Abelson & Company and an associate professor at Texas A & M University, two-thirds of all top performers use a geographic farm.

Realtor® Klaus Huckfeldt of Palm Springs, California defined a geographic farm as "any number or group of homes in a residential neighborhood, subdivision or development that you service on a continued basis." A geographic farm could include two or three small areas at opposite ends of town. What matters is that they have similar housing prices, styles, and residents.

The benefits of a geographic farm are obvious. First, it's easy to manage. You can drive through your farm and count the real estate signs. You also can look at the conditions of homes, locate neighborhood schools, even pinpoint street potholes. When you walk into a local drugstore or McDonald's, you meet potential prospects.

Second, geographic farming creates synergy. That is, as your signs start popping up all over the neighborhood, things will snowball. People will start talking about you and the homes you're selling. The more people talk about you, the better the chance that they'll call you when it's time to sell or buy a home.

Benefits of
Geographic Farm
1. Easy to manage
2. Develops synergy
3. Easy to research
4. Your signs say "Success"

Third, researching a geographic farm is fairly easy. Data kept by the multiple listing service (MLS), U.S. Census Bureau, county tax assessor and other institutions is often by address. Public domain records like these can tell you the average income of people in your farm, average home size, average number of people in the family, average ages, and other important facts. Some of this information is even broken down block by block.

SOCIAL FARMS

While less common than territorial farms, social farms can also be profitable.

A social farm can be formal or informal. Formal social farms are created by "farming" a group of people who belong to the same organization, such as a church, folk dance group, sailing organization, Elks' Club, or volunteer society. Compiling lists for formal social farms is as easy as grabbing a membership directory. Typically the social farmer joins the organization and becomes one of its most visible members.

Informal social farms, on the other hand, are developed by you. You could create an informal social farm of your friends and relatives. Or people who play at the local public golf course. Or people who play the piano. The point is that the people have something in common which gives you a way to access them. Examples of other informal social farms, which also are described as "niche markets," include:

1. ethnic groups,

2. single people,

3. older people,

4. members of the gay and lesbian community,

5. people with disabilities.

According to Julie A. Bleasdale, in the article *"Think Globally, Sell Locally,"* in the June 1992 <u>Real Estate Today</u>®, ethnic groups are a great niche market.

<u>Ethnic groups.</u> According to the Urban Institute and the U.S. Bureau of the Census, at least 20 million Americans speak a first language other than English. Eleven million speak Spanish as their primary language. Three million Asians speak little or no English.

American Demographics magazine predicts that by the next century one-quarter to one-third of all Americans will belong to racial or minority ethnic groups.

Targeting an ethnic group means designing culturally appropriate marketing materials and learning cross-cultural etiquette. To reach the rapidly growing market of Hispanic buyers, for example, Coast Federal Bank in Los Angeles offers a free Spanish language video to guide them through homebuying. In Danville, California, Coldwell Banker agent Marsha Golangco makes sure to present Japanese clients with her business card in both hands with her name in Japanese facing them. She also has her name printed in English on the other side. When Japanese clients hand her their business cards, she always takes a few seconds to read them as a sign of respect.

The October 1993 Real Estate Today® magazine profiles the following, in *"Specializing An Outlet for Bigger Profits"* by Warren Berger, as examples of Realtors® practicing niche marketing:

Single buyers. Claudia Deprez founded Florida Singles Real Estate in Palm Beach Gardens. She hosts homebuying seminars for singles at hotels and sends direct mail fliers to members of singles organizations and dating services. She also has enjoyed plenty of free media coverage through a local newspaper column. Singles account for 60% of her business.

Older buyers. Linda Brunson of Clements, Realtors® in Dallas markets to senior citizens. While she admits that the effort so far has been only been moderately successful, she has no doubt that it eventually will work. Her primary marketing tools have been seminars and information fairs for seniors. Her company developed a senior-oriented sales training course for its agents and promotes its specialized services in magazines and newspapers directed at seniors.

Members of the gay and lesbian community. In Chicago, RE/MAX saleperson Jim Anderson combines social and geographic farming by targeting the gay community as well as several neighborhood areas. About half his business comes from the gay and lesbian community, which he markets in newspaper ads and through direct mail under the slogan, "Your community real estate professional for the gay and lesbian market."

People with disabilities. In Tucson, Arizona, Craig Runyon of Prudential Aegis Realty considers himself a specialist in helping disabled buyers find homes. He belongs to several organizations that assist disabled people and often speaks at local clubs or business luncheons. He also created a newsletter about housing for the disabled.

> " *Even if you're on the right track, you'll get run over if you just sit there.*
> —Anonymous "

In his advertisements to the general market, he always includes a wheelchair logo and the line, "If you have special needs, call us." Today half of Runyon's sales come from buyers with disabilities.

In Huntington Beach, California, James C. Anderson was "swamped with business" after less than a year with Century 21-Berg Realty when he tapped the niche market of hearing-impaired buyers and sellers. Hearing impaired himself, Anderson markets hard-to-sell homes within earshot of railroad tracks, freeways, or airport runways to deaf buyers. He distributes fliers to churches and to clubs and organizations serving the hearing-impaired and he uses a Telecommunications Device for the Deaf in his home and business.

Other niche markets include professional women, single parents, families with small children, working mothers, members of religious groups, and members of computer clubs.

Disadvantages of Social Farm

1. Hard to manage

2. Limited marketing appeals

3. Hard to research

Managing a social farm can be more difficult than a geographic farm. First, prospects' homes often are scattered, which makes driving through one area and looking for real estate signs impossible. It also is difficult to create neighborhood-oriented marketing appeals. For example, the potentially powerful appeal that home values have risen 20% in a specific neighborhood over the past year is useless in a social farm. On the other hand, if home values have risen 20% across the city, this appeal could be useful in a social farm.

On the positive side, social farms allow you plenty of opportunities to meet potential prospects in settings that give you the chance to get to know each other. In a recent survey by the National Association of Realtors®, one out of every five homebuyers used a real estate professional they knew. But even more homesellers — one out of every two — chose a real estate professional on the basis of a personal relationship.

Because members of a social farm usually chat with each other, the same synergy found in a geographic farm can develop. And the more people talk about you, the more likely they are to call you. However, with a social farm, not many prospects will notice all your "sold" signs.

The biggest problem with social farming is research. To farm effectively, you need information about people's homes, incomes, ages, homebuying histories and other factors. Most of that information is only available by address.But you will find a partial solution in the "Survey" script in Chapter 15. You also can rely on more general, citywide information such as that provided by your local board.

The unseen benefit of a social farm is that you'll probably have some fun cultivating it. After all, there is more to life than sales, listings and board meetings.

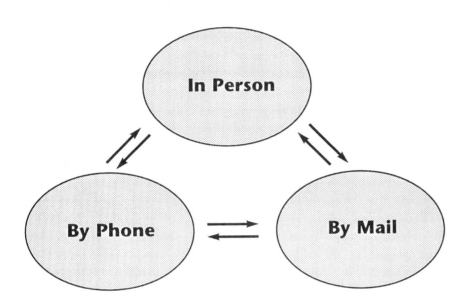

**Benefits of
Social Farm**
1. More opportunities for
   personal contact
2. Develops synergy
3. FUN

Reaching the Farm — The three main ways to reach your farm are: in person, by phone, and by mail. Ideally these three work together.

THREE WAYS TO CULTIVATE YOUR FARM

You can probably think of hundreds of ways to reach your farm, but the three most common are by: (1) face-to-face contact, (2) phone, and (3) mail. This can be called the "farm marketing mix."

Here's a good example of how the three together can help you.

In the monthly newsletter he mails to his farm, Agent Ralph Lewis writes a few catchy descriptions of new listings in the area. Within a day or two, one of the 250 prospects who received the newsletter calls Ralph for more information. Now renting, she's interested in owning a home.

Over the phone, Ralph finds out the kind of home she's looking for, price range, size of her family, and what special features interest her most.

The next evening, Ralph is at her apartment, with descriptions of five or six homes that fit her needs. He begins showing her homes and, within a few weeks, he writes up an offer. The deal goes through.

Unfortunately, things rarely work out that easily, but communication is at the heart of every sale.

Because every farm -- and every farmer -- is different, it's good to experiment with different types of communication. For example, prospects in your farm might respond more positively to a phone survey than to a mail one. Or maybe it's best to send it first, then call. The exact mix depends on you and your farm. It's also true that what's most effective one time might not be the next. Don't be afraid to test different methods.

FARMING—HOW MUCH IS A CALL WORTH?

To figure out how much farming can benefit you, look at how much one lead can be worth.

Let's say that you're making cold calls two days a week, two hours a day. For simplicity's sake, assume you call 15 people an hour and for every 15 calls, you set up one appointment. That adds up to two appointments a day, four appointments a week, 16 appointments a month.

Out of these 16 appointments, you close one sale, giving you a commission of $1,500 (assuming an average sales price of $100,000, with an average gross commission of 3%, and a 50/50 agent-broker split).

Looking back, you can see that for the 240 calls you made in the month (30 per day times 8 calling days per month), you make one sale. That means each call is worth about $6.25 ($1,500 commission divided by 240 calls) to you.

The figures we used are probably lower than what would actually happen. But the point is to think that you're getting paid not by the sale, but by the contact. And every contact means $6.25 in your pocket.

Usually, you should be able to count roughly on one sale for every 10 appointments you set, which would make each contact worth even more.

So farming by phone can be very cost effective.

About This Book

This book focuses primarily on the second element of the farm marketing mix -- the phone -- and particularly on "cold calls" used to generate pre-qualified leads.

If you're relatively new to farming and, in particular, farming by phone, this book will not only help you develop the right techniques, it will also help give you vitally important self-confidence. If you're already doing a lot of farming by phone, keep reading. Even though some of the material may be familiar, you'll find a few new tips to save you money and time.

> *Stay with your goals. Consistency is better than constant change.*

In the next two chapters, we've created an eight-step, two week plan for choosing and organizing a farm. While two weeks may seem like a lot of prep time, you'll reap the rewards for years to come.

But remember no one type of marketing effort stands alone. Mail, phone, and personal contact all work together to help you reach your goal of increased sales and listings. In fact, some studies show that following up a letter with a phone call can generate 10 times the response of a letter alone. Throughout this book, you'll see references to our other book, *How To Farm Successfully—By Mail*, which can help you farm by mail. Together, these books will give you a real head start on successful farming.

PRACTICE EXERCISE ONE

1. Reflect on your personal beliefs about selling.
   Think about sales in your career which have come out of an established relationship and those based on convincing.
   Which group of people have you been able to maintain long-term relationships with?
   Which have been your best clients?
2. In which situation do you feel most comfortable -- socializing with a group of people or talking to people about your work and ideas?
   How are you different in each situation? In which are you most effective?
3. How different are you when "selling" than when "yourself"?
   Would you like to be more "real" when selling?
   If so, how could you accomplish that?
4. Think about conversations you've had when rapport sprang up with the other person.
   Now think about conversations when no rapport existed.
   What were the differences between the two?
   How would you explain them?
5. How do you feel about the phone?
   How comfortable are you speaking on the phone?
   Whom are you most comfortable speaking with?

CHAPTER 2

SIZING UP YOUR FARM

> *Tough times never last, but tough people do.*
> —Robert Schuller

A TWO-WEEK PLAN FOR ORGANIZING YOUR FARM

In this chapter, we'll show you how to evaluate a potential farm based on your income goal. The statistics you need are simple ones used in everyday real estate matters. By the time you finish, you'll have a realistic farm size based on the average value of homes and turnover in your farm.

Day 1

STEP 1 — LOOK AT YOUR PERSONAL INTERESTS

Whether you choose a geographic or social farm depends on a number of factors. One of the most important is you.

Take five minutes and ask yourself the following questions:

SELF-QUIZ	YES	NO
1. Do you now belong to any organizations which you could use as a social farm? For example, are you active in the local PTA? Youth soccer? Sierra Club? A hospital volunteer group?	☐	☐
2. Are there organizations you would like to join which you could use as a social farm?	☐	☐
3. Do you enjoy the social atmosphere of these "club" environments?	☐	☐
4. Do you belong to an ethnic group that could serve as your farm?	☐	☐
5. Do you have any special housing needs that you share with others?	☐	☐
6. Would you prefer working with one group of people who have unique needs?	☐	☐
7. Would you prefer working within a more heterogenous neighborhood?	☐	☐
8. Is the neighborhood where you live a potential farm area?	☐	☐
9. Does your neighborhood have good, well-segmented tracts that you could farm?	☐	☐

If you answered "Yes" to questions 1 through 6, start thinking about ways you could effectively manage a social farm. If you answered "Yes" to 7, 8, or 9, consider a geographic farm. But the decision process isn't over yet.

Now think about three potential farm areas. Don't put constraints on your thinking. Start with what you like — areas you find interesting — people you'd enjoy knowing better. Pick three potential farms and write brief descriptions of them on a notepad. Look at the potential farm's approximate size, house value, turnover, and demographics of residents. Is this a group you could feel comfortable with and relate to? If you dislike golf, for example, it would be unwise to choose a golfing club for a social farm. Or if you're into country music, pick-up trucks, and cowboy boots, marketing luxury estates in an exclusive division may not be for you.

Take a drive through the three areas you're considering. Or if you're thinking about a social farm, stop by some of the places where you'd find potential prospects.

After thinking about your needs, narrow your choice to one potential farm. If this is absolutely impossible, then you'll have to perform the next step for each of your alternatives. By the time you finish, however, it's highly likely that one choice will stand out.

> *There is no "one perfect way." Options always exist — if you have the vision to look for them.*

DAY 2

STEP 2 — CALCULATE THE FARM SIZE YOU NEED

Most real estate books recommend farming a two to three-year-old area with 200 to 500 homes, depending on the average selling price and turnover. The assumption is that higher priced homes and higher turnover take more work, which means your farm should be smaller.

Rather than basing this important decision on general assumptions, why not run some numbers about the area you're considering farming? What follows works best for geographic farms because it relies on figures available by neighborhood or through your Multiple Listing Service (MLS). But you can also use it to guide your thinking about a social farm. Although you won't have average selling prices and turnover, perhaps you can estimate these figures from city or board figures.

So grab a pencil, some scratch paper, and your calculator.

Before beginning, collect the following statistics:

1. Total number of co-op sales you made last year and total number of own sales. The purpose is to calculate your average commission.

2. Selling prices of all homes sold in your potential farm over the last twelve months.

3. Total number of homes in potential farm.

Remember that it takes six months for a farm to begin producing and then the increases are gradual. This means that you'll need additional revenue from outside your farm, particularly the first year.

The first step in these calculations requires that you set a target goal in farm income from commissions. Be realistic. Everything else builds on this.

INCOME GOAL: $_____

Now figure out your average commission rate. This depends on how many of your listings you expect to sell yourself and how many will be co-op (MLS). Look at your past history. If you sold 20 homes last year, with 15 co-op sales and five on your own, your average commission percentage was:

Your total # sales last year:	20

co-op sales multiplied by commission percentage
15	x	.03 (3%) =	.45

own sales multiplied by commission percentage
5	x	.06 (6%) =	.30
		Add =	.75

$$\frac{Sum}{\# \text{ of sales}} = \frac{.75}{20} = \quad .0375$$

Average Gross Commission Percentage = 3.75%

Now figure it for yourself:

# of sales you get a year:	___
# co-op sales:	___
# other sales:	___
(# co-op) x .XX (% comm) =	___
(# other) x .XX (% comm) =	___
Add above two numbers =	___
<u>Sum of above numbers</u>	___
# listings you get a year =	___
AVERAGE COMMISSION PERCENTAGE:	_____

Next, we need the average selling price of a home in your farm. Just grab the MLS records for the past year and write down the selling price for every home in your farm. Add the prices so you have a total sales volume, then divide by the number of sales. For example, if 40 homes in your farm sold last year for a total of $4,000,000, the average selling price was $100,000. Now do it yourself:

Selling price: _____
                                        _____
                                        _____
                                        _____
                                        _____
                                        _____
                                        _____
                                        _____
                                          (etc.)

Total sales volume: $_____
Total # homes sold last year: _____

$$\frac{\text{Total sales volume}}{\text{Total \# homes sold last year}} =$$ _____

AVERAGE SELLING PRICE: _____

Next take the average selling price and multiply it by your average commission percentage to figure out what you're likely to get for a listing. If you average commissions of 3.75% and the average home sells for $100,000, you'll make $3,750 on a sale. Do it for your prospective farm:

Average gross commission percentage: _____
Average selling price: _____
Avg. gross commission percentage x
average selling price =   _____
AVERAGE INCOME PER LISTING: $_____

Knowing your average income per listing, divide your income goal by it to find out how many listings you need.

For example, if your annual farm income goal is $60,000 and you make an average of $3,750 per listing, you'll need 16 listings.

Do it for your farm:

Income goal: _____
Average income per listing: _____

$$\frac{\text{Income goal}}{\text{Average income per listing}} =$$ _____

 # OF NEEDED LISTINGS: _____

Now you have your:

Income goal   _____
Average commission percentage   _____
Average home selling price   _____
Average income per listing   _____
# of needed listings   _____

It's time to figure out how large your farm needs to be. First calculate your farm's turnover. Half the work is done, as you've already determined the number of homes sold last year. Just divide that by the total number of homes in your farm. For example, if 88 homes sold in an area with 720 homes, the turnover rate is 12.2%.

Now compute the turnover rate for your farm:

homes sold last year =   _____
Total # homes in farm =   _____
$\dfrac{\text{\# homes sold}}{\text{Total \# homes}} =$

                                                 _____

ANNUAL TURNOVER RATE =   _____

Knowing the turnover rate and the number of listings needed to reach your income goal, you can now figure out the right size for your farm. To get it, just divide the number of needed listings by the turnover rate. If you needed 16 listings in an area with 12% turnover, then you'd have to farm 133 homes.

needed listings =   _____
Turnover rate =   _____
$\dfrac{\text{\# needed listings}}{\text{Turnover rate}} =$

                                               _____

FARM SIZE AT 100% LISTINGS =   _____

The above number assumes you'll get all the listings in your farm. Since it's unlikely that will happen, decide what percentage you can expect. Remember that you can probably count on 20% of the listings your second year of farming, 50% the third year and 75% in future years.

EXPECTED PERCENTAGE OF LISTINGS = _____

Now take the farm size at 100% listings and divide it by your estimated percentage of listings. This will give you the actual size of the farm you'll need.

Farm size at 100% listings =   _____
Estimated percentage of listings=   _____
$\dfrac{\text{Farm size at 100\% listings}}{\text{Estimated percentage of listings}} =$

                                               _____

ACTUAL FARM SIZE NEEDED =   _____

In the appendix, you'll find a blank worksheet that takes you through the above steps.

DAY 2

STEP 3 — CHECK OUT YOUR COMPETITION

Go back to the multiple listing service records and check who listed homes sold in your farm over the past year. If one company or agent had 75% or more of the listings, think hard about farming that territory. But if four or five agents crop up repeatedly, go for it. Just make a commitment to keep up your efforts for a year.

You also might want to drive around your real estate farm and look for signs. If 10 homes for sale carry the same sign, chances are good that another farmer is firmly planted in that ground. But if the 10 homes have three or four different signs, the neighborhood could be ripe for plucking.

FINAL THOUGHTS ON SIZING UP YOUR FARM

While it's important to let income goals guide you in selecting your farm size, also consider the following:

First, manageability. Will you be able to serve your farm in person, on the phone, and through the mail? If your farm has 1,000 homes -- if you plan to call each homeowner four times a year -- and if each call takes three minutes, you'll have to set aside 12,000 minutes -- or 200 hours.

On the other hand, if you mail to your farm, the U.S. Postal Service grants a fairly significant discount if you mail to 200 or more homes. These bulk rates can save you 40% on postage costs.

If you combine phone and mail marketing, 1,000 homes might be manageable, but most agents restrict their farms to 200 to 500 homes.

Finally, remember to keep your income goals reasonable. It will take several years for your farm to become a primary income source.

PRACTICE EXERCISE TWO

1. How realistic are you in setting sales goals?
    Are you all pie-in-the-sky?
    Or do you come down too hard on yourself and set goals beneath your capabilities?

2. How hard are you willing to work and how much of yourself will you put on the line?
    Can you extend yourself emotionally every day to make cold calls?
    How will you handle the high rate of rejection?

3. What can you do to make this process easier for yourself?
    Can you "treat" yourself before or after calling?

4. What is the worst that can happen when you farm by phone?
    How would you respond to this?

5. Can you make a genuine commitment to farming?
    Do you have the stamina to undertake activities day after day, month after month with relatively little pay-off for at least a year?

CHAPTER 3

STAKING OUT YOUR FARM

> *It is not enough to have the courage to do the right thing— it must also be done in the right way.*
>
> —*Anonymous*

DAY 3

STEP 4 — COLLECT REAL ESTATE INFORMATION ON YOUR FARM

Go back to the multiple listing service or county assessor's records on the homes sold in your farm last year. Check back a few more years and see how the total number of homes on the market has changed. Is real estate in the area on an upswing or a downswing?

Now look at average selling prices over the past five years. Calculate the average annual appreciation. Do significant differences exist from year to year?

Also ask these questions: How different are the average listing price and the average selling price? How long do most homes stay on the market? Can you tell whether homes with two or three bedrooms or those with four or more sell better?

From descriptions of the houses, look for special features. Do a lot of homes have views? Screened porches? Three-car garages? Drive around your farm and study it. Do houses along any street stand out?

If appropriate, call or visit the offices of builders and developers of your farm. Ask which house models characterized each construction phase and how, why and if the designs changed over time. Find out which were most popular and why. Note the reputation of builders and developers in your farm.

If brokers in your area don't use MLS, you'll have to take a trip to the county courthouse and examine property records to collect information on your farm.

DAY 4

STEP 5 — COLLECT GENERAL INFORMATION ON YOUR FARM

Visit your local newspaper office or library and ask to see back issues of the paper. Look through the local news section for the past few years and see whether your farm is featured in any stories. If it is, you can probably get an idea of current issues in your farm and who the community leaders are. It's a good idea to make personal contacts with community leaders, as they usually have extensive networks of friends and associates who often turn to them for real estate referrals. You also should stop by the local chamber of commerce.

Other relevant information is available from agencies such as the U.S. Census Bureau. It keeps statistics on monthly housing costs, income, marital status, family size and other demographics. This should be in the reference section of your city library. You also can make specific data requests to the Census Bureau and purchase the information directly on computer tape, CD-ROM or microfiche. For individuals, however, this may be prohibitively expensive.

Your local newspaper office, library and chamber of commerce are good sources of information. You can also use the U.S. Census Bureau and the Department of Labor and Employment Statistics as well as local homeowners' associations and prominent tract builders.

At the library, you should also find statistics compiled by state agencies. In Alaska, the State Dept. of Labor and Employment Statistics issues a report on employment figures and trends by subregional areas that includes housing statistics such as foreclosures, number of new loans, rental housing availability and rates, and average prices for two-, three- and four-bedroom homes. It also outlines cost of living changes in major cities as well as average annual wages and pay scales.

Many local governments have planning departments that track similar changes. You may want to request a meeting with a city manager or local supervisor to ask specifically about issues concerning your farm.

You also can check with local homeowners' associations and promininent tract builders, if your farm is in a development.

DAY 5

STEP 6 — MAP OUT YOUR FARM

Get a big map of your farm. If possible, use subdivision plats or parcel plats of the area from the county courthouse. You want a map that shows each property.

Now mount it on the wall. Use colored push pins to mark all the real estate activity. You might follow this color scheme:

Red — Others' listings
Green — Your listings (keep these handy!)
Yellow — For Sale By Owners
Black — Sold within last year

Do the homes cluster in any particular area? Are a number of homes on the same block for sale? Have recent transactions been in one neighborhood? Where are the FSBOs?

> *Business is like riding a bicycle. Either you keep moving or you fall down.*
> *—John David Wright*

Also mark local schools, shopping areas, parks, recreation facilities, sports arenas, public transportation lines, police and fire stations, government offices, churches, hospitals and anything else of interest in your farm. By the time you finish, you should be able to look at the map and understand how your farm is laid out, how it functions and what's on the market. If you're working with a social farm, mark points of interest to potential clients. For example, you'd note marinas if your farm was a sailing club.

Within the next ten years, most major brokerages will probably have mapping software. Geographic Information Systems (GIS) can give detailed information about any property and its surrounding area. Punch in an address and GIS will identify it on the map while providing a profile of its history including previous sales prices, utility costs and tax information. It also measures distances to points such as shopping centers and schools.

Unfortunately, learning these programs is not easy.

DAYS 6 - 11

STEP 7 — CREATE YOUR FARM FILES

The amount of time it takes to create your farm files depends on whether you use a computer and whether you have access to computerized property records.

For each home in your farm, you'll need the following information:

SAMPLE FARM FILE

Name:
Address:
Owner-occupant: Renter: Absentee landlord:
Phone number: (h)   (w)
Best time to call/visit:
Home model:
Bedrooms/baths:
Date purchased: Purchase price:
Parcel #:
Land sq. footage: Building sq. footage:
Special features:

Number of adults in home: Number of children:
Schools:
Occupations:
Notes:

Contact Record:

Date	Type	With	Remarks
_____	_____	_____	_____
_____	_____	_____	_____
_____	_____	_____	_____

As you work your farm, you'll want to add prospect and property information to these files. You'll also want to record whenever a resident responds to one of your mailings. You should record each response in two places: the individual farm file and the mailing response record described in Chapter 15.

When you first meet someone who lives in your farm, ask them how long they've lived in the neighborhood, numbers and ages of children, property details, their likes and dislikes. If you can't take notes during the conversation, stop a minute when you leave and write down what you remember. Enter the information in your farm file as soon as you get back to your office.

It's the attention we pay to little things — promotions, births, weddings, even the championship of a child's soccer team — that lead up to big things. Like the commission on selling a house.

You start compiling your farm files by getting names and addresses. Because most information is kept by address, the following applies particularly to geographic farms. With a little work, however, you can also use it for social farms.

Title Insurance Companies — In some areas, title companies and occasionally Boards of Realtors® will provide complete farm rosters and mailing lists to real estate agents and brokers for no charge or for a nominal fee. They do this, obviously, to promote their own services and develop relationships with the real estate sales community. Some, however, provide only "property profiles" which are useful for establishing comparable housing prices but not for creating farm lists. You can also find valuable information in quarterly reports prepared by some Boards of Realtors®.

In setting up your list, your local title company, Multiple Listing Service (MLS), homeowners' associations, county administrative offices, and/or outside services should be helpful.

Title company data usually comes from county offices and typically does not contain phone numbers. For these, you'll need a reverse phone directory. To use reverse directories, you look up addresses and find residents' names. Pacific Bell updates its directory every six months for most cities, every three months for major metropolitan areas. There's no one time of the year when directories are issued.

But unlike your local phone book, these aren't free. Pacific Bell customers have to lease the directory, paying anywhere from $39 to $132 per edition.

Reverse directories also are available from the following private companies:

Haines Directories, 216-243-9250
Stewart Directories, Inc., 410-628-5988
Cole Directories, 800-228-4571

One problem you could run into is a rash of unlisted numbers. If you do, there's no way you can get the numbers out of the phone company.

But be creative. If you have a substantial percentage of unlisted numbers, why not consider a special mailing to these prospective clients, offering a small premium if they return a prepaid card with basic information: size of family, size of house, occupation, and phone number?

Going this route, one thing you can be sure of is that they haven't had many other agents calling them. So the extra effort may pay off.

Most title company data contains owner rather than occupant information. In creating your farm list, it's important to note who is an owner-occupant, renter, or absentee owner.

You'll know a house is rented when the owners' legal address differs from the parcel address. However, in some cases, this will be only a mailing address or a post office box. To find out if the owner lives at the property, look in a reverse phone directory. Check the home's address and see if the occupant's name matches the owner's. If it does, the owner lives there. If not, someone else does. Write down the renter's name, too.

Because they are often overlooked by other farmers, absentee owners and renters represent potential gold mines for you.

Multiple Listing Services (MLS) — In addition to data provided by title companies, you may be able to get roughly the same information through your local board or MLS. Again, this data will be from county records and therefore will most likely not contain telephone numbers. Before using this information, check with your local board or the MLS to make sure you have the rights to use it for farming.

Homeowners' Associations — Many building projects with some form of cooperative ownership (typically called "common areas") maintain lists of residents. Often this includes phone numbers. Because such information is not public, your access to it is limited. If, however, you're farming an area and come to know association members, you can always ask someone to pass one on to you. Be aware, however, that such directories do not typically break down owner-occupants and nonowner-occupants.

County Administrative Offices — If title company, MLS, or homeowners' association data are not available, you may have to undertake the chore of researching county records yourself. While this may take some time, it should pay off. At the County Assessor's Office, you'll not only find information about property ownership, you'll also find information about all property transactions in the area, including For Sale By Owner and bank foreclosures. These probably wouldn't appear in MLS information.

For farming purposes, the County Assessor's office in our home county in Nevada provides a "Parcel by Street Address List" that gives owners' names. The Assessor's office also sells street address labels for 10 cents each plus 3 cents for special selections.

In our Assessor's Appraisal Record, housing details such as square footage of the land and building, year of construction, outside drawing or photo, number of bedrooms and baths and number of fireplaces are listed.

The third useful item from the Assessor is the Sales Data Bank, which reports on all real estate sales in the area, including For Sale By Owner and private sales.

While not all County Assessors will provide information in the above formats, your Assessor should have owner names, property listings by street address and parcel number, parcel maps and appraisal records. In some areas, you can pay about $1 for field books with this information or spend less than $100 for computer print-outs.

In the Country Clerk-Recorder's Office, you'll find information about deeds, mortgages, liens and foreclosures. This information is often difficult to use, as it's by book and page number instead of owner name.

You also can get addresses from Voters' Registration lists.

Outside Services — Some outside firms compile county owner-ship data. The largest nationwide is TRW REDI (800/345-7334). Covering more than 300 counties in 34 states, it supplies maps, aerial photographs, and ownership information to thousands of real estate offices. Standard available property information includes land use, legal description, mailing address, owner's name, parcel number, property location, assessed value and taxes and exemptions. Depending on the county, TRW REDI also can tell you a property's latest sale date, sale price, year built, zoning, garage type, number of bedrooms, number of bathrooms and other characteristics.

You could use this service, for example, to ask for all the residental homes valued between $100,000 to $150,000 in a farm area, together with their phone numbers. You also could ask for the names of all veterans or widows/widowers. TRW REDI brings together information from a number of public sources, which makes it easy for you to use.

For an annual fee, TRW REDI will provide you with information on microfiche, in print directories, through on-line services or on CD-ROM.

In addition to real estate-oriented services such as TRW REDI, you can get residential data through outside mailing list services. Your local Yellow Pages will direct you to suppliers in your area. With these brokers, you can specify criteria such as age, income, marital status, years in home, renters, etc.

One problem with these lists is that they're often available only for one-time use. To get the best price from a broker, decide in advance how many times you want to mail the list and rent it for that number up front. List prices vary, but Rocco Erker and Gregory Erker in *The Real Estate Professional* quote the going rate as $65 per thousand names.

When dealing with an outside list rental company, find out its information sources. Often it's telephone directories, which mean the data will describe occupants rather than owners. While this is important, you also will need property owners' names.

Another problem with mailing list services is that they typically have 3,000 to 5,000 name minimums. If you only need 500 names, you'll have to pay a premium.

A final consideration about dealing with an outside list compiler is the time lag between collecting and publishing the information.

Fortunately, updating your list is easy, as you'll see later.

Social Farms

If you work a social farm, your approach to getting names, addresses, and phone numbers will, by necessity, be a little different.

Most organizations and clubs publish membership lists with names, addresses, phone numbers, family members, and whatever information they think is important. If you join an organization or club, you should have no problem getting a membership list.

If the club or organization does not maintain a membership list, suggest that they do. In fact, you might even volunteer to create it for them. If the information is already in their files, you can just enter it into a computer database. If they don't have the information, probably the easiest way to get it is through a mailing to members. You can look up the addresses and phone numbers of those who don't reply in local phone directories. If possible, try to find out who owns homes and who rents them.

Computerized Farm Files

Personal computers are not required for effective farming — after all, agents have been farming for a lot longer than computers have been affordable.

But they certainly can make your job easier. If you already have a personal computer, farm with it. If you're thinking about buying a computer, do it. Consider a portable or notebook computer which you can take to open houses and on sales calls.

Many general mail lists and data-base management software programs are well-suited to your farming needs. In addition, programs designed specifically for real estate exist. If you're new to computers or not comfortable with them, you probably should look at real estate software first. It may be a little more expensive than more generic data management programs, but it's worth it. Above all, make sure that whatever software you choose is user-friendly. You don't want to spend a lot of time learning it when you could spend the time farming.

The best software programs combine a data base, communications module for making and tracking calls, word processing and automated scheduling. Below is a sampling of available programs. The following list is not a recommendation — just an idea of what's out there:

Howard and Friends
Sanderson Data Systems Compatibles
P.O. Box 527
Suquamish, WA 98392
206/698-6452

On-Line Agent
On-Line Software, Inc.
International Office Center
600 Holiday Plaza Dr.
Matteson, IL 60443
800/996-6547

Power Prospecting
Innovative Software, Inc. Compatibles
3345 Industrial Dr., Ste. 10
Santa Rosa, CA 95403
707/577-0581 or 800/707-5767

REALTY 2000
NDS Software Compatibles
P.O. Box 1328
Gardnerville, NV 89410
800/421-3069

Top Producer
Top Producer Systems, Inc.
10651 Shellbridge Way, Ste. 155
Richmond, BC, Canada V6X 2W8
800/444-8570

Contact Pro
Actoris Software Corp. Macintosh
1100 Centennial Blvd, Suite 248
Richardson, TX 75081
214/231-7588

Real Estate Connections
RealData, Inc.
78 N. Main St.
South Norwalk, CT 06854
203/838-2670

Sales Management Solution
Impact Solution
135 Cumberland Road, Suite 203
Pittsburgh, PA 15237
412/367-8833

Computerizing your list will allow you to divide your farm into a number of groups: owner-occupants, absentee owners, renters, senior citizens, families with small children, former clients, etc. You can also target residents of specific streets or blocks. This allows you to further tailor marketing messages, which makes them much more effective.

It's good to talk to people who already computerize their farm files and ask for software recommendations. You also can call the Real Estate Brokerage Managers Council (312/670-3780) for suggestions.

How to Create Computerized Farm Files

When you start working with these programs, you'll come across two important, and possibly confusing, terms: records and fields.

A record is all the data associated with a single prospect. In the simplest case, this includes the prospect's name, address, city, state, ZIP code and ownership status.

A field is one of the elements in a record such as the name, address, city, state or ZIP code. In short, fields make up records and records are composed of fields.

You'll also read about "sortable" and "nonsortable" fields.

At the very least, you'll want to be able to sort your farm records by owner's last name, ownership status and by ZIP code (for postage). Other "sortable" fields you might want to include are street, city, last and next contact dates and perhaps home size.

When creating fields, always include an extra sortable field or two in case you want to add one later.

As for labels, your local computer store will sell ones that fit into your printer's tractor feed. These typically come one-, two-, three- and four-across. Four-across are usually the cheapest.

Whenever working on a computer, always remember to make a backup of your data and store it in a safe place. You can lose a lot of time and hard work if you don't.

Manual Farm Files

If you can't afford a computer, start with manual records and plan to convert to computer later. Do it as soon as possible, as you'll soon discover how quickly your mailing labels will become obsolete and how often you'll need to update them.

In keeping manual files, you'll need two sets of records:

1. a master index card file,

2. peel-off mailing label sheets.

For the index card file, follow the format on page 30. Keep this file in alphabetical order by prospects' last names. This will make it easy to grab their cards when they call.

While some Realtors® use 3-by-5 cards, others prefer 4-by-6 cards which can accommodate more notes. Frankly, we'd opt for the latter. The more you know and write down about the people who live in your farm, the more you'll have to talk about. And the more you have to talk about, the better the chances are that you'll develop a relationship and eventually get a listing.

To save time and trouble, we recommend using peel-off mailing labels for your master file cards.

All you have to do is type a master of your mailing list on blank paper in the proper format to align with the labels, then have it copied onto peel-off label sheets at your local quick printer.

You probably also should have the printer copy the basic form for your index card, so you don't have to type hundreds by yourself.

Under "Notes," jot down objections the prospect raises to your sales presentation when you call. Also note the outcome of the call. Knowing what objections people raise, as we'll see later, can be a key to finding their "hot buttons" in buying or selling their home.

Finally, remember how important it is to keep track of whom you call and when. There's nothing quite as embarrassing as calling the same person twice in one week and delivering the same opening line.

> *We cannot do everything at once, but we can do something at once.*
>
> —*Cicero*

Checking Your List

Updating Your Directory

If the phone numbers in your farm file are from a reverse or street address directory, even with twice-yearly updates, some of the numbers will be wrong.

If you're using numbers from a commercial list broker or a membership roster published once a year, chances are even better that you'll strike out.

That's why it's important to regularly clean and update your records.

Before You Call

Before you even approach the phone, it's a good idea to send out a direct-mail letter requesting address correction service through the post office (see *How To Farm Successfully—By Mail* for letter ideas). You can verify the address by writing either "Return Postage Guaranteed" or "Address Correction Requested" on the outer envelope.

With "Return Postage Guaranteed," the post office will return undeliverable letters to you for a fee. With "Address Correction Requested," they'll provide you with the recipient's new address — for an additional fee.

Either way you'll be able to find out whether an address is correct, hopefully get the new address, look up the new phone number from information or a reverse directory and update your files.

If you call a home in your farm and hear a recording giving a forwarding number, first check your local telephone directory to identify the new neighborhood by the first three digits of the phone number. You'll then know if they moved two blocks away or across town, which could affect your decision on whether to follow up. Under these circumstances, it's also a good idea to check a reverse directory for the name of the newest occupant.

During Your First Call

On your first call to a prospect, verify the information you have in your farm files and fill in the blanks for the rest.

For example, ask about the children's names and ages; number of people in the family; special features of the home; hobbies; how long they've lived in the neighborhood; why they chose that particular house; and the story of how they bought it. You may want to follow the "Survey" phone script to collect this information.

But never call without doing some homework. Prospects will be impressed if you show you've gone to some trouble to dig up information on their home. For example, you'll know by the Assessor's Record what year they bought the home and what price they paid. A few minutes of extra work and you can find out the average mortgage rate for that year. You should have this type of information in your files before you ever touch a telephone dial pad.

Finally, keeping up-to-date records is a good incentive for maintaining a regular schedule of farming by phone.

DAY 12
STEP 8 — DEVELOP YOUR MARKETING PLAN

Your Marketing Strategy

To successfully farm, you must develop a marketing strategy. This means positioning yourself. Look at your goals, strengths and weaknesses, competition, target market, their needs, and economic trends.

Jay Conrad Levinson in *Guerrilla Marketing: Secrets for Making Big Profits From Your Small Business* recommends, "Ask yourself basic questions: What business are you in? What is your goal? What benefits do you offer? What competitive advantages? When you know the true nature of your business, your goal, your strengths and weaknesses, your competitors' strengths and weaknesses, and the needs of your target market, your positioning will be that much easier to determine, your strategy easier to plan."

Here's a sample strategy for a real estate farmer:

The purpose of my real estate business is to get and sell a majority of the residential listings in the Castle Pines neighborhood. This will be accomplished by positioning myself as a real estate specialist who can provide excellent service because of my in-depth knowledge of Castle Pines and its real estate market. My target market is Castle Pines residents. Marketing tools will emphasize telephone calls supplemented by personal visits and direct mail. From time to time, I will also organize special promotions. My niche is that I make Castle Pines my priority and study every aspect of life that affects its real estate values and marketing. My identity is one of expertise, experience, reliability and responsiveness to client needs. Ten percent of my income will be allocated to marketing.

> " The harder you work, the luckier you get.
> —Gary Player "

As a farmer, you position yourself as a real estate specialist marketing to a particular group of people. That group has defined needs, desires and values. You take the time to find out what these are. Then you develop skills and language that are responsive to them.

The real farming pro takes the needs and desires of prospective clients seriously. That doesn't mean that you neglect developing expertise. It does mean, however, that when you express that expertise, you do so by showing prospective clients how it will benefit them. Your approach isn't "I am so good," but rather "This is how I can help you."

> " I never thought of acheivement. I just did what came along for me to do -- the thing that gave me the most pleasure.
> —Eleanor Roosevelt "

Now write your seven-sentence strategy:

Name_____

Date_____

MARKETING STRATEGY

_____
_____
_____
_____
_____
_____
_____
_____
_____
_____
_____

Once you have a marketing strategy, the next step is to create a media plan for a year. This book focuses on the telemarketing component of that plan, but we also recommend our other book, *How To Farm Successfully—By Mail*, for tips on effective direct mail approaches. Because the books feature sample telephone scripts and direct mail letters built around the same offers, you can decide whether to make a particular offer over the phone or by mail.

In summary, here is how you can size up and stake out your farm in two weeks:

TWO-WEEK PLAN FOR ORGANIZING YOUR FARM

DAY 1 Look at your personal interests.

DAY 2 Figure out required farm size based on your income goal. Check out your competition.

DAY 3 Collect real estate information on your farm and its residents.

DAY 4 Collect general information on your farm.

DAY 5 Map out your farm.

DAY 6 to Day 11 Shop for computer software and create farm files.

DAY 12 Develop your marketing strategy and media plan.

Your Telemarketing Plan

In writing your media plan, remember that not even the best farming efforts will pay off for at least six months.

Based on the 28 phone scripts in this book, we've outlined sample telemarketing components for your plan. Review them carefully and adapt them to meet your own and your farm's needs.

In the plan, we assume that you're farming new territory. That's why the first few scripts consist of introductions. The next scripts establish you as a real estate specialist. You then move into more specialized offers, all of which are designed to enhance your reputation for caring about your farm and for professionalism.

When you farm, plan to contact prospects by phone every other month. During the in-between months, plan to send direct mail letters or make door-to-door visits. Many of the scripts will facilitate this, as they provide opportunities for face-to-face meetings.

SAMPLE TELEMARKETING PLAN

Month	Telemarketing Scripts	Page
1	Introductory script with premium	198
3	Survey script	207
5	Information kit (select best)	227
7	Seminar script	201
9	Good times/bad times script	212
	or Home evaluation script	223
11	Booklet script (select one)	246
13	Annual report	219

Our telemarketing plan is only a general guideline. If, for example, your farm area is hit by a rash of burglaries, you may want to offer the "Home crime-stoppers" or "Neighborhood watch" kit instead of the "Fire protection" kit. During the spring, you may think that the "Garage sale" kit would generate more responses than the "Vacation" kit. If you're willing to experiment, you can divide your farm in half and test two offers to see which works best.

Throughout the year, also plan to use the specialized telemarketing offers featured under "announcement scripts," "invitation offers," "special circumstances," "follow up referrals" and "client farm" as opportunities arise.

One of the biggest advantages of farming by phone is that it enables you to respond to circumstances quickly and at minimal direct cost.

PRACTICE EXERCISE THREE

1. Read the scripts in Chapter 15. Then write your own telemarketing plan.

    Name_____

    Date_____

    Farm_____

Telemarketing Plan

Month	Telemarketing Script	Page
1		
3		
5		
7		
9		
11		
13		

SECTION TWO

Why Telemarketing Works

CHAPTER 4

Telemarketing:
Wave of the Future

> *To be successful, you have to keep moving.*
> *After all, no one stumbles on something*
> *sitting down.*
>
> — *Anonymous*

In the article "Give Your Cold-Calling Skills a Workout" from the March 1994 *Real Estate Today®*, Julie A. Bleasdale reports on two agents who swear that cold-calling is the hottest way to generate new business.

Tom Klapsa of Vero Beach, Florida, told Bleasdale that when he entered the real estate business, he'd lock himself in a room and make hundreds of cold calls. After nine months, he had 60 listings — just from cold calls. Today he tries to make 20 cold calls a day — he gets 25 listings a year as a result.

Andrew Lacey of Spartanburg, South Carolina, spends about 10 hours a week making cold calls. He said to Bleasdale, "Two years ago I closed 60 transactions. Then I began calling FSBOs, expired listings, and buyers and sellers I had worked with." The next year, he closed 160 transactions.

What Is Telemarketing?

Telemarketing is the planned, professional and measured use of the telephone in sales and marketing.

In the U.S., telemarketing began to take off during the energy crunch of the '70s. Companies were looking for alternatives to personal sales calls — and the gas-guzzling cars it took to make them. Personal sales calls also incur expenses for hotels, meals, and entertaining. While these costs have risen steadily, the relative cost of telephone service has declined. Telephone service is less expensive now, both in real terms and in relation to the rest of the economy, than ever before.

In 1982, revenues from telephone marketing surpassed direct mail. That gap has kept widening. By 1990, half of all goods and services sold in the U.S. were done so over the phone. Today the average face-to-face sales call costs more than $200. The average telephone sales call costs about $3.50.

EXPENSES OF FACE-TO-FACE CALL
VS. TELEPHONE CALL

Face-to-Face Call:	Telephone Call:
Staff time	Staff time (minimal)
Automobile	Phone charges
Meals	
Missed appointment time	
Hotels	
Misc. (parking, tolls, etc.)	

TIME COST OF LOCAL FACE-TO-FACE CALL
VS. TELEPHONE CALL

Face-to-Face Call:

Drive to appointment: 30 minutes
Wait: 15 minutes
Meeting: 30 minutes
Drive back to office: 30 minutes

Telephone Call:

Dial number: 10 seconds
Conversation: 3 minutes

Telephone sales calls can save both time and money compared to face-to-face sales calls.

Realizing telemarketing's advantages, many companies over the past 10 years have scaled down their outside sales forces, installed more phone lines, and increased inside telephone sales staffs.

Versatile, inexpensive, and easy to use, selling by phone can generate leads, keep customers happy, qualify prospects, research a market, target an audience, personalize a sales approach, and help arrange appointments.

With the phone, you can immediately assess the effectiveness of your sales message and build trusting relationships with your farm prospects.

Types of Real Estate Telemarketing

Real estate telemarketing can be divided into two types of calls: (1) outgoing and (2) incoming.

Outgoing Calls

This book focuses on the most difficult type of call, outgoing or "cold" calls. While many agents fear making cold calls, their fears are groundless.

Through outgoing calls, you can contact prospects, recruit buyers, keep in touch with sellers, make listing appointments, follow up referrals, bolster direct-mail results, strengthen ad campaigns, and do whatever else your creativity can dream up.

Incoming Calls

Types of incoming calls include a person inquiring about a newspaper ad or "for sale" sign, a prospect responding to a farm letter, a renter thinking of buying, a friend referred by a happy client and, of course, complaints.

All too often we take incoming calls for granted. Yet these are among the hottest leads you'll ever get. So be careful to handle them properly. For tips, see Chapter 16.

Advantages of Telemarketing

Selling by phone makes a lot of sense. It takes less time than a face-to-face meeting. It costs less than either a meeting or a letter. And it gives you fairly close personal contact with prospects. It also is harder for a prospect to say no over the phone than it is to say no after reading a letter.

Advantages of using the phone are that it . . .

Projects a Positive Image

When you dial a telephone number, the person on the other end is one step removed from you. That means they can't see how you look or what you're wearing. While you may think face-to-face contact would be an advantage, what if the prospect disapproved of your hair color or style of clothing?

In face-to-face encounters, some authorities suggest that 55% of a listener's response is based on the speaker's body language or mannerisms. The tone of voice, accent, and other vocal features convey 38% of the message, while only 7% is tied to the actual words. By eliminating visual "triggers," you force prospects to respond only to what they're hearing. If you can develop a pleasant tone and pleasing telephone personality, you can lay the groundwork for a number of very positive relationships. And you're much more likely to impress prospects with what you know.

Increases Your Flexibility

In real estate, many calls are spent trying to set up appointments. But agents can also use the phone to:

<u>Quickly Touch Base with Clients</u> — With almost everyone in this country buying or selling a home every five years, maintaining healthy relationships with former clients is critical. Especially when you consider that more than half of all Americans move to a new home less than 10 miles from their previous one. Yet 75% of the people who buy or sell real estate never hear from their agent again.

<u>Expand Your Sphere of Influence</u> — Using the phone makes it easy to follow up on referrals. In fact, anyone with a telephone becomes a potential prospect.

<u>Target Specialized Groups</u> — You can develop customized phone scripts for FSBOs, expired listings, renters, and absentee owners (see Chapter 15).

<u>Pre-qualify Prospects</u> — Ask the right questions over the phone and you won't waste time meeting with people who aren't serious

about buying or selling. You might also target prospects for further calls or send them literature and flag them for future follow-up.

Solve Problems — Often help is only a few seconds away, if you know the right person to call.

Conduct Informal Research — The telephone is great for doing surveys that can help you better target your marketing efforts (see Chapter 15).

Lets You Reach More People in Less Time

In face-to-face selling, salespeople average one interview for every five contacts. Over the phone, that ratio drops to one in 10.

But the difference is that each phone contact takes much less time. On a good day, a face-to-face sales rep may see five to eight prospects. On the phone, a sales rep can call 20 to 25 numbers an hour and probably talk to 15 prospects. From 15 contacts, even an inexperienced sales rep will get perhaps one or two appointments; pros can set up one appointment from every five contacts.

If you farm 300 homes and plan to drop by each house once a month, you'd have to visit 10 homes a day, seven days a week. Over the phone, you could make the same number of contacts in less than half that time. After all, it takes only 10 seconds to dial a number.

Gives You Immediate Feedback

One of the best things about the phone is immediate feedback. You have a sense of the person to whom you're talking and they have a sense of you.

Unlike direct mail, where you hit hundreds of homes with the same message, the phone allows you to individualize and improve messages. If a prospect offers an objection, you can overcome it right on the spot. You also can ask a prospect about his or her real estate needs and get ideas about how to better serve your farm.

By the end of several phone sessions, you should have a good idea of what offers motivate people in your farm and how you can best present them.

Keeping careful records allows you to evaluate and sharpen your skills. Just regard each call as an opportunity to do better.

Promotes Organized Professionalism

Well-organized agents can take notes, refer to the Multiple Listing Book, check the computer screen, and schedule appointments — all while talking on the phone.

> " *Things may come to those who wait, but only the things left by those who hustle.*
> —Abraham Lincoln "

If you have more than one phone line, you can get immediate answers to questions. Just put a prospect on hold and make a quick call.

Skillful use of the phone makes you appear knowledgeable and self-confident. The person on the other end will never know how many papers are spread out in front of you.

Saves You Money

For most of us in real estate, the majority of calls are local, which minimizes the expense. Moreover, brokers often pay these monthly service charges.

Even when you consider post office discounts for bulk mail, it's cheaper to let your fingers do the selling.

Builds Personal Relationships

Farming by phone lets you initiate and nourish personal relationships that often lead to long-term clients.

One important difference between telemarketing and direct mail is that you begin relationship building with a prospect from the moment he or she picks up the phone.

Imagine the impact you can have if you start talking about the great addition on a prospect's home; or the terrific paint job they did last summer; or the garden that's their pride and joy.

If you sound sincere and friendly, a prospect is more likely to remember your conversation and be willing to meet with you.

Disadvantages of Telemarketing

Before starting to farm by phone, it's important to weigh the disadvantages.

High Rejection Rate

It's tough to pick up the phone knowing that nine out of every 10 people on the other end will tell you no. Being able to handle rejection separates top commission earners from run-of-the-mill agents. Professionals don't take this rejection personally; they just move on to the next call with their enthusiasm and optimism intact.

More Impersonal Than Face-to-Face Visits

Although farm calls are one step removed from the personal contact of face-to-face visits — you can make that distance work for you. Remember that the phone helps reduce the effects of stereotypes and prejudices.

You Must Persist

Farming by phone only works if you set a schedule and stick to it. This isn't easy, especially when you've had eight "no"s and you're dreading picking up the phone again.

It's also tough when you run into a string of busy signals or no-one-at-homes. In these cases, keep accurate records and call back later. Attention to detail is time-consuming but necessary.

Making the Telephone Work for You

Two keys to making the telephone work for you are to have the right attitude and to set aside time for prospecting.

Check Your Attitude

Before you start farming by phone, think about your attitude. Is it easy for you to call people? Are you comfortable asking questions over the phone? Are you comfortable answering questions over the phone?

To succeed at farming by phone, you should be positive and confident. You need to feel good about what you're selling, the company you represent, and yourself as a professional. You need to feel confident that you can sell your services, solve problems and get information that people need.

Think of the telephone as a professional tool. Study how you use it and what it can do for you.

Spend 75% of Your Time Prospecting

Most agents in your office probably spend 75% of their productive time doing paperwork and only 25% looking for new clients and selling.

Wasted time is why the average full-time real estate salesperson only makes about $26,000 a year.

To become a top performer, you must turn around these percentages. Plan to spend 75% of your time prospecting — much of it with time-saving phone calls — and cut your paperwork to 25% of your time.

In the long run, this is the only way to build a solid income base.

> *When I relate to the best part of a person and ignore all the other parts of that person, he starts presenting more and more of the best part of himself to me and the problem sort of goes away.*
>
> —M. Kenneth Oshman

PRACTICE EXERCISE FOUR

1. Take a piece of paper.
   Go back to your last work day and break down how you spent your time. How much did you spend prospecting?
   How much did paperwork take up?
   How much did you waste?
   If you're not happy with how you spent your time, what can you do to adjust the percentages?
2. List the advantages of farming by phone.
   List the disadvantages.
   Which are most important to you?
   Why?
3. Think about whether you'd feel comfortable farming by phone.
   Read over how the two agents used "cold calling" to get listings.
   Can you see yourself setting aside 10 hours a week for "cold calls"?
   How about five hours a week?

CHAPTER 5

Successful Phone Strategies

> *Every one minute you spend*
> *in planning will save you at least three*
> *minutes in execution.*
>
> — *Crawford Greenwald*

Before you start farming by phone, take a moment to think about what you intend to accomplish.

To succeed, you need a strategy — one that gives you realistic, achievable goals and, at the same time, puts you in the right frame of mind.

In the end, what you think and how you react can make a bigger difference than what you actually say.

Your Greatest Telephone Challenge — You!

In telemarketing, your greatest challenge is not the person on the other end of the line. It's you.

Be Open to Rejection

It's tough to call strangers. To be effective, you can't come across as stiff, wooden or locked into a scripted presentation. You have to express personality, warmth, caring, and professionalism. That makes it a lot easier for you to feel personally rejected when someone turns down what you have to offer.

For anyone selling over the phone, rejection is a fact of life. In telemarketing, the average close ratio is about 10%. That means nine out of every 10 people will say "no." But that's okay. The phone puts you in touch with such a large number each hour that all you need is for one or two to say "yes."

Still — expect the best. Then, as Norman Vincent Peale writes, "In doing so, you bring everything into the realm of possibility."

Let Your Fear Work for You

If you're afraid every time you sit down to make cold calls, that fear will show in your voice. Prospects will become uncomfortable and find it easier to turn you down.

When you feel nervous, let your nerves work for you. Channel your nervousness into energy. Make it sound like enthusiasm. Don't avoid fear — face it and use it.

When a prospect rejects you, it's okay to feel a momentary disappointment. But then remind yourself that they're not rejecting you. They're just not interested in what you're offering. The next time you call, things may be different. When you hear "no," think about what might have motivated the person to say it. Think about how you could have handled the conversation differently. Learn from the experience and keep your sense of humor.

> **"**
>
> *It takes as much courage to try and fail as it does to try and succeed.*
>
> *—Anonymous*
>
> **"**

The truth is, people are more approachable on the phone than you'd imagine. According to Jay Conrad Levinson in *Guerrilla Marketing: Secrets For Making Big Profits From Your Small Business*, only 7% hang up on all telemarketers. Forty-two percent hang up on some telemarketers. A rousing 51% listen to all telemarketers!

Don't Limit Yourself

Unlike people on salary, you have no income ceiling. And with real estate playing such a key role in most Americans' finances, endless opportunities stretch ahead of you.

But all too often, it's easy to limit our vision and circumscribe our goals. Setting your sights too low and thinking negatively about yourself can tie you down even more tightly than a lack of leads.

To move ahead, be objective about yourself. Recognize your strengths, acknowledge your weaknesses, and design a sales strategy that works for you.

Be Prepared

It's easy to throw together a list of numbers and think that's all you need to farm by phone. Don't kid yourself.

First, remember that you're positioning yourself as an expert. You're not just peddling houses or listings; you're a competent, knowledgeable agent whose primary interest is helping your clients make sound real estate decisions. For that to come across, you can't fake it. You have to know your facts, and those facts must be current.

Off the top of your head, you should be able to describe the latest listings, available financing programs, new developments in the area, average mortgage rates, average home values, average rental values, and pending legislation that affects real estate.

Once you master this, you'll be amazed at how much you know and have to talk about. Plus, you'll have the added advantage of a big boost to your self-esteem.

If you think that following a schedule would crimp your style, think again. Planned or not, we all live on schedules. If you don't sketch out your time in advance, you probably waste a lot more of it than you realize.

Set an Overall Objective

As you organize your farming by phone, think about your overall objective. Rather than going for the once-in-a-lifetime sale, set your sights on something manageable. Getting to know prospects —

setting up meetings — finding out information — these objectives are realistic.

Plan Ahead

In Section One, you worked out an overall telemarketing strategy. Now examine it more closely.

In most areas of the country, June and July are good prospecting times. That's when employees take time off, kids are out of school, and people are more willing to contemplate moving. Another good month is February, after the hectic pace of the holidays slows down.

So consider scheduling some farming by phone during the last week of January and at the beginning of June.

If you've been in real estate more than a year, you already know which months are busy and which are slow. Plan to spend the "slow" months generating leads for more productive periods.

If you're planning to follow up a direct mail letter with a phone call, wait three to four days after it arrives. That gives the homeowner time to open and read it, but not forget it.

Of course, other opportunities arise during the year. Maybe your firm is planning a big ad campaign the last week in March. Or a Little League team you sponsor is in the play-offs. Or a rash of fires breaks out in the neighborhood. The week after any of these events would be a good time to get on the phone.

If you plan in advance, you won't find yourself scrambling for prospects.

Draw Up a Daily Plan

You should probably restrict your calling to 20 calls an hour, two hours a day. Whenever your voice begins to lose its enthusiasm, it's best to stop. Even telemarketing pros fade fast after four hours.

In deciding when to call, certain times are better than others. "Fringe" times — mid-morning, late afternoon, or weekends (except Sunday before noon) — are generally good. Avoid calling before 9 a.m. or after 9 p.m., unless you've made prior arrangements with someone.

If you don't have a touch-tone phone, get one — preferably with a redial button. If you have only one phone line, order call waiting. Then you won't have to worry about missing calls while you're prospecting.

If you have a computer with contact management software and a modem, you can mark or tag all the names on your target list and

> *Business, more than any other occupation, is a continual dealing with the future; it is a continual calculation, an instinctive exercise in foresight.*
>
> —Henry R. Luce

have the automatic dialer call each one in sequence. Your computer will keep track of the date, time of the call, and name of the person called as well as issue a report when the process is complete. Dialing one number takes 10 seconds, and every second you save adds time you can spend selling.

Calling 20 numbers an hour, two hours a day, five days a week, adds up to 200 calls weekly. If your farm has 300 homes, it will take you a little more than a week to reach all of them — two weeks, if you add a few days for callbacks. Try to reach each number at least six times. Keep track of messages left, telephones unanswered, busy signals never reached, calls completed and appointments made.

For each prospecting appeal, fill out a Farm Call Plan.

Farm Call Plan

Date:_____

Farm Area:_____

    1. Number of homes in farm:_____

    2. Hours calling per day:_____

    3. Number of calls per hour:_____

    4. Calls per day:_____

    5. Number of days to reach farm:_____

    6. Add 2 days for call-backs:_____

Follow-up:_____

_____

_____

Notes:_____

_____

_____

The Farm Call Plan worksheet helps you determine the number of calls you need to make to reach your entire farm with an appeal.

Set a Performance Goal

Each day you spend prospecting by phone, set a goal. Most of us would probably use making a certain number of calls as our objective. Don't do that.

Set a *performance goal*. At the start of each phone session, tell yourself, "I'm going to schedule two appointments today." Or "I'm going to get five referrals."

Then don't stop until you do it.

Make Short Calls

Since most people have a telephone attention span of only four minutes, keep your calls short — three to four minutes. But you can

> *"I must do something" will always solve more problems than "Something must be done."*
>
> *—Anonymous*

still make them warm and personal. General time limits help you be more efficient and productive.

Call Everybody and Keep Moving

As you work through your prospect list, you'll probably find yourself wanting to skip certain names. That's a no-no. Being committed means sticking to your plan.

Another trick is to keep moving. If you're feeling great because you just lined up an unexpected interview, don't treat yourself to a cup of coffee or brag about it to other agents. Start dialing another number. Your best chance to set up another appointment is right then. As the old saying goes, "Strike while the iron is hot."

On the other hand, if you find yourself running into a string of rejections, don't stop to feel sorry for yourself. Keep dialing. Giving into a few twinges of self-pity can easily mushroom into an overwhelming sense of self-criticism and negativity. You simply can't afford to waste that energy.

Track Your Progress

As you make your calls, keep track of how you're doing. Note the results of each call in two places: the prospect's file (hopefully, on your computer — otherwise, an index card) and a master list, or Call Response Tally, that you keep by your side.

The Call Response Tally shown above allows you to keep track of calls as you make them.

Call Response Tally

Date:_____

Farm area:_____

Time of day:_____

Number of calls:_____

Calls completed:_____

Busy signals:_____

Left message:_____

Call-backs:_____

Referrals:_____

Objections:_____

Appointments:_____

Follow-up:_____

_____

_____

Notes:_____

_____

_____

Your tracking need not be elaborate or formal. Just use old-fashioned scratches (////) on the appropriate lines.

If you spot a pattern showing that something isn't working, stop and make changes. For example, you may notice that you're running into a lot of busy signals at a certain time of day. Just switch your calling time.

Whenever you reach a prospect, have his or her file in front of you. Jot down notes as you talk.

If a prospect raises an objection, note it. At the end of your prospecting session, you'll be able to see immediately the primary objections to your offer. Then you may want to adjust your phone script or write a handful of appropriate responses to keep nearby.

You can also spot patterns indicating that your offer is working. Call-backs, referrals, and appointments are signs that you're heading in the right direction. Over time you'll see these numbers improve.

Follow Through

When you hang up from your last call for the day, your farming isn't over. Block out a half hour for follow-up. Maybe you promised to send someone listings on new homes. Or a caller requested information on a financing program. Or perhaps you found a prospective seller who'd like a brochure on your company.

If you want to make a terrific impression, follow up right away. Get the material in the mail that night and make a note to call again three or four days after they receive it.

Return Calls Promptly

In real estate, it's especially important that you promptly return calls. Making a prospect wait a few hours or a few days to hear from you — some agents don't get around to returning calls for a few weeks! — can utterly destroy their trust in you. In effect, you're telling the prospect, "You're not important enough for me to call back right away."

If you find your schedule so packed that returning calls immediately is impossible, then set aside 45 minutes to an hour each day just for this. Return calls in the evening, if you have to.

Other Time Management Tips

It's a good idea to schedule a drive through your farm at least once a week. Look for new "for sale" signs, "for sale by owner" signs, remodeling projects, and anything else. As soon as you get back to the office, note your observations on the homeowners' (prospects') files.

The Successful Sales Presentation

Certain qualities characterize every successful sales presentation.

<u>Reflects Prior Planning</u> — You have to know your business so well that you have a good answer for anything a prospect asks. Your approach needs to be smooth, confident, and so well practiced that it sounds extremely natural.

<u>Positions You as an Enthusiastic Expert</u> — If you love your business and you're good at it, you can't help but transfer those feelings when you talk over the phone.

<u>Reveals a Philosophy of Selling</u> — This is crucial, because it differentiates you from everyone else calling with a sales pitch. You help people find out what they really want, then make sure they get it. That's a lot different from approaching each prospect as your next commission check.

<u>Creates a Sense of Urgency</u> — Sometimes it's hard to push for quick action. But you can think of offers that have deadlines or limited quantities. You also can convey urgency with your choice of words and tone of voice.

<u>Sounds Spontaneous and Sincere</u> — It's ironic that the more you practice selling, the more spontaneous you can sound. Although it may seem that you can't "turn on" spontaneity and sincerity, the fact is that you can. Some years back, *Time* magazine listed a series of thoughts to ponder. Our favorite was, "Sincerity is not the measure of truth." Sincerity is something we can practice.

<u>Is Always Honest</u> — A good agent never fails to point out material drawbacks that may affect a sale. And if a buyer asks about something that slipped by in a seller's disclosure statement, the agent always gives an honest answer. Misinforming or misleading clients is more trouble than it's worth. Especially in a business where reputation translates almost directly into commission dollars.

<u>Avoids Stereotypes</u> — Before prospecting, relinquish all your stereotypes and preconceptions. A used car salesman may collect rare antique stamps. A college professor may spend his weekends coaching Little League. A housewife may be the financial whiz who invests and multiplies her doctor-husband's six-figure income.

In sales, you can't afford to offend or write off anyone. And if you make up your mind to like people, they'll like you back. When people like and trust you, you won't have to worry about getting business.

The Power of Positive Thinking

Thinking about calling, writing and visiting 300 homes in your farm each year can be overwhelming.

Just take it one step at a time.

The first step is to *believe* in yourself. Don't expect a spouse, partner, lover, child, colleague, or anyone else to give you the strength you need. Chances are no one will be around when you hang up the phone after a "no" or walk away from a door that closes behind you.

To succeed in sales, you have to believe that you can make it — and you can't let anyone diminish that belief. Top salespeople feel this in their bones. But they're not arrogant about it. Every great salesperson has a genuine interest in and concern for the people they do business with. They remember people's names and faces; they write down their hobbies and important information about their families. Often they remember birthdays. Yet they also focus on meeting their own personal goals.

Get Ready

Times have changed and the days of door-to-door peddling are disappearing. But even with the increased reliance on the phone, relationships still come first.

To best prepare for farming by phone, do the following:

Decide to make a definite number of calls each day.

Schedule a definite time period to make your calls.

Set a performance goal for yourself, with a certain number of appointments or referrals you want to have by the end of the session.

Finish all the calls on your list each session.

Keep track of how you're doing with a Call Response Tally sheet.

Strike while the iron is hot. When you get an appointment, dial another number quickly.

When you run into a dead end, dial another number quickly.

Don't stop to analyze your results during your session; wait until the end of the day.

Finally, and most importantly, every time you pick up the phone, believe that you're going to get a "YES!" Be enthusiastic and show it. You'll find it's contagious.

> *One of the greatest discoveries is that a person being can alter their life by altering their attitude.*
> —Anonymous

PRACTICE EXERCISE FIVE

1. Listen to your voice as you talk on the phone.
   Is it enthusiastic?
   Does it go up at the end of sentences or down?
   What attitude does your voice convey?

2. Listen to yourself during business calls.
   How different are you than during personal calls?
   What types of questions do you ask?
   What kinds of replies do you get?
   Are you happy with the way you handle business calls in general?

3. Invent a new question for yourself to use on the phone.
   Try it.
   See what kind of response you get.
   Is this the type of response you wanted?

4. Think about your ability to organize your time.
   If you write up a schedule, will you stick to it?
   If not, how can you make it easier to follow?

CHAPTER 6

Selling Yourself Over the Phone

> "
>
> *No bird soars too high,*
> *if it soars with its own wings.*
>
> —*William Blake*
>
> "

In real estate, everyone starts at the same gate. You run the same course, have the same opportunities, and often work the same neighborhoods. Some agents wind up in half-million-dollar homes, while others struggle to pay their monthly bills.

Why do some people succeed and others don't? Because successful agents know that the most important part of selling is selling themselves.

The Prospects' Point of View

One key to successful selling is remembering that prospects aren't interested in you; they only care about what you can do for them.

When you call a prospect, they're asking themselves, "Is this person good for me? How can he or she help me?"

All too often, we boast to prospects about our great sales record, awards, and million-dollar deals.

Most prospects couldn't care less. Sure, it helps build our credibility — a little.

But prospects really want to know whether we genuinely care about them — about their housing problems, finances, needs, obligations, and families.

It's up to us to show that we can offer valuable services. We demonstrate this not by focusing attention on our accomplishments, but on how we can help them.

Here's an example of two ways to approach the same prospect:
Example 1:

"I'd like you to know that last week I sold the Smith home down your street for a great price!"

Example 2:

"Just last week, I had the pleasure of helping the Smith family find a new home — you know, they just had a beautiful baby boy and they desperately needed an extra bedroom. The new home is just what they were looking for."

After the first example, the prospect is thinking, "So what? You may think you're a hotshot . . . but you're not going to sell my home!"

After the second example, the thinking might go, "Here's someone who really cares about her clients."

66

People have a way of becoming what you encourage them to be, not what you nag them to be.

—*Anonymous*

99

No matter how good the deal, it's emotions that drive home sales.

People aren't looking to buy properties, they want what the properties can do for them.

That may mean brightening their financial outlook, increasing their sense of security, giving them a feeling of achievement, making them more socially acceptable, or bolstering their self-esteem.

To be a success, you must learn to look at your business from the prospects' point of view. Then phrase your conversation in terms of their wants, needs, and dreams.

The Magic Word — "You"

One word you never have to worry about overusing is "you."

In a 15-minute interview, insurance salesman Frank Bettger said "you" or "yours" 69 times.

All too often, real estate professionals concentrate on demonstrating their superior knowledge. They do so not only in their words, but in their voices and mannerisms.

Many agents don't realize it is possible to be both humble and confident. Next time you're on a call, catch yourself every time you say "I." Try to use "you" as many times as possible. Watch how the listener's response to you changes.

Focus more on what others need from you than on what you need from them.

Sometimes while prospecting, you'll sense that it's not the right time to talk about real estate. Maybe you should talk about the prospect's job, hobbies, or children. Within limits, go with your intuition. Listen to people. Find out their needs. One top telemarketer recommends spending only 20 to 30% of a call talking — and 70 to 80% listening.

What to Say

Research demonstrates that the first four minutes of a face-to-face meeting are crucial. In that short amount of time, participants form opinions about each other.

Over the phone, you have just 15 seconds to make the right impression. And 100% of that impression hinges on how you come across verbally.

Create Warmth

Some studies suggest that just by a speaker's voice over the phone, listeners can tell with 90% accuracy whether the speaker feels positively or negatively towards them.

When you're talking, the listener picks up on a lot more than your words. How you feel about yourself — and about them — is reflected in your voice. Think of all the times you've picked up the phone and as soon as you heard "Hello" — you knew there was a problem.

Instead of putting listeners off, you can use your voice to create a sense of friendship and warmth.

Assume Control

How will you react if someone responds to your offer for a free home market evaluation with, "I'm not going to sell my home. Who do you think you are, bothering me like this? I'm busy. I don't have time for people like you."

If you reply,

"I'm sorry I bothered you,"

and hang up, you'll lose control. But if you say,

"I appreciate the fact that you're busy. I can see by the way you take care of your home that you use your time wisely. That's why you especially might be interested in finding out what all those hours you've put into your home are worth. In the long run, it could save you time and money."

— now the ball is back in your court. Sometimes even experienced salespeople lose control and credibility in about 10 seconds.

It happens when they dial a number, greet the prospect, then right off the top utter, "Do you want to sell your house?"

Sales is not a pushing contest. It's a matter of friendly persuasion. Do yourself a favor and tell yourself that you'll *never* start a call this way.

Being in sales means facilitating the process by which clients discover their own needs. Sure, you give prospects reasons to buy or sell their homes. But instead of telling them what to do, you offer friendly, solid information. You guide them through the decision-making process and help them rationalize what they want. Yet the decision is theirs.

Words Do Matter

Look at the difference the way we say things can make. For example, when showing a house to a prospective buyer, you could say,

"Look at this lovely garden."

Or you could say,

"Just imagine the colorful azaleas and roses you'll have blooming here this summer."

The first is a bland general statement; the second plucks at the prospect's imagination, conjures up warm pictures, and psychologically hints at ownership. In sales especially, you need to think before you speak. Certain words just work better than others.

What a difference it would have made in the Gettysburg Address if Abraham Lincoln had started off, "87 years ago . . . " instead of the famous "Four score and seven years ago . . . "

Here are a few rules of thumb for selecting words:

Use Active Words

Always try to use active words instead of passive ones. This simple trick can greatly strengthen your speech.

For example, don't say, "The letter will be mailed today." Say instead, "I'll personally drop it in the mailbox this afternoon."

Here are more examples:

"A park is being built up the street."

"The County Parks Department is building a park up the street."

"You'll only be able to receive this offer for a limited time."

"This offer is good only until the end of the month."

"The living room can always be repainted."

"You can always repaint the living room."

Avoid Weak Words

Avoid what some of us call "weasel words": *if, if you like, if I may, might, possibly, rather, very, little.*

Use strong words: *You can, You have an opportunity, substantial, choice, powerful, impressive.* Just make sure your words are warm and clear and paint desirable pictures in the listener's mind.

> **“**
> *What people hear can be different than what you say.*
> **”**

Appeal to the Senses

Use words that have sensory appeal. For example: *peace, tranquillity, spacious, fragrant, cozy,* and *comfortable.* Think about these words especially when you're describing property.

If someone starts talking to you about a "starter home," what do you conjure up? Probably a two-bedroom cracker box with a pint-sized yard, maybe one tree, and on a busy street. Not very appealing, is it?

Describe the same property as a picturesque dollhouse or a charming country cottage, and watch your phone start to ring.

Speak in a Conversational Tone

No matter how much preparation has gone into your prospecting script, it's important that you sound natural. All too often when a salesperson calls, you can tell the speech is "canned."

Colorful, descriptive words are good; so are personal words that draw listeners into the conversation. Phrases such as "isn't it?," "wouldn't it?" and "couldn't it?" can easily get listeners personally involved.

False compliments are out. Using them only tells the listener that you're insincere and can't be trusted.

Also avoid anything that starts with: "Don't you know . . ." or "Let me tell you about . . ." or "My friend . . ."Using that kind of language tells the listener that your attention isn't really on them, but on yourself. For a listener, it's actually a put-down. That's something most people won't put up with. At least not from you.

Weed Out the Negatives

To prospects, it's important that you be positive. So weed out critical comments. Instead of saying,

> *"That house needs a lot of work,"* try

> *"Because it's a fixer-upper, you can get a great price break."*

Or instead of

> *"The carpet is old and needs replacing,"* try

> *"It will cost very little to replace this carpet with something brighter."*

But be careful not to come across as "Pollyannish" or falsely cheerful.

Also avoid certain words, such as "buy" and "sell." People don't like to buy houses, they like to own homes.

Look at the difference in these statements:

"I can help you sell your home."

"I can help take care of finding a new owner for your home."

The first emphasizes the weighty chore of selling; the second sounds pleasing to the ear and to the imagination.

These differences are quite subtle and some of you may think it's making a mountain out of a molehill. But believe me, the words you use make a difference.

BAD WORDS	GOOD WORDS
Cost	Value
Price	Worth
Down Payment	Initial Investment
Buy	Belongs
Purchase	Own
Contract	Assurance
Decision	Choose
Difficult	Easy
Drawbacks	Results
Liability	Appreciate
Expensive	Valuable
	Proven
	Proud
	New
	Trust
	Comfort
	Fun
	Profit
	Save
	YOU

Learn to turn around the bad words with good words, and see how the image you send over the phone changes for the better.

Keep It Simple

Keep your words and phrases simple. For you, words like wrap-around mortgages, trust deeds, title insurance, and disclosure statements may be old hat. But not to most of your prospects.

You want to make yourself understood without putting prospects in the humiliating position of asking, "Could you explain that, please?"

Rather than ask, most people will hang up and spare themselves the embarrassment.

Also never ask a prospect, "Do you understand?" Who's going to admit they don't? With that kind of language, you patronize prospects (not good for business!).

Keeping things clear is actually a hallmark of genius. If you read Abraham Lincoln's speeches or Thomas Jefferson's letters, you'll see that the greatest minds have always had the ability to express themselves simply.

When we use fancy words, the only people we're impressing are ourselves.

What's in a Name?

Everyone's name is important. Addressing a prospect by name is a sign of respect.

You can actually kill a call in the first few seconds if you don't use a name.

In fact, it doesn't hurt to address the prospect by name frequently. Just avoid going overboard.

If the name is extremely unusual, you may want to ask about it. There could be an interesting story behind it.

Using prospects' names also helps remind you that your farm is made up of real people, with individual needs and dreams, who deserve your personal attention.

Making the Right Offer

Always have a solid and simple offer ready.

Never call a prospect without a good offer.

Some offers that work well in direct mail farming are: free home evaluations, information kits, open house invitations, and For Sale By Owner kits.

Over the phone, you can tailor each offer more personally. Perhaps you have buyers looking for a ranch home in the Whispering Pines area of your city. Checking in your reverse directory, you find the names and phone numbers of every owner of a shingled ranch in the area.

Your calls might go something like this:

Agent: *Good evening, Mr. Bernard. This is Greg Jones with Star Realty here in Pottstown. Do you have a minute to talk?*

Prospect: *Well, just a minute.*

Agent: *Mr. Bernard, I was wondering if you could help me. You see, I'm trying to help a nice young cou-*

ple, Linda and Edward Smith. Edward is an engineer for Hughes Aircraft, and Linda is a paralegal. Edward has just been transferred to this area from Tucson, and they're very concerned about finding a home in a good school district for their two wonderful children. Knowing that the schools in Whispering Pines are among the best in the city, they've decided to look only in our neighborhood. I was wondering . . . do you know anyone who might be thinking about selling? Maybe one of your friends or neighbors?

From a call that begins like this, agents have had the good fortune to find someone who's seriously thinking of selling. Chances are that from 15 or 20 calls, an agent will get the names of four or five people who have at least mentioned selling.

But even if no names are forthcoming, agents making this type of call will impress prospects with the personal attention they give clients. They also show that they're not afraid to take risks.

Compare this approach to the agent who calls and starts off with, "We have several people interested in buying in this neighborhood. May we show your property?"

To the listener, that's a slap in the face. The likely response is, "Who is this agent anyway? My house isn't for sale. Who do they think they are?"

In dreaming up offers, be imaginative and creative. But be real. Offer something genuinely valuable.

In Chapter 15, you'll find sample scripts for a number of situations: introducing yourself to a farm, offering free home evaluations, offering information kits, offering information booklets, announcing listings and sales, inviting prospects to open houses, offering assistance to For Sale By Owners, getting expired listings, converting renters to buyers, getting relocations, appealing to absentee owners, following up referrals and keeping in touch with past clients.

Below are examples of circumstances when the offers would be appropriate.

Home Crime-Stoppers Kit — Not long ago, there was a terrible murder nearby.

Make sure your offer has substance.

The next day, enterprising security companies were knocking on doors and ringing up a lot of sales. If they had thought of it, Realtors® could have done the same thing. They could have offered a Home Crime-Stoppers kit, with leaflets, coupons, and the names and addresses of local security companies, insurance companies and police departments.

Pulling the kit together would've taken a few days. But the Realtors® could have done cooperative deals with insurance companies and police departments. Most would have had appropriate brochures already available.

Then all the Realtors® would have had to do is call each home, talk a little about the tragedy, and offer a free kit.

It would've gone like hotcakes.

Offers like this (you'll find a number of sample scripts in Chapter 15) help you several ways. First, they demonstrate your personal concern for farm residents. Second, they link you with important community resources. Third, they're a great way to get to know prospects. Just deliver as many kits as you can right to prospects' doorsteps. And be sure your name and telephone number are prominently displayed.

Income Property — Perhaps your farm is in an affluent area where homeowners can afford rental or income properties. If you have a listing on a nice four-plex with good financing, why not call a few high-end prospects in your file and see if they're interested?

Financing — You know that turnover in your farm is low and many homeowners bought when mortgage rates were around 13%. From the prospects' files, you can find out the year each home was purchased. Why not call those who bought when rates were high and see if they'd be interested in owning larger homes for about the same monthly payment? Or maybe they'd be interested in refinancing. Either way, you have a reason to call. Especially if there's a larger, more expensive home on the market just a few blocks away.

Renters — When driving around your farm, you spotted a courtyard of Spanish bungalows that you know are rentals. Judging from the current market, you'd guess each tenant pays around $700 a month. For about the same amount, they could own homes. Since renters don't always realize the tax and other advantages of home ownership, why not call and tell them?

Prospect Interest — Several years back, a friend spotted a house she fell in love with. It had gingerbread trim, a massive stone fireplace, and walls of windows overlooking a mountain canyon. She insisted the agent contact the owner to see if he was willing to sell. To her surprise, he didn't say no.

Remember, most houses change hands every five years. If a buyer suffers from love at first glance, follow it up. The owner might not be willing to sell now; but four years down the road, the buyer may still be interested, even if he or she has bought another home.

<u>Free Home Evaluations</u> — Offering a free home evaluation can work especially well if a prospect has just finished building a new garage, adding an extra bedroom, or putting in a pool. Every home-owner likes to know the value of what they've done.

As you can see from all these examples, farming by phone can be more personal and timely than farming by mail.

Can Telephoning Work for You?

Being a good salesperson usually isn't a natural gift; you have to cultivate the right skills. Doing so takes time and effort.

If you read the biographies of this country's greatest salespeople, you'll see that many of them started out with two left feet, one of them in their mouth.

Years ago, Lee Iacocca launched his career as a fumbling sales representative. In his autobiography, *Iacocca*, the plain-speaking and straight-shooting former Chrysler Corporation chairman remembers,

> *"Some people think that good salesmen are born and not made. But I had no natural talent. Most of my colleagues were a lot more relaxed and outgoing than I was.*

> *"For the first year or two, I was theoretical and stilted. Eventually I got some experience under my belt and started to improve. Once I had mastered the facts, I worked on how to present them. Before long, people started listening to me."*

Success takes commitment and hard work. That's what separates the winners from the losers.

Have a specific purpose. Avoid trying to be everything to everybody.

PRACTICE EXERCISE SIX

1. The next time you're talking on the phone, pay attention to what you're doing with your body.
   Are you fumbling around?
   Tapping your fingers on the table?
   Or are you totally focused on the conversation?

2. Make a list of words you frequently use in conversation.
   Show it to someone close to you and see if they can add a few.
   For every "bad" or negative word on the list, think of a good, positive one.
   Practice adding those words to your conversation.

3. Go back over the past week.
   Write down all the situations when you could have made a prospecting call.
   Did you do it?
   Why or why not?
   Now write down all the prospecting call situations that could come up in the next week.

4. For a day, monitor your language during your calls.
   Make a mark every time you use the word "I."
   Make another mark every time you use the word "you."
   Which do you use more frequently?

CHAPTER 7

Tips on Telephoning

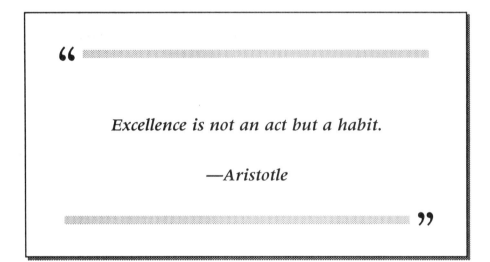

Excellence is not an act but a habit.

—Aristotle

Like every other form of communication, telephoning has its own rules of etiquette.

All of us recognize phrases such as "Call me back," "Hold on," "Just a minute, please," "Could I take a message?" and "All our representatives are busy now. Please stay on the line and we'll be with you in a moment," as associated with the phone.

In this chapter, we'll look at telephone courtesy as well as how to develop an effective telephone voice.

Where You Are

Your surroundings when you make prospecting calls are important.

If your desk is one of 15 crammed into a small, high-ceiling, noisy room with elevator music playing in the background, consider calling from home.

During your conversations, you must focus totally on what the prospect is saying. You can't have people shoving notes in front of your face, kids clamoring for your attention or a radio taking your mind off what you're saying.

If you call from home, make sure that the background stays quiet. In other words, don't have someone running a vacuum cleaner while you're trying to concentrate. Background noises not only distract you, they also distract the person on the other end.

As a general rule, call from a comfortable and pleasant environment where you feel relaxed. Keep your farm files nearby, and be sure your desk top has plenty of room for spreading out papers and taking notes.

When to Call

You can find all kinds of recommendations on the best time to call people in various occupations. They're interesting, but not for you.

When farming by phone, you call people at home. The Direct Marketing Association's *Guidelines for Ethical Business Practices* says that all telephone contacts should be made during reasonable hours. Generally, that's from 9 a.m. to 9 p.m.

Time of Day

The best time to reach people who work is from 5 p.m. to 8 p.m. Then you have a good chance of catching them between getting home and taking off for a meeting or social engagement.

Although you might think people don't like being disturbed during these hours, you'd be surprised.

With the huge variations in when we eat and the short amount of time meals usually take, I hardly ever interrupt anyone in the middle of dinner. If I do, I just set up a time to call back.

If you're calling people who don't work, the best time is between 9 a.m. and 10 a.m. By then, children are off to school and the parent at home is usually cleaning up.

Afternoons are generally a bad time to call, unless you're trying to reach retirees.

Days of the Week

Avoid calling on Friday. By then, most people aren't thinking about "business." Monday through Thursday is fine. Saturday morning is also good. On Sunday, people sleep in or go to church. Restrict your calling from 1 p.m. to 8 p.m.

If no one answers or the line's busy, make a note and call back later. Try busy signals again after 15 minutes.

Whatever you do, don't just call once or twice. Try six times to reach each number. If they're hard for you to reach, chances are they're also hard for other agents to reach.

Persistence pays off.

Courtesy Counts

Erastus Wiman once said, "Nothing is ever lost by courtesy. It is the cheapest of the pleasures, costs nothing, and conveys much. It pleases him who gives and him who receives, and thus, like mercy, is twice blessed."

When it comes to telephone manners, I've been put on hold for more than 10 minutes . . . talked to people carrying on two conversations at once . . . and had friends wash dishes or play computer games as I talked.

Common courtesies we pay attention to in person seem to slip by the wayside over the phone.

> *I never lost a game. I just ran out of time.*
> —*Bobby Layne*

Who would you rather talk to? Someone who:

Puts you on hold	*or*	*Gives you full attention*
Chews gum or eats candy in your ear	*or*	*Talks clearly*
Talks above your head	*or*	*Speaks simply*
Puts you down	*or*	*Builds you up*
Has a chill in their voice	*or*	*Speaks warmly*
Talks to someone else in the background	*or*	*Focuses only on you*
Doesn't answer your questions	*or*	*Gives you clear answers*
Interrupts you or finishes your sentences	*or*	*Lets you speak your mind*
Talks about themselves	*or*	*Talks about you*

Courtesies, such as saying "please" and "thank you," paying attention, not interrupting, and not talking too much, are just as important over the phone as they are in person.

In essence, treat people the way you would like to be treated.

Use Hold Buttons Sparingly

Every time you put a caller on hold, you tell them that the other person calling is more important. Only use the hold button in extreme emergencies. If you do, don't stay away longer than 15 seconds.

When you come back, don't dismiss the interruption with a curt, "Sorry to keep you waiting."

Instead give a full apology: "I'm sorry, Mr. Smith. Thank you for waiting."

It's also a good idea to summarize where you left off. Hopefully you can recreate the mood of the moment when you left.

Use Prospects' Name Frequently

William Shakespeare's famous line, "A rose by any other name would smell as sweet" does not apply to people. A person's name is important. And if you're calling someone you've never met, don't start off on the wrong foot by using their first name.

Nowadays most people are casual about names. They are relaxed about people they're doing business with using their first names. But you'll still find the types who write to Ann Landers complaining about someone calling them Marie or George instead of Mrs. Berrenger or Mr. Husman.

So use names carefully.

Say "Please" and "Thank You"

"Please" and "thank-you" never go out of style. Say them often.

Know When to Stop Talking

A salesperson can never know too much, but they can talk too much.

Knowing when to keep your mouth shut isn't easy. But talking too much, especially when you have nothing to say, can kill a relationship with a prospect.

Let the prospect talk. They'll feel good and so will you, when you get the appointment.

Never Interrupt a Prospect or Finish Their Sentences

When you interrupt a prospect, you're saying, "That thought isn't important. Listen to me, you turkey."

When you finish a prospect's sentences, you're telling them that you already know what they want to say and that they'd better hurry up.

Pay Attention

Often we think we can hide the fact that we're not paying attention. Don't fool yourself.

Prospects can tell if your mind is someplace else during your conversations. Especially if you have to ask them to repeat something.

Pay attention. It's worth it.

Never Argue

Instead of arguing with a prospect, twist their objection around into an advantage. Chapter 11 will help you do that. For now, remember never to argue with a prospect. It's okay to disagree, but always give the prospect a little credit.

If you have a quick temper, you may have to work on this. But engrave this rule in stone: Never argue with a prospect. If someone does get angry with you, Cal LeMon recommends the following in *Assertiveness: Get What You Want Without Being Pushy:*

- don't be funny
- don't argue
- listen
- use the person's name
- slow down
- lower your voice
- sit down
- negotiate

Keep It Short and Simple

Most phone conversations with prospects last three to four minutes. If they go on any longer, prospects become bored.

Three or four minutes may sound short, but you can pack a lot of powerful words into them. The key is to plan what you want to say, have appropriate responses ready, and keep the conversation on track.

> *To be creative, if you talk less and listen more you will do very well.*
> —Claude Rosenberg

You can be friendly without being long-winded.

Never Hang Up First

Write "Never hang up first" beside the rule, "Never argue." If you hang up last, the prospect won't feel jilted when a last-minute question pops up. Wait until you hear the other receiver placed back down — then do it yourself.

Watch Your Favorite Words

On a plane not long ago, I counted the number of times a flight attendants said "Sure."

"I'd like a Coke."   "Sure."

"Do you have any lemon?" "Sure."

"What about a glass of milk?"   "Sure."

She must have used the word 50 times in five minutes. We all have pet words that others can find annoying. Watch your speech for a few hours and see what yours are. Then try to minimize your use of them on the phone. Too many "Sure"s or "okay"s or "Uh-huh"s in a conversation will make it sound like you're not really paying attention.

If You Call at a Bad Time, Reschedule the Call

Sometimes the phone rings at the wrong moment. For example, a prospect may just be sitting down to dinner. Or in the middle of an argument with a child. Or writing up a business report. Don't be put off if a prospect sounds distant.

If you sense that it's a bad time to talk, it probably is. Ask for a time when you can call back. This gives you an edge, as you'll be calling back by invitation. And since the person will probably feel badly about cutting you off the first time, they'll be more likely to listen to you.

Soften Your Words

Here are a few tricks to make you sound more pleasing over the phone:

Don't Say This:	Say This:
Hold on.	Just a moment, please.
We must have . . .	May we have . . .?
You ought to . . .	Perhaps you could . . .
Sorry to keep you waiting.	Thank you for waiting.
Good-bye.	Thank you for your time.
Who's calling?	May I ask your name, please?
What's your name?	And your name is?

Secret of Success

Over the phone, you can use your voice to create an image of self-confidence, intelligence, and caring.

Often telephone salespeople sound bored with their jobs, as if they are going through the motions and following directions step-by-step.

That's not exactly the way to make people think you're inspired, creative, and good at what you do.

Your voice is an instrument that you can use to play a humdrum, ordinary tune, or you can fill it with valleys and peaks.

Over the phone, a good sales voice is:

- clear
- well paced
- friendly
- sincere
- confident
- relaxed
- cheerful

Your phone manner should be professional and courteous, but always persuasive.

Talking over the phone is not the same as talking in person. Because the listener can't see your hand movements or facial expressions, your voice becomes a portrait of your personality. Your voice has to make gestures, carry your facial expressions, and tease out responses.

It has to be full of lightness and darkness, softness and determination, playfulness and professionalism, smoothness and rhythm. In other words, your voice has to convey the real you.

Here are some tips for tuning up your voice.

People remember quality.

Put a Smile in Your Voice

Before you make a call, smile — big. Putting a smile on your face puts a smile in your voice. That's the best way to make yourself sound pleasant, lively, enthusiastic, and expectant. Keep smiling throughout each call.

Intonations can also help. They not only add interest and sparkle to your voice, they help convey meaning.

Here's a simple example:

"JUST A moment."   (The voice falls at the end.)
"JUST A MOMENT."   (The voice rises at the end.)

The first example makes the person listening feel that they're bothering the speaker.

In the second example, the speaker sounds eager, warm, and pleased to help the listener. Which impression would you prefer?

Slow Down Your Speech

Your speaking pace is more important over the phone than in person. If you talk too quickly, your words will run together and the listener will have a hard time understanding you.

But if you talk too slowly, the listener could feel frustrated and wonder, "Why doesn't this slowpoke hurry up?"

At the beginning of a call, talk a little slower than normal. Experts say 140 to 150 words a minute is ideal.

Talking slowly helps the listener concentrate better and understand what you're saying.

Lower Your Voice Pitch

Some of us have high-pitched voices; others have low-pitched voices.

Actress Katharine Hepburn used to have a terrible time with voice pitch. Whenever she became excited, her voice would soar upwards and hit jarring, displeasing notes.

With the help of a voice coach, through singing, she learned to control the pitch.

In direct-response broadcast advertising, deep male voices are almost always used, primarily because they have authority and believability.

You don't have to go so far as to mimic their deep voices, but remember that the deeper your voice, the more confident and knowledgeable you sound.

Speak Directly into the Phone

A simple but easy-to-overlook trick is this: Don't hang the receiver below your mouth. Keep it about a half inch directly in front of your lips. Talk straight into it. That's the only way to make sure your voice is clear.

Listen to Your Own Voice

How does your voice sound on the phone? Does it sound confident? Caring? Sincere? Natural?

How many times have you heard your own voice and not recognized it?

That's because when you talk, the sound comes back to you through bone vibrations in your ear. You don't hear yourself the way the rest of the world does. Everyone else hears your voice as it's carried through the air.

All of us can improve the quality of our voices.

The first step is to ask someone objective to evaluate your voice. Does it sometimes sound tinny? Abrasive? Harsh? Grating? Does it have enough resonance?

When checking your voice, look for problems with sloppy pronunciation, misplaced breathing, a monotonous tone, or maybe dropping the end of every sentence. These problems are common and easily corrected. Just listen to yourself and practice making your voice better. Use a tape recorder so you can hear yourself the way others do.

Enunciate Clearly

English is full of hard-to-pronounce words. Strung together, some words become almost impossible to say.

If you mush words over the phone, listeners will have problems understanding you. Articulate each and every sound clearly. You'll feel better about what you're doing and you'll spare prospects the embarrassment of asking you to repeat yourself.

By recording and listening to your own voice, you can improve tone and pronunciation.

Always practice enunciation in front of a mirror. See if you can read your lips while you talk. Some of us, like me, are lazy and tend to move our lips as little as possible.

Sounds that are especially difficult to enunciate are *s, t, d, p,* and *b.*

For starters, practice reading the following paragraphs in front of the mirror:

> *When the snow falls, the sleighs glide across the glen, their slick blades skimming over the shiny surface of the ice. A popular pastime for people of all ages, sleighing stirs a sense of nostalgia.*
>
> *Fur-lined coats, steaming cups of coffee, the chirping of birds, the glistening patches of snow . . . all make beautiful memories.*
>
> *Today in the roofed and covered rinks where children on skates practice their pirouettes, there is no cool breeze blowing through their hair or chill nipping at their noses. Something good is gone.*

These paragraphs will help you practice your enunciation.

When you have this down pat, you should be able to clearly read your lips while pronouncing every word.

Voice Matching

One trick phone pros use is to match their voices to the listener's. If the listener's voice is soft, they soften their voice. If it's brusque and businesslike, they turn into Mr. or Ms. Efficiency.

Matching voices helps create rapport. Match a listener's volume, tone, tempo, pitch and cadence. You'll make them feel more comfortable and you'll feel more comfortable, too.

Another trick is to echo back a prospect's words. This also helps build a sense of trust.

For example, if a prospect says,

"I'm not sure we're interested in looking at any houses."

You could reply,

"But if you look at these houses, I think you'll find . . ."

Instead of the word "look," you could've used "see" or "visit." But each word is slightly different. By using "look," you're showing that you're on the same wavelength as the prospect.

Telephone Tips Wrap-Up

Miss Manners' amusing approach to etiquette hides a gem of truth: **The little ways we treat people often make a big difference.** Being kind and polite is often even more important on the phone than in person.

Before you begin farming by phone, make sure you're in a comfortable, pleasant environment, where you feel relaxed and there are no background noises to divert you.

When considering the times to schedule your calls, make them during the evenings Monday through Thursday, on Saturday morning, or on Sunday afternoon.

Then polish up your manners. Over the phone, courtesy requires that you *never* do the following:

- Put a prospect on hold unless absolutely necessary
- Interrupt or finish a prospect's sentence
- Let your mind wander
- Argue with a prospect

- Be long-winded
- Hang up first

With your voice, you create a portrait of yourself in sound. You want that picture to be cheerful, relaxed, confident, sincere, clear, and pleasing to the ear.

If you listen to your voice and you're not happy with it, ask someone objective to help you. Work out the kinks by practicing in front of a mirror.

Every good actor knows that you can smooth away a heavy accent, find a better pace, add emotion and warmth, or learn to pick up and bounce back the voice of another person. All it takes is practice.

Finally, the voice with a smile in it is the voice that sells. To have a smile in your voice, put one on your face. See how much better it makes you feel.

PRACTICE EXERCISE SEVEN

1. Think about where you're most likely to make prospecting calls.
    Is it a comfortable, quiet environment?
    Do you feel successful and productive in that environment?
    If there are distractions, what can you do to eliminate them?

2. During telephone calls, practice getting into an immediate voice match through your volume, tone, tempo, pitch and cadence.
    See how and if the other person's response to you changes.

3. In one day, count the number of times salespeople address you by your first name.
    What effect does it have on you?
    Do you think it will have the same effect on prospects you call?

4. Tape record your voice for three minutes.
    Play it back twice, each time taking notes.
    Examine the tone, pace of delivery, voice quality, resonance, pitch, enunciation, and type of language used.
    Think about how you could improve it.

SECTION THREE

Your
Farm Call
Scripts

CHAPTER 8

The Prospecting
Call Script

> " *Effort and courage are not enough
> without purpose and direction.*
>
> — *John F. Kennedy.* "

Don't let the word "script" frighten you. We're not talking about a canned spiel that you mechanically deliver. A script enables you to strike up a conversation with a clear purpose, direction, flexibility, and consistency.

Think of it as the path leading to your goal. In this case, the goal is setting up an appointment or building a relationship or getting to know your farm. With a good road map, you'll spare yourself many detours and distractions.

You not only need to know what you want, you also have to know how you'll get there. A script can help.

What a Script Can Do for You

First, write scripts that fit your prospects' needs and wants.

If you farm an area full of young families, write a script that focuses on the ease of owning a larger home. If you farm an exclusive area, plug the advantages of income property.

Using a script is helpful because it:

Gives You a Plan of Action

With a script, you'll never start off a prospecting call with, "Do you want to sell your home?" By building scripts around creative, innovative offers, you can make prospects want to meet you or take advantage of your services. It's not as hard as it may seem, but it does take a little thought. Doesn't anything in life that's worthwhile?

Helps You Overcome Objections

If you have a script, you can predict 60% of a conversation.

The other 40% is up for grabs, but it's unlikely anyone will throw you a totally unexpected curve ball.

After a few sessions of farming by phone, you'll notice the same objections and responses cropping up over and over.

Based on your script, you can figure out how to respond to each objection. You can also anticipate questions, come up with alternatives, and sketch out answers — all before you ever dial a number.

You'll be surprised at how thorough preparation helps you feel more confident and self-assured.

Makes Your Presentation Consistent

In each call, there's the danger of going off track. Someone may start talking about their problems with a neighbor, a disagreement with their partner, or a sickness they've recently suffered.

When that happens, be empathetic. But don't lose your focus.

A script helps you get the conversation back under control because you know exactly where you want it to go next.

But be careful: Sometimes it is important to let people talk. When you listen to their troubles sympathetically, they'll remember you. Play each situation by ear. Be friendly, but be focused.

Provides Logical Organization

In any conversation, how often do your thoughts follow each other logically?

Most of us tend to believe we usually make perfect sense. But often we don't.

When farming by phone, you don't have time to be long-winded. You've got to have your approach down pat.

In this friendly art of persuasion, you build a case using conversational remarks, questions, and logical arguments. You have a dialogue with a prospect and give them reasons to take up your offer.

Making people recognize their own needs is difficult. Telling them they need something which you can offer won't do it. You have to be a gentle, smart, and confident persuader.

Stresses Benefits over Features

Sales experts love this language. All it means is that you focus on how people use things, not the things themselves.

In other words, when you're trying to sell a house, you don't focus on the 30-year roof or the copper gutters or the 6,000 square feet.

Property	Feature	Benefits
123 Main St.	shade trees in backyard	where family can have picnics
	wood trim	makes house feel warm & cozy
	huge basement	where kids can play without bothering the parents

Make up an index card on each listing and convert the features into benefits.

You sell the shade trees gracing the spacious backyard where the family can have picnics — the charming wood trim that makes the house feel warm and cozy — the huge basement where the kids can play without bothering the parents.

People don't buy houses — they own homes that express who and what they are.

Off the tops of our heads, it's easy to concentrate on the facts. With a script, you can have the mental pictures ready. Separating benefits from features won't be a problem, because you will have thought through the features and already converted them into benefits. You'll even have notes right there before your eyes.

Yields Better Results

If a novice salesperson can get one or two appointments from every 20 calls and a pro averages one appointment from every three or four, we obviously learn from experience.

Selling yourself by phone takes much more than a pleasing personality. It requires thought, practice and skill.

That's why the first year or so in any sales job is often a real struggle. You can't know all the little things you can do that will make a huge difference in your commissions.

But learning them can be a real thrill. And when you prospect by phone, you'll see the results immediately.

And if you're good now, by the time you finish this book, you'll be even better.

Why You Need Scripts

Basically, a script helps you organize your thoughts and allows you to weed out extraneous information. It helps clarify the direction and focus of your conversation.

When using a script, you'll sound smoother and more knowledgeable. You'll have ready answers to prospects' questions and immediate responses to their objections.

With so much help at your fingertips, you'll feel more self-confident than ever before. But remember, no script is ever finished.

Scripts have to work well over time. If a script isn't, look for what's wrong and change it. Use different words. Revise the offer. Add a 30-day deadline. Tell a story. Make one change at a time and see what happens.

Remember the Boy Scout motto, "Be prepared." Make that your motto, too.

Script Formats That Work

Most telemarketing companies use one of four types of scripts:

Word-for-Word Scripts — Like a machine, the person using this type of script reads the words automatically. Listeners can tell, too. Usually this rigidity is only appropriate with highly technical products or when legal requirements dictate a by-the-book approach.

Logical Flow Scripts — These scripts have some word-for-word sections, but they also allow the salesperson some freedom. Maybe they have scripted lines at the beginning to introduce a product or service. But then they move right into more personal, open-ended material.

Prompt Scripts — These put the facts at the salesperson's fingertips. They're helpful if you expect questions that need explicit answers, but don't want a rigid structure.

Call Outline Scripts — This is the type of script most often used for farming. The scripts follow a general outline, with important points noted for reference. They leave lots of room for personal interaction. In telemarketing lingo, these scripts are *rapport builders*.

Script a Conversation

Don't think of your scripts as something you absolutely must get through.

Scripts only provide you with appropriate openings and quick responses to keep conversations going.

They give reasons to get to know prospects and ask about their needs and desires, so you can figure out the best ways to help them.

A lot of fluffy phrases or high-talking words don't belong in your scripts. Keep scripts simple and person-to-person. Try to make your conversations flow naturally and don't let prospects even guess that your next sentence is staring up at you.

Elements of a Good Script

When you sit down to write a script, these are the areas to cover:

The Opening

In the next chapter, you'll find out more about how to write the opening. For now, think of it as the way you set the stage for the rest of the call. Begin with a friendly and casual greeting, letting the

> *A person's work is a portrait of that person.*
> —*Anonymous*

prospect know right away who you are and what company you represent.

The Attention-Getting Remark or Reason for Calling

If you're not feeling too sharp, you can try to launch the conversation with something like, "I understand you just moved into your home. Could I ask you a few questions?"

In the sample scripts, we recommend this approach if you're just getting to know your farm. While it can provide invaluable information, it's not the best offer for attracting prospects.

Look through the sample scripts and see the variety of attention-getting remarks we used.

The Benefits of Listening

Once you've gotten the prospect's attention, you have to keep it. Begin selling the benefits of what you're offering.

Always use language that reflects the prospect's point of view and you'll soon turn their attention into interest.

Avoid being long-winded. Some experts recommend sticking to only two or three benefits. Otherwise prospects might find your offer confusing.

The Questions

Use questions to find out what motivates your prospect.

Once you demonstrate that you're genuinely interested in helping a prospect, you begin building a trusting relationship. By asking specific questions, reflecting back a prospect's words, and matching the tone, pace and inflection of their voices — you increase their sense of rapport.

Through questions, you can dig out what motivates a prospect. It may be money or security or status or comfort. Right on the spot, you can revise your offer to meet their individual needs.

The Objections

Objections are opportunities. The prospect is keeping the conversation going and inviting you to respond to their concerns. Expect objections. Welcome them. The prospect is telling you their feelings. Take them seriously and think through your responses.

Some objections will crop up repeatedly. Prepare answers for them and study how they work. Other objections, you'll hear less often. Be prepared for those, too.

If you run into someone who doesn't offer any objections, beware. You want prospects to tell you how they feel. That's the only way you can develop a mutually trusting relationship.

The Critical Close

During the close, you ask the prospect to take you up on your offer. That may mean getting them to agree to a free home evaluation, receive an information kit or booklet, drop by an open house, attend a seminar, or give you a referral.

Sometimes you'll present the offer to a prospect within the first 30 seconds of the call. Or you may wait until two minutes into the call. Start to close when your intuition tells you that the time is right.

If you don't learn to close, you'll be on the phone forever.

And if the prospect doesn't seem to hear you the first time around, try again. First-time closes hardly ever work.

Be patient and be persistent.

The Wrap-Up

Your last 15 seconds of a call can be as critical as the first 15.

During these final moments, confirm whatever you agreed upon, check addresses and phone numbers, repeat promises you made, make sure the prospect has your name and number, and thank them for their time.

If the prospect didn't take you up on your offer, you may want to review their major objection, repeat your response, and thank them for their time. It's also a good idea to let them know that they'll be hearing from you again. Remember — your job is to build relationships and this will take more than one call.

In summary, a good farming call has the following characteristics:

- gets attention
- stimulates interest
- arouses desire
- makes the offer

Instead of thinking of a script as a sales presentation, treat it as a "persuasive interview." In an interview, you have give and take. Remember that many sales pros let prospects do 70% to 80% of the talking.

How to Use a Script

A good script is only about three minutes long. But it takes hours of preparation. This is especially true when you start farming by phone, as you'll need to practice handling objections and making the close. Over time, your prep time will decrease. But you'll always need to write your scripts thoughtfully.

Some people prefer to type their scripts on long pieces of paper. They staple the pages and put them in binders or on flip charts.

That's okay for the word-for-word scripts, but not other types. You, for example, need more flexibility.

Many real estate agents use 3-by-5 index cards. Each has one or two sentences and is color-coded. You might use colors like this:

Script Section:	Color Code:
Opening	Blue
Attention-Getting Remark, or Reason for Calling	Orange
Benefits	Pink
Objections	Yellow
Close	Green
Wrap-Up	White

You may want to slip the cards into plastic covers and keep them in an indexed three-ring binder or on a large Rolodex.

That way you can flip quickly to the section you need next. Remember, during a phone call, you don't have a lot of time. Another advantage of the cards is that they're easy to revise and update. If you change a sentence, just take out the old card and slip in the new one.

It's a good idea to keep the old ones in a file. Every so often, you can take them out to see how your approach has changed over time. It's a good way to learn.

Having the "benefits" of the home evaluation offer on a pink card in front of you as you talk helps organize your thoughts quickly during a telemarketing call.

Home Evaluation Offer

Benefits:
- assess how much equity you have to use
- better understanding of your financial net worth
- calculate probable profit if you sell
- it doesn't cost you a dime — the evaluation is free
- quick and easy — only takes an hour

In *Guerrilla Marketing: Secrets For Making Big Profits From Your Small Business,* Jay Conrad Levinson recommends typing scripts single-spaced on one page. In the first paragraph, you introduce yourself. The second is your attention-getting remark and the reason for the call. The third paragraph highlights benefits of your offer. In the fourth paragraph, you make the close.

Levinson describes the ideal telemarketing script as containing about four interest- creating comments and flowing directly to the benefits. He also suggests that you build rapport right away with questions.

It's probably best to save the computer for your files and record-keeping. Usually only word-for-word scripts are kept on computers.

Although we recommend the index cards, use what feels most comfortable to you.

Practice, Practice

If you want to come across as smooth, relaxed, and polished, you have to practice.

Think of yourself as a pianist. Behind every flawless performance lie hours of pounding away at the keyboard.

To practice, you'll need a tape recorder — just the standard $30 cassette version will do. Once you've written your script, slap in a cassette, and push the "record" button.

Read it the way you would speak it, then play it back.

First listen to the sound and quality of your voice. Is it pleasing to you? Can you spot things you'd like to improve? Ask someone else's opinion, too.

After you've critiqued the sound, think about the content. Does the script seem to flow naturally? Are there places where it's rough, or sounds a little staged?

Work those out. Then practice the script with a friend willing to role-play.

You should also draw up a list of the most common objections you'd expect.

With your partner's help, act out several scripts. Play the agent first, then switch over to the prospect.

After a few times, you'll be able to spot the weaknesses in your script and fix them. You also may want to run the script by a few other agents in your office.

As you practice, be assertive but not aggressive. Knowledgeable but not conceited. Warm but still professional.

> *Most people don't plan to fail — they fail to plan.*
> —*Anonymous*

By the time you finish, you should have developed an almost instinctive response to any possible objection or question.

Your goal is: No matter where the prospect pulls away from the conversation, you should be able to gently and persuasively get them back on track. Guiding them along with you, keep heading for the close. After a time, you'll become so good at it you won't even realize what you're doing. And neither will your prospect.

Don't Be Afraid to Change

Once we've written something, changing it can be hard. But remember your goal. And don't be afraid to keep improving what you've written.

If your scripts are not working as well as you'd like, consider asking someone in your office to evaluate them. It's probably best to choose an agent who's familiar with farming by phone.

Also think about making the following changes:

Simplify Your Offer

Sometimes we forget that what's clear to us isn't always clear to listeners.

For example, suppose you're asking:

"Mrs. Page, you've owned your home for six years. Would you be interested in a free home market evaluation?"

Now she's wondering:

"What on earth is she talking about?"

But she says:

"I don't think so. Good-bye."

Consider this approach:

"Mrs. Page, you've been in your home for six years. Wouldn't you like to know how much your home is worth today?"

Then sail straight into the benefits of knowing her home's value in the current market.

Add a Sense of Urgency

You can quote all the benefits in the world, but if you don't give prospects reasons to act upon your offer now — they never will. You

> *Be tolerant of ambiguity. Our world is full of gray areas.*

may not even notice that you failed to create a sense of urgency — until you start tallying your results!

Here are examples of offers with urgency:

Adding urgency to an offer can improve your results dramtically.

"You know, Mr. Bellflower, experts are saying that rates will only stay this low a few months. If you'd like a larger home for the same amount of money, it's important to start looking as soon as possible."

"Dr. Smith, I only ordered 30 kits. People are snapping them up. If you'd like one, you'd better order it now!"

"Ms. Lane, I'm only offering free home evaluations until the end of the month. My appointment book is filling up quickly. Could we set up an appointment for Friday?"

Most urgent offers are built around either being available only for a limited time or in limited quantities.

Strengthen the Close

There are many ways to close a call. Just an extra word or two can strengthen a close.

Instead of:

"Which would be more convenient, Wednesday or Thursday?"

Try:

"I'd love to show you what's new on the market. I can be at your home Thursday evening. Is seven o'clock all right or is eight better?"

Soften the Lead-In

If you think you may come across as too pushy, try softening your open.

Instead of leading off with a factual statement, try something more open-ended:

"Mr. Keil, have you ever thought about how you could use the equity built up in your home to make more money?"

Change the Offer

Changing the offer involves more work than any other change. But it can also make the most difference.

If a poorly received offer focuses on size, switch to finances. If it's security, go for special features. If it's convenience, try prestige.

There are hundreds and hundreds of types of offers. Try to pinpoint what works best with the majority of your farm residents.

Final Thoughts on Scripts

Now we've begun to zero in on the specifics of farming by phone.

First, we discussed the importance of writing a script. Not a word-by-word script, but more like a play-by-play — a general guideline to keep you on track.

Why should you use a script? Because a script:

1. Gives you a plan of action
2. Helps you overcome objections
3. Makes your presentation consistent
4. Helps you organize your thoughts logically
5. Helps you keep the prospects' perspective in mind
6. Produces better results

Every script needs certain elements. They are:

1. An opening
2. Attention-getting remark or reason for calling
3. Benefits of listening
4. Questions
5. Ways to overcome objections
6. A close
7. A wrap-up

Keeping elements of your scripts on index cards gives you the flexibility to quickly find the right words at the right time. You also might want to consider a one-page, single-spaced typed outline.

PRACTICE EXERCISE EIGHT

1. Take a property you have listed.
   Write down six features of the property.
   Now take each feature and convert it into two benefits.
2. Pick up your tape recorder.
   Select a sample script from Chapter 15.
   Now read the script into your tape recorder.
   Play back and analyze it.
   Make changes so that it feels more natural to you.

CHAPTER 9

The Opening

> *Persistent people begin their success*
> *where others end in failure.*
>
> *— Anonymous*

Getting started on the right foot is important, especially if you don't want a receiver banged down in your ear.

In the first 15 seconds of a farm prospecting call, you have to capture the prospect's attention, identify yourself and your firm, give the reason for your call, and prevent your prospect from hanging up.

The Critical First 15 Seconds

During the first 15 seconds of a call you should:
1. *Use the prospect's name.*
2. *Introduce yourself and the firm you are representing.*
3. *Ask for a moment of the prospect's time.*

Some clever salespeople try to weasel their way into a call by avoiding saying who they are and why they called.

This only frustrates prospects.

Today telemarketing experts agree: Identify yourself right off the top. Don't try to lure a prospect into talking to you, especially when you want a mutually trusting relationship to develop. If you trick them into talking to you, how can they ever believe you again?

Use Your Prospect's Name

Almost the first word out of your mouth should be the prospect's name.

If a child answers the phone, ask for Mr. Smith or Mrs. Smith. Pick one or the other, but don't let the child do it for you.

More often than not, you won't be sure who answers. A good way to start is by asking, "Mr. Smith?" with an uplifted voice.

If it is Mr. Smith, he'll say, "Speaking."

If it's not, the person will either go find him or tell you he's not in. In that case, you may ask to speak to Mrs. Smith.

Using the prospect's name as a question makes you sound upbeat and enthusiastic.

If the prospect's name is hard to pronounce, fumble your way through it. Chances are that he or she will correct you and when they do, write it down phonetically so you can keep referring to it throughout the call.

Introduce Yourself and Your Firm

As soon as you establish that you're talking to the right person, introduce yourself. Usually the best way is to give your name, then the name of your company.

If your company has a strong advertising campaign or is known for a particular quality, you may want to mention it. But avoid any trite sayings like, "This is Joe Jones with Smith Realty, the sell-more-homes people."

Only introduce your company first if your personal name is unusual or hard to pronounce. In that case, you might also add a little phrase to help someone remember it.

For example, you might say, "I'm with Dickinson Realty and my name is Jeffrey Christmas — just like the holiday."

But keep it short.

Your greetings should be friendly, warm, and casual, without a hint that you're trying to sell something.

Your tone should also be purposeful and direct, but not aggressive. Remember that you establish the tone of the conversation by what you say and how you say it.

Ask for a Moment of Your Prospect's Time

With introductions out of the way, you repeat the prospect's name, then politely tell him or her how long you expect the call to take.

Here are some convenient introductory phrases:

"Mr. Michaels, do you have a few minutes?"

"Mrs. Williams, is this a convenient time to talk for a minute or two?"

"Mr. Smith, could you give me a few moments of your time?"

Almost everyone will say yes. If they don't, ask for a time when you can call back. They'll probably ask what you want to talk about and, in a second, you'll be into your script.

At this point, some overeager salespeople try to prolong the pleasantries with "How are you today?" While some people will disagree, I think this is a fatal error. If a stranger is calling, I know they really don't care how I am and I don't want to tell them. All I want to know is why they called.

Of course, if you've been farming a turf for awhile and know your prospects personally, some pleasantries would certainly be appropriate.

Boiling it down to the basics, the first few seconds of each call should go like this.

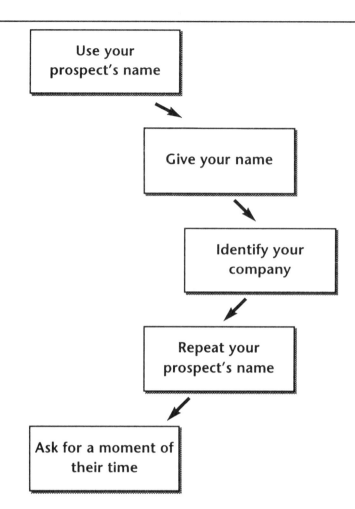

What to Say Next

Now comes the critical moment. If you come across as wanting to sell the prospect something, forget it. You haven't even started the persuasion process.

But if you can lead the prospect to believe that you want to talk about something important to him or her, they're likely to pay attention.

There are a number of ways to start prospecting conversations. Usually you try to do one of two things: (1) convince him or her of the benefits of listening or (2) establish rapport.

The approach you choose depends on your personality, the prospect and the offer you're making. If your goal is to get to know your prospects better, building rapport is good.

But if you want them to take you up on an offer built around something like financial security or a safe home, go for the benefits-of-listening approach.

Here are a few suggestions.

The Benefits-of-Listening Approach

This approach takes you directly into the heart of the offer. Lead off with your strongest benefit. You might begin like this:

"I'd like to talk to you about reducing your monthly mortgage payment."

"If you'd like to start having your money work for you instead of your landlord . . ."

"I'm calling to tell you about something that could give you and your family financial security."

For a softer approach, try a thought-provoking question such as:

"Have you ever wondered what you would do if . . . ?"

"Have you ever stopped to think about . . . ?"

"Do you want your family . . . ?"

If you decide to plunge right into benefits, be sure to describe them in terms of how they can help improve the prospect's life.

Give your prospects a sense of power. Offer them an opportunity to take decisive, positive action. Help them see the difference your offer can make in their lives, and you'll see a difference in your life, too.

> *How much you care matters more than how much you know.*

Some agents prefer a two-step approach. They start with a rapport-building remark, then move onto benefits.

The Rapport-Building Approach

Here are some hints for rapport-building openings.

Refer to Your Mailing(s) — Many real estate agents send a regular newsletter or other mailings to their farms. If this is the case, you can refer to them in the first few moments of the call.

For example, if last month's newsletter had a big spread on home improvements, mention it. Then lead into a related offer — perhaps a free market evaluation based on some remodeling you spotted while driving by.

But be sure that you mention the newsletter for a reason. Don't just use it to enhance your credibility. Remember, your prospects don't care nearly as much about your credibility as they do about what you can do for them.

Refer to an Ad Campaign — If you're handling a new development, condominium complex, or vacation time-sharing concept that has received extensive media attention, ask if they've seen the ads or TV spots.

Maybe you can mention a catchy phrase or good-looking footage that will help the prospect remember it.

But quickly follow up with something more substantial. Avoid such generalities as,

"Have you ever considered owning a second home?"

Instead, try something such as,

"Did you know that despite the recent tax revision, there are still considerable tax benefits to owning a second home?"

Mention a Referral — Nothing opens more doors for you than a good referral. You can't start off any better than,

"You know Andrew Thompkins, don't you? He suggested that I give you a call."

Immediately you create the first link in building your relationship with the prospect.

Announce a New Listing — All of us are curious about our neighbors and neighborhoods. If you have a new listing, call nearby neighbors and let them know you're handling it (see Chapter 15 for a sample script). You can take the opportunity to ask if they know any prospective buyers.

You also can invite them to upcoming open houses.

Make a Personal Reference — If you know anything at all about the person you're calling or their home, use that information at the beginning of the call. You could try something like,

"I read in the local paper the other day that you recently were promoted — congratulations!"

Or,

"I drove by the house the other day and saw the new paint job. It looks terrific!"

The more genuine and complimentary you can be, the better.

Refer to a Recent Neighborhood Event — Use these openings with special offers — for example, the "Home Crime-Stoppers" kit we mentioned a few chapters back. Your lead-in might be,

"Were you aware of the recent rash of robberies on the 500 and 600 blocks of Rocky Road?"

Offers like these tie you into the neighborhood and strengthen the perception of you as part of the community. And that's what you want.

In certain cases, however, be careful. You don't want people to think you're capitalizing on someone else's misfortune. Life insurance salespeople, for example, have garnered bad reputations for passing out business cards at funerals.

<u>Ask a Favor</u> — Some sales experts recommend that you start off by asking the prospect for a favor — for example,

"I wonder if you could do me a favor?"

This approach is hard for prospects to refuse. But it can come across as mildly deceptive. Instead of using it at the top of the conversation, we recommend falling back on it when an obstinate prospect refuses to budge. When you've given up and see no hope of changing the prospect's mind, ask them to do you a favor and tell you what you did wrong.

Sparking Their Interest

Once you've captured a prospect's attention, the next step is converting attention into interest. Prospects become interested in an offer when you demonstrate how it can benefit them personally.

Remember that as soon as you identify yourself on a call, the prospect starts wondering about you. They ask themselves: *Why should I listen? What is this all about? Is this legitimate? Is this agent sincere?*

Most often, you'll be greeted politely, but with a hint of suspicion.

It's not hard to dispel this type of suspicion. The right tone of voice and the right words can go a long way. Just remember to stay focused on what the prospect needs and wants.

Emphasize the Greatest Benefits

As a real estate professional, you point out to prospects what you perceive as the biggest advantages of your offer.

Often agents start conversations by emphasizing financial benefits such as lower monthly mortgage payments, moving up to a larger home, or capitalizing on the appreciation of the prospect's current residence.

Repetition can actually increase your offer's attractiveness, so don't be afraid to make the same offer to the same homes more than once.

But remember that financial benefits aren't as motivating to some prospects as they are to others. Just as some of us like jazz and others prefer rock and roll, different offers appeal to different prospects. See which offers appeal most to your farm residents.

And when you find a winner, stick with it. Don't be afraid to make the same offer to the same homes more than once. Many of your prospects will forget the offer as soon as they read or hear it. Repetition actually increases your offer's attractiveness, as long as prospects don't become bored. Usually a prospect needs to hear a piece of information five or six times before boredom sets in.

Also don't be surprised if an offer that works perfectly one day stops working the next. People are not always predictable. Just try a new offer.

One final note: While you generally want to use your biggest benefit at the beginning of the call, it's often best to save your second biggest benefit for the end — especially if the first benefit generated interest.

Saving a benefit for the end of a call can greatly strengthen your close.

Keep Your Opening Short and Direct

In addition to describing the benefits a prospect will enjoy by taking up your offer, your opening needs to be short and to the point. Why? Because people lose interest — fast.

And the minute they lose interest, you've lost them. So keep on target and lead the prospect through a logical sequence that ends with your offer.

Stress How You Can Help Them

As a friendly persuader, you not only want to encourage prospects to act, you also want them to ask you to help.

But don't play yourself up too much. Build in little motivators, with things like using the word "we." Or toss in a phrase about how "I helped your neighbors down the street." Or "You know, the Jones got wonderful financing."

Select words and ideas that build you up without making you sound boastful.

It helps if you assume from the beginning that the prospect is going to use your services. Couch all your language in those terms. It's simple, subtle and it works.

Get a Dialogue Going

Real estate is very personal. Selling it isn't like selling drill bits.

Every homeowner, every renter, every absentee owner has her or his own perspective on your business. They also have stories: how they bought their first home, why they bought their current home, what kind of home they want in the future. They can tell you about the helpful or the harmful mortgage broker . . . the appraiser who down-valued their home . . . the loan officer who got them a terrific rate.

Ask them about these stories. You'll learn a lot about them as individuals and about your farm in general. Talk to your prospects and let them know that their stories are important to you.

Keep your own stories for sharing with your friends.

Explain the Advantages of Owning a Home

Here are some very practical reasons why people should own homes.

Protection Against Inflation

How many times have you heard, "If only I had bought that house way back when?"

Real estate investments over the years have kept pace with, or in many areas even exceeded, the inflation rate.

Just the other day, I heard about lots which sold for $5,000 when the land was being developed. Ten years later, the average lot price is $150,000. Quite a dramatic return, isn't it?

While homes generally aren't sold as investments, one logical reason for owning a home (versus renting) is its appreciation.

Tax Benefits

With Congress closing many tax loopholes, home ownership has remained a significant tax write-off for millions of Americans.

This argument is especially effective with renters, many of whom would be surprised at the tax savings if they could deduct mortgage interest.

And when people move up into larger homes — with larger mortgages — interest deductions also increase.

Low Initial Investment

While most lenders prefer 20% down, many times a buyer can purchase a home for as little as 10% (or even 5%) down. Even that percentage can be reduced with seller financing.

Putting $9,000 down (10% of a $90,000 house) or $850 a month sounds a lot more palatable than paying almost $100,000 for a home.

Huge Potential Market

In Japan, homes are handed down through generations. This greatly shrinks the housing market.

In the United States, on the other hand, houses change hands almost as quickly as cars. Here people are more interested in getting the equity out of their homes than in handing down a heritage. That creates a lot more real estate activity.

Personal Independence

Having your own home gives you personal and, to a degree, financial freedom. You can decorate it, add on, take away, put in a garden, and basically do whatever you like as long as you don't violate local statutes.

Home ownership offers many advantages. Explain these benefits to your prospect.

A long time ago, I was renting a small stucco home with an ancient kitchen featuring enormous solid wood cabinets and a wonderful tile sink.

Four years after I moved in, the owner sold the property.

The new owner thought my lovely, character-filled kitchen was an atrocity. One day he told me that he intended to modernize it. I asked him not to. I came home from a trip a month later to find a kitchen with cheap butcher block cabinets and fluorescent lighting.

I decided on the spot that it was time to own my own home.

Forced Savings

Home ownership is a wonderful way to have a place to live and build equity for the future.

Paying rent just puts money in a landlord's pocket. Owning a home puts money in your own pocket.

It's a painless, easy way to prepare for retirement, especially considering that people over 55 don't have to pay taxes on their first $100,000 in profit from their homes.

Flexibility

Often a big objection to owning a home is the lack of flexibility. Some people think that ownership ties them down.

Homeowners can always rent out their homes — and have you manage the rental! Some rentals even generate positive cash flow.

Remember, Americans usually move once every four to five years. Owning a house really isn't an albatross.

Trade-In Value

When we trade in cars, we usually trade up to bigger and better models. The same is true with houses. Of course, tax law encourages us to do so.

It's a lot easier to move up to a dream house by "trading up" than saving pennies in hopes of accumulating a huge down payment.

Describe the Unique Features of a Home

Now that we've reviewed the advantages of home ownership, let's move on to why people pick certain homes.

The primary reason: people always look for larger homes.

Consider it the result of the "law of rising expectations." It's human nature to want something bigger or better than what we have.

In looking for a home, the first thing people notice is, of course, the price. Generally, they have a fixed idea of what they believe they can afford to pay.

But when a home wins their hearts, it's because of the benefits provided by certain features — buyers look for these benefits and are willing to pay for them.

Popular features include:
- location
- brick patios
- landscaping
- skylights
- tile or shake roofs
- hardwood floors
- fireplaces
- large closets
- swimming pools
- picture windows
- modern baths
- modern eat-in kitchens
- laundry rooms
- views

When prospective buyers walk through a home, features like these conjure up dreams. English Tudor architecture may stir fantasies of kingship. A pool could represent a commitment to get in shape. An eat-in kitchen could be a symbol of family togetherness.

People buy homes because their hearts tell them to. The things that move their hearts include love, security, recreation, economy, privacy, warmth, convenience, investment, and the very human desire to own.

Because everybody falls in love with different houses for different reasons, your toughest job is figuring out how to make that magical moment happen for each and every one of your buyers.

The Value of Referrals

Listings are the bread and butter of a real estate professional. Referrals are the steak and potatoes.

Referrals can give you more productive leads than anything else. Farming is particularly good for generating leads. People in a social group or neighborhood tend to know and talk to each other. If one person finds an agent they like, they're likely to recommend the agent to others. Never minimize the importance of referrals in sales, and never forget to ask for them.

In fact, every time you talk to someone who is not in the market to buy or sell a home, ask if they have a friend, relative, or neighbor who is.

Referrals work for you in two ways. They:

1. Provide the names of prequalified prospects.
2. Increase your credibility by establishing an immediate personal link to a prospect through the mutual friend or colleague.

Referrals Get Good Names for New Prospects

If someone gives you a prospect's name, it's likely that the prospect has mentioned buying or selling. Maybe they said something casually at a party or at work. Maybe the person knows the prospect just had a baby and needs more room. Whatever the reason, the person making the referral thinks you can help the prospect.

If you maintain warm, positive relationships with clients, you should find referrals making up a larger percentage of your business each year.

But even when you have a stable income base, set aside time for prospecting. This will keep your skills sharp and keep you up on marketplace trends.

Conventional sales wisdom is that every time you close, get three referrals. Some real estate professionals ask their clients to call the referrals after the deal closes. Then they follow up.

> 66
> *Your reputation is as much a part of you as anything else.*
> 99

When a home wins a buyers heart, it is because of the benefits provided by certain features.

If a person can't think of any referrals, prod their memory with questions like,

"What clubs do you belong to?"

and

"Is there anyone in your club who might be interested in a new home?"

If they're don't want to call themselves, that's okay. Just ask if it's all right to use their name when you call.

And remember, once you have a name, call as soon as possible. Chances are that your client has been talking to them about the home they're buying or selling — you want to strike while the impression is fresh.

Also, don't overlook the possibility of referrals from someone who just stops by the office.

One real estate agent got caught up in a messy divorce where the wife tried to list the home. It turned out she couldn't give it to him on her own, but her attorney was interested in income property. The next day, the agent signed up the attorney as a client.

Remember that every person you meet knows a couple hundred or more people whom you don't know. That adds up to a lot of potential clients.

Referrals Strengthen Your Presentation

Using a referral with a prospect strengthens your presentation by creating immediate rapport, giving you specific examples to discuss and increasing your credibility.

<u>Building Rapport</u> — Using a referral to begin a call is great. Right from the start, you and the prospect have a mutual friend in common.

Remember the old adage: It's not what you know but who you know that gets you places.

Having someone refer you means that they valued your service. That gives you a good feeling. And that good feeling will come through in extra self-confidence radiating from your voice when you call the prospect.

<u>Giving You Specific Examples</u> — With a referral, you have a specific example of services that you provided. You can tell the prospect exactly how you helped the person who made the referral and why that person thinks you could help the prospect. The referral gives you a strong starting point for building a relationship.

A referral also provides accountability. The prospect may think that you'll report back to the person who made the referral. They'll probably treat you differently than if you called out of the blue.

Referrals also can help during prospecting calls. If you get into a tight spot, you can always refer to someone else's situation. For example, they might say,

"We just can't afford it right now."

You could respond,

"I understand why you feel that way. So did the Witherspoons, until they saw how easy it was to use the equity in their home to move into a much roomier one. They said they never would have dreamed it possible to be living the way they are now."

Any debater knows that specifics always strengthen an argument. When we hear about good things happening to other people, we like to think they could happen to us, too.

Keeping track of stories to use on prospecting calls is a good idea. Jot down a few to slip into your script binder. They could work wonders.

Building Credibility — People in your farm can't go to the library and look up statistics on local Realtors® to see who does the most business.

I don't think that would matter much anyway.

What people look for is a real estate agent who puts their interests first — the kind of agent who takes the time to give them personal, one-to-one attention. You can't put a yardstick to this kind of service. But you can make a very effective statement about it through word of mouth. Some salespeople ask clients to sign letters of referral. They prepare them, then whip them out and ask for a signature when the sale is concluded.

Recommendation letters can be useful during face-to-face interviews. You can leave them for prospects to study. It's a good idea to carry five to ten recommendation letters in your briefcase at all times.

When you're farming by phone, though, letters won't work.

However, a reasonable variation is to ask a prospect if he or she would like to talk to some of your clients. Of course, you should clear this with your clients first. Try to match up the prospect with a client in a similar situation. For example, if the prospect is a woman looking for her first home, find a client in a similar situation. And don't give out any client's name too often.

Try this approach if you have a prospect right on the edge of doing business with you and you need a little extra incentive. Simply offering to put prospects in touch with former clients implies that you can be trusted.

So when you farm by phone, have six to ten phone numbers of clients who will give you recommendations.

If you give out a recommendation number, call the prospect back the next day to see what happened. Then use the opportunity to repeat your offer.

Finally, promise yourself that you'll get three referrals at the close of every sale. Start building your farm the smart way.

Building Trust

Buying or selling real estate is about trust and relationships. Your relationship with a prospect begins the first time you speak together on the phone. One of your primary goals is to get the prospect to trust you.

The secret of turning prospects into clients is to cultivate their trust in you.

You achieve this through having the right facts, figures, and approach, as well as through your tone of voice and choice of words.

With a child, trust is instinctive. With most adults, it's something you have to win.

With prospects, you win trust by showing that you understand their needs, that you have the ability to meet their needs, and that you're genuinely interested in their best interests. Sound familiar?

Building trust requires care because small missteps can destroy it in an instant.

For example, if you're caught in small white lie on the first call, there won't be many others.

Or, if you promise to do something and don't follow through, trust breaks down. You may think they won't remember, but they will. And they'll resent it.

Trust is always earned.

Final Points

During the first 15 seconds of a prospecting call:

- Use the prospect's name.

- Identify yourself and your company.

- Repeat the prospect's name.

- Be courteous and let them know how long the call will take.

Now you have to choose between a rapport-building or benefits of listening approach. Either can work well. Your choice depends on your own personality, the person you're speaking to, and the nature of your offer.

When you can, start a call with a referral. Referrals can:

- Expand your farm directory by giving you new names for prospecting.

- Strengthen your presentation by creating rapport at the beginning of the call, giving you specific examples to use during it, and in general increasing your credibility.

PRACTICE EXERCISE NINE

1. Work out how to introduce yourself.
   Decide if you want to add on an identifying phrase after the company name.
2. Go through the sample scripts and study the opening remarks. Mark whether they represent a benefits-of-listening or rapport-building approach.
3. Considering your farm and the demographics of residents, list what you would consider the three most significant advantages of home ownership.
4. Right now, think of three people you can call and ask for referrals. Do it.
   Don't forget to write them thank you notes (see *How To Farm Successfully — By Mail* for sample).

CHAPTER 10

Questions Keep the Conversation Going

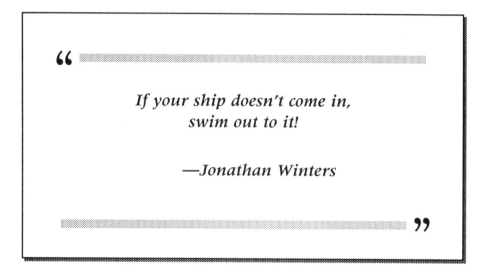

> *If your ship doesn't come in,*
> *swim out to it!*
>
> —Jonathan Winters

Throughout a prospecting conversation, it's important to keep up the momentum. Because you initiated the call, that's your responsibility. Don't expect the prospect to start chatting merrily.

To break down a prospect's initial resistance and create a warm and inviting atmosphere over the phone, nothing works better than questions.

Questions take some of the burden of talking off you and put it on the prospect. You get to know each other, which is what you want.

How to Spot a Potential Seller or Buyer

After a call's initial pleasantries, your first goal is to find out if the person you're talking to is a genuine prospect.

You can't tell just by asking, "Are you interested in selling your home?" or "Do you plan to buy a home any time soon?"

Here the rule of thumb is simple: Virtually every adult in this country uses, buys, or sells real estate. Therefore, your prospects are limitless. If someone isn't interested today, try again in six months or a year. Keep working your farm until it pays the returns you want.

You can tell how good a prospect is by asking questions. Too many agents give up as soon as they hear a prospect say, "I'm not interested."

If you take the path of least resistance, don't expect to become a real estate star. The prospect might be interested; he or she just might not know it yet.

You could respond to

"I'm not interested"

with anything from

"Have you ever considered that . . . ?"

to a simple and direct,

"Why?"

At the start of the call, you primarily want to get the conversation going. Don't think to yourself, "I've got to find out if this person is interested in buying or selling a home." Think instead, "I'd like to get to know this person. Someday he or she could become a client."

If you've stated your reason for calling and the listener doesn't seem interested but is willing to continue the conversation, keep it going with questions.

What Questions Can Do for You

Questions work for a number of reasons. The most important is that they encourage a two-way conversation.

Help You Stay Out of an Argument

If the prospect says something you don't agree with, find out why they feel that way. Ferreting out the reason could tell you a lot about the prospect.

Then validate the prospect's feelings. Don't think that the whole world has to agree with you. Give people room to express themselves and they'll feel good about their relationship with you. In the long run, being positive with someone will take you a lot further than being negative. Remember that on farming calls, what matters most is how the prospect thinks and feels, not how you think and feel.

Keep You from Talking Too Much

By asking questions, you reduce the danger that you'll monopolize the conversation. Too many salespeople talk too much. Questions protect you from this.

Let You Get to Know Each Other

When you ask questions as a real estate professional, you should cover the basics. For example:

- Does the prospect own or rent a home?
- How many people live in the house?
- Is the prospect single, married or living with someone?
- How many children live there?
- How old are the children?
- What kind of work does the prospect do?
- How long has he or she lived in the home?
- Does the prospect tend to move every few years or so?
- What does he or she like about the neighborhood?
- What does he or she dislike about the neighborhood?
- What does the prospect like about the home?
- Does the prospect have financial resources outside of his or her employment?
- Would the prospect someday like to invest in real estate?

Phrase these questions so they don't come across sounding threatening, but merely as "I'd like to get to know you better."

Questions like these help fill in the gaps in the prospect's file. To know what kind of home a prospect might be interested in, you have to know what kind of lifestyle they have and what they value.

Once you have a handle on a prospect's lifestyle and interests, you'll know your best sales strategy.

Help the Prospect Clarify His or Her Thinking

You can use questions to help a prospect think through an issue. Many prospects will not have the information you do about the real estate market and the value of their home. Some won't even know what their options are until you tell them.

It's easiest to tell people things through questions. Questions encourage rapport and sharing. They demonstrate your concern for helping the prospect make the best decision.

Help People See What They Really Want

When I began looking for a home, I wanted a fixer-upper on a big lot, with room for a pool, lots of windows and at least one large tree. I wound up with a rebuilt house on a big lot where I can never put in a pool, almost a forest of trees, and skylights.

The lesson is: People seldom know what they really want — at least when it comes to buying a home.

As you get to know someone, you'll develop a sense of what really matters to them and what doesn't.

Someone may think they don't want to sell their home, but if they could buy that big white Cape Cod down the street — and pay only $50 more a month — they'd do it in a flash.

Your responsibility is to make prospects aware of real estate opportunities about to pass them by.

Make the Prospect Feel Important

Having interviewed hundreds of people, I know how flattering it is to have someone ask you questions about yourself.

Very rarely does anyone reply, "It's none of your business."

If someone does, don't take it personally.

People like to talk about themselves. They like to tell the story of how they found that special house and of all the trouble they went through to get it.

Listen when prospects talk to you, and you'll never be wondering what on earth to say next. The person who asks questions is the person who never stops learning.

It's trite but true — the more you learn, the more you earn.

When you ask questions, you show your prospect that you care about what they think. This makes them feel important.

Two Kinds of Questions

A long time ago, Socrates said that you can sell more by asking people than by telling them. Basically you can ask two types of questions: (1) open-ended and (2) close-ended.

Open-Ended Questions

Open-ended questions can't be answered with a yes or no. They're probing questions which require a prospect to give you information.

Used to keep conversations flowing, open-ended questions start with words like these:

- Who
- What
- Where
- When
- Why
- Which
- How

Reporters use open-ended questions frequently.

By posing questions certain ways, you can direct a prospect's thinking. But the prospect will never know it.

If you ask a question in a voice filled with interest and enthusiasm, it's much more likely that the prospect will answer back the same way. If you pose a question matter-of-factly, expect a crisp and clear response.

More often than not, you'll probably ask open-ended questions at the beginning of a call. Remember that your goal is to build relationships — and open-ended questions are a great way to do that.

When you're asking these questions, don't be afraid to feed back a little information about yourself — not boastful information, but the kind that friends exchange when they're getting to know each other.

If you open up, people will open up to you. Don't spill out your problems, but let your personality come across. And you'll see others showing you their true colors, too.

Close-Ended Questions

Close-ended questions can be answered with yes or no. Use these when you want more control in a conversation or need to get the prospect back on track.

Often in telemarketing, close-ended questions are used to take sales orders, confirm information, or set up visits. They're highly structured and sharply reduce rapport-building.

Close-ended questions begin with words like:

- Is
- Do
- Has
- Can
- Are

Close-ended questions have several useful variations — the paraphrase and the tie-down.

<u>The Paraphrase</u> — When you ask this type of question, you echo back the prospect's own words.

An example of a paraphrase question.

Agent

In your income bracket, I'm surprised you haven't considered the possibility of investing in rental properties. May I ask why?

Prospect

Because of all the headaches of managing them.

Agent

Suppose you found a way to enjoy all the financial benefits of rental properties without the headache of managing them. Then wouldn't you agree that rental properties are a sound investment for someone like yourself?

Similar to matching the prospect's voice, repeating their words increases your rapport and facilitates communication. People love their own words. And they think just the way they talk.

The Tie-Down — Sales experts and trial attorneys use these a lot. With tie-downs, you don't leave much room for variation in answers.

You can spot a tie-down in phrases like these:

- Aren't you?
- Don't you agree?
- Wouldn't it?
- Haven't you?
- Won't you?
- Isn't it?
- Can't you?

Tie-downs are popular for reducing sales resistance, and they work because they help people see things in a different light. The beauty of them is that if you say something, the prospect may doubt it. If the prospect says it, it becomes true.

In addition, tie-downs help your prospects say the one word you want to hear — "yes."

When to Use Open- and Close-Ended Questions

The best way to farm by phone successfully is to intertwine open- and close-ended questions. Use the former to build your relationships and warm up the conversation. Use the latter to keep the conversation on target and zero in on your close.

If you start a conversation with close-ended questions, you'll regret it; because if you give someone a chance to say no before you present your arguments, the odds are two to one that they will.

At the beginning, use open-ended questions. Find out how the prospect really feels about your offer. Figure out the prospect's situation from their responses. Then step up the pace of the call and zero in on the close with one or two tie-down, close-ended questions.

Switching back and forth between open- and close-ended questions is the best way to keep your conversation flowing while maintaining control.

To sharpen your skills at picking out close- and open-ended questions, try your hand at this list.

1. Have you lived in this area long? *Close (C)*

2. Why did your family choose this neighborhood? *Open (O)*

3. Don't you think this is a wonderful neighborhood for raising children? *(C)*

4. Do you ever take your children to the nearby city parks? *(C)*

5. How large is your home? *(O)*

6. Is it bigger than your previous house? *(C)*

7. What do you look for in a house? *(O)*

8. Are you originally from this area? *(C)*

9. If you could move anywhere in the city, where would it be? *(O)*

10. With interest rates dropping so quickly, wouldn't you agree that now is a good time to buy? *(C)*

11. What do you like best about your home? *(O)*

12. What things would you change about it? *(O)*

13. Do you believe that real estate is a good investment? *(C)*

14. Have you considered the tax benefits of owning a second home? *(C)*

15. Why is it important for you to own your own home? *(O)*

To see how easy it is to switch from close- to open-ended questions, look at these examples:

Close: *When you look for a home, are there any special features that are important to you?*

Open: *When you look for a home, what special features are most important to you?*

Close: *Is it that your family must have three bedrooms?*

Open: *How critical is it that your family have three bedrooms?*

Close: *Did you use a Realtor® to find your current home?*

Open: *How did you find your current home?*

Close: *Do you like colonial-style homes?*

Open: *What style of home do you and your wife prefer?*

Sometimes you'll want to get the prospect back on track — and keep him or her from wandering too far from the subject of your open-ended questions. In this case, switch from open- to close-ended questions:

Open: *When, during the week, is the best time for us to get together?*

Close: *Would Thursday evening be a good time for us to meet?*

Open: *What kind of people do you think would be interested in this offer?*

Close:	*Do you know anyone who might be interested in this offer?*
Open:	*What did your last Realtor® not do for you?*
Close:	*Do you feel you got adequate service from your former Realtor®?*
Open:	*What advantages do you see in renting?*
Close:	*Do you want to be renting nine months from now?*

Learn to Listen

Listening well is an art that too few of us bother to practice.

If you want to succeed in real estate farming by phone, learning to listen is important.

To listen well, you have to be strong enough to let the other person talk.

That sounds easier than it is. It involves more than learning to keep your mouth shut. It also involves putting your ego to rest, at least during the call.

But if you improve the way you listen, you'll also improve your number of appointments.

What to Listen For

Listen for two things: (1) the content of what the person is saying and (2) the feeling behind the content.

People reveal their feelings in the words they choose, their vocal inflections, their pauses, and the sincerity they convey.

Inflections are key to unlocking feelings. Take, for example, the following sentences:

Depending on the vocal inflection, the meaning changes. If the emphasis is on "don't want," probe for the real reason.

> *We are generally more persuaded by the reasons we discover ourselves than be those given to us by others.*
>
> —Blaise Pascal

I DON'T WANT to buy a new home.

I don't want TO BUY a new home.

I don't want to buy A NEW HOME.

Listen not only to what people say, but also HOW they say it.

If "to buy" is underscored, maybe they'd like a house, but don't want the burden of owning one.

If the voice rises on the words "a new home," the person may be feeling a lot of financial pressure.

But maybe not. They may feel pressure that they interpret as financial when it's not. Maybe talking to you for a few minutes could change their perception.

One area where you need to be a little hard of hearing is when the prospect says no. "No" and "yes" can mean many things.

Never take what people say at face value. Look for what they're really saying. When a prospect says they want a big house, they may really just want each child to have their own room. Or they may want a big house to impress colleagues at work. Or enough bedrooms to accommodate a steady stream of visitors. Listen well and try to figure out the reason behind the reason.

Along with listening well goes not being afraid of silence. During any call, silence can be a wonderful way to cut through a maze of words and get to the heart of the matter.

Most of us feel uncomfortable with silence. But silence can be your friend.

To a prospect, your silence can be a sign of understanding and patience.

For some people, answering certain questions can be difficult. They may need some time to come up with answers. Give them that time. Don't interrupt.

Only a big person knows how to give others attention and concern. Listening well is not a passive activity. It's full of dynamics that can help increase your commissions.

Good listeners give encouraging feedback. Sometimes they offer reassurances, with warm, positive words or even silence. Other times they encourage prospects through confirming their viewpoints and agreeing with them. Asking questions demonstrates your interest in a prospect.

Good questions start with phrases like these:
- What do you mean by . . .
- What would you need to . . .
- What's the difference for you . . .
- What would that look like . . .
- What would you accomplish . . .
- What are you saying . . .
- How would you . . .

> 66
>
> *The most important thing in communication is to hear what isn't being said.*
>
> —*Anonymous*
>
> 99

- Why is that important to you . . .
- Tell me a little about . . .
- Give me some idea of . . .
- Fill me in on . . .

Good responses start with phrases like these:

- I see your point . . .
- I know what you mean . . .
- I understand . . .

During your calls, look for verbal hints that reveal what the prospect is like. Jot them down. File them away. Over time, you'll find you're becoming a pretty good judge of human character.

The more you know about someone, the better you'll be able to guess at what point they'll enter the real estate market.

Don't worry about trying to carry on brilliant conversations. Focus on listening instead.

Helpful Transitions

Making smooth transitions, especially in response to a prospect's objections, is critical to successful farming by phone. Transitions can help a conversation stay on the right tone and keep it moving. They're especially useful when a prospect raises an objection, as they allow you to show sympathy for it.

"I understand" or "That is a good point" are transitions that indicate you're listening, but not necessarily that you agree. Other good words are "appreciate," "agree," and "know." They can make you sound warm and friendly.

More useful phrases include: "Sounds good, doesn't it?" and "What do you think?" You also can transition by paraphrasing what the prospect is saying. For example, you could say something like, "Dr. Worth, based on what you've told me about your home, I believe that I can help you . . ."

Weed little negatives such as "don't understand," "dislike," and "don't you know" out of your speech and you'll find them disappearing from your mind, too.

Final Points

Useful for softening a conversation's tone, digging out relevant information, and steering the prospect where you want them to go, your questions should begin right after you capture a prospect's attention.

Asking questions is good because it:

1. Keeps you out of arguments
2. Prevents you from talking too much
3. Helps you get to know a prospect
4. Clarifies a prospect's thinking
5. Helps prospects see what they really want
6. Makes prospects feel important.

During farming calls, you ask either open- or close-ended questions.

Open-ended questions give a prospect room to respond. They start with words like "what" or "who" or the powerful "why." They're good for finding out more about the prospect and for building rapport.

When you want more control over the conversation, use close-ended questions. Geared towards yes or no answers, these questions are usually asked toward the end of the call leading up to the close.

Often telephone pros vary the two types of questions to give rhythm and pace to a call. Otherwise, a string of open-ended questions can sound like an interrogation, and a cluster of close-ended ones makes the agent seem pushy.

Whatever types of questions you ask, remember one thing: **listen to the response.** All too often we miss clues as to how someone really feels and thinks because we take their words at face value. Tune in to the feeling behind the words and you'll be heading in the right direction.

PRACTICE EXERCISE TEN

1. Write 10 open-ended questions and 10 close-ended ones.
   Figure out how and when you could use each during a prospecting call.
2. The next time you're involved in a conversation with a friend, family member or co-worker, practice listening.
   Cut back on what you say and practice empathetic listening.
   Does your listening make a difference?
3. Practice asking questions in all kinds of situations.
   If you're in a store, ask a clerk a question about a product.
   If you're in a restaurant, ask the waiter questions about the food.
   How do people respond to your questions?
4. Listen to the questions you ask during business calls.
   In which category do most of them belong?
   Under what conditions do you use each type?
   Do you think you could be more effective if you changed your questioning strategy?

CHAPTER 11

How to Handle Objections

> *Peoples's best successes come after their disappointments.*
>
> —Henry Ward Beecher

Remember that an objection is not the same as rejection.

Be glad when someone raises an objection. It means you've gotten to first base. They're at least willing to talk to you and to listen to what you have to say.

As we said earlier, hardly anyone will flat-out say "no" or even worse, hang up on you. People are just too polite. So they offer excuses, or "objections."

To top real estate professionals, an objection really says, "You haven't convinced me yet. What else do you have to add?"

Most of us resist change and prefer the status quo. When someone proposes a new idea, our initial response is almost invariably, "no." But give us a few logical arguments and some strong incentives, and many of us will at least consider change . . . especially when we're persuaded that it's in our best interests.

Basic Guidelines

When handling an objection, remember that how you respond is just as important as what you say.

If you reveal even the slightest trace of hostility, a prospect will instantly pick it up.

Be pleasant, positive, and a good conversationalist. Avoid negative words or attitudes.

To see how positive you are naturally, tape record a conversation with a family member or friend.

Listen to it looking for negative words and phrases. Most of us who consistently express negative attitudes are not aware of it.

If you find you're more negative than you'd like, start pausing before you speak. Mentally switch gears and make the effort to look on the bright side.

When you're talking on the phone, do the same thing. If you bad-mouth your competitors or are unfailingly critical, the only person the prospect will think poorly of is you.

If the prospect offers an objection, it's easy to respond negatively. Avoid that temptation. Always respond positively.

It's also good to give prospects choices. When you ask for an appointment, give them a choice of times. They'll feel more in control.

When you come head-to-head with an objection, follow these guidelines:

1. Listen to the objection fully.

2. If you don't understand it or want more information, ask a question.

3. Bridge the objection with a transition.

4. Respond to the objection.

5. Make sure the prospect understands your response.

6. Move right on.

One key to handling objections is to answer them fully but not allow them to derail your conversation. Keep steering towards the next benefit of your offer. Don't give the prospect time to keep digging into the objection — unless the prospect insists. But always try to maintain your conversation's momentum.

The Six Most Common Objections

You probably think that if you make 300 calls, you'll run into 300 different reasons why people don't want what you're offering.

That won't happen. Your daily Call Response Tally will show the same objections cropping up over and over.

Most objections in real estate farming center around six themes:

1. I can't afford it.

2. It's not what I want.

3. I already have an agent.

4. I have to talk it over with someone.

5. We want to do it ourselves.

6. I'm not interested.

These objections arise in response to any real estate offer, whether it's for an information kit or a free home evaluation.

If the unusual happens and someone tells you, "I'm not interested," then slams down the phone — forget it. Make a note to call them back in a month or so. But don't throw their file away. You may have just caught them at a bad time.

If the person says, "I'm not interested" and stays on the line, the ball is in your court.

Dealing with objections takes skill because it runs counter to our natural instincts. When someone disagrees with us, our natural response is to tell them they're wrong. As a real estate professional, you can't do that.

But you can help prospects see things differently through offering new information, a change of perspective, or another angle.

> **❝**
>
> *Success can be measured more by obstacles overcome than be pinnacles achieved.*
>
> *—Anonymous* **❞**

Remember that your goal isn't to change someone's mind. You want them to *reevaluate* the situation and *decide again,* based on whatever new slant you've provided.

That may sound simplistic, but it's crucial. If you think you're trying to get someone to change their mind, you'll demonstrate that in your tone of voice and choice of words.

But if you think of overcoming an objection as attempting to persuade a prospect to reconsider a position, you'll come across as more understanding and compassionate.

When dealing with objections, you throw out facts, testimonies, examples, and details that provide logical arguments against them. But you do so with a positive spirit. And you let the prospect themselves tell you how to structure your approach.

That's one reason why it's a good idea to start farming calls with open-ended questions.

These will provide clues as to the prospect's personality type and values. Ask what clubs or groups they belong to. What their interests are. See if they have any hobbies.

To overcome objections, you need to appeal to a prospect's own set of beliefs, values, and standards — not your own.

Look for the Real Objection

As surprising as this sounds, the first objection you hear usually is not the *real* one.

You might think, "Why not?"

Because off the top of their heads, most prospects won't know their real objection. They probably have a negative feeling, but can't quite attach it to a reason. Or they may be trying to protect themselves. It's hard to reveal yourself to a stranger.

To discover the real objection, many agents respond to an initial objection with something like, "In addition to that, are there some other reasons?" or "Could you give me some examples . . .?"

The second objection is usually the genuine one. When you hear it, focus on responding to it.

But don't ever make prospects think they are wrong — even when their objection is utterly invalid. Let your prospects think they're figuring it out for themselves. Just guide their decision-making.

Hit the "Hot Button"

If a prospect grew up in urban concrete, maybe they hanker for a yard full of shade trees. Or if they spent their childhood rising to the rooster's crow, maybe they dream of sweeping city lights from a penthouse suite.

If you can key into a prospects' dreams, you'll become a top performer in no time.

One young couple looking for a house never mentioned they'd like a pool. But each time I showed them one, their eyes lit up. Of the original batch of listings I showed them, only two had pools. After finding this hot button, we switched gears and had them on their way.

All of us have secret hot buttons.

It doesn't take hours of conversation to figure out what people really want. Sometimes you'll know in the first few minutes of a call — that is, if you ask the right questions and give your full attention to the answers.

Phrases That Turn an Objection Around

To effectively respond to objections, turn negatives into positives.

Once I heard about a woman whose husband drove her crazy. Every night he would methodically go through the house, checking every door and window to make sure it was locked. He did this even if his wife had just locked them.

Finally, she couldn't stand it anymore. How could anyone live with a man who was so picky?

But then she realized that being picky was what had taken him so far in the business world. As a bank president, he had to pay careful attention to details. The characteristic that drove her nuts was the secret of his success.

Once she saw it that way, his fanaticism never bothered her again.

To twist around an objection, you don't need a laundry list of all possible responses. But you do need to clue into what a prospect is really saying — and you need a few all-around answers to help take the wind out of objections.

More often than not, you can transform a prospect's objection into the main reason to take up your offer.

When you discover a prospect's true objection, you find out about their motivation. That helps you decide what approach to use. And chances are that the prospect has no idea they've given you such valuable information.

In handling objections, a few good phrases can work magic.

"Feel, Felt, Found"

These three words are among any salesperson's oldest and dearest friends. They trigger feelings that will facilitate conversation and make it easier for you to close.

Suppose a prospect said,

"I'd love to own a new home. But we just can't afford it right now."

Using "feel, felt, found," you'd say,

Use language that makes your prospect feel you understand their point of view

"I know how you feel. Many people have felt that way. But with the new kinds of financing available, people have found they can afford houses they could only dream of owning before."

This approach makes a prospect feel he or she isn't the only one with the problem. And, as the agent points out, solutions exist that others have taken advantage of.

Little "Yes"s Lead the Way

When you run into a stone wall of resistance, start chipping away at the edges. Hitting it head-on is useless — you'll only wind up with a skull fracture.

But if you start courting a reluctant prospect, getting them to agree with you on minor points, by the time you reach the major point, the prospect is much more inclined to go along with you. Here's an example:

Prospect: I've had this home for five years and I'm not about to sell it now.

Agent: But, Mr. Hoskins, wouldn't your family enjoy living in a more spacious home?

Prospect: I suppose so.

Agent: Couldn't you use some extra room?

Prospect: Yes.

>   Agent: *If moving into a larger home could wind up sav-*
>   *ing you money over the next few years, wouldn't*
>   *you be interested? You are interested in saving*
>   *money, aren't you?*
>
>   Prospect: *Isn't everybody?*
>
>   Agent: *Mr. Hoskins, I'd be happy to show you a way you*
>   *and your family could . . .*

With a carefully thought-out string of questions, the agent draws in the prospect and gets them to agree. Finally, the prospect can come to only one conclusion.

The next time someone raises an objection, pass it right back to them with a question. Then keep the questions coming until they see the light.

Questions often help prospects realize that their objections were of no consequence after all. Using this approach helps prospects work out in their own minds why they should take up your offer. This approach is gentle, friendly, and it works. Remember, little "yes"s can pave your way to a successful close.

"If You Were"

If you try this approach, be 100% sincere. Otherwise, you'll not only fail, you'll also eliminate your chance to try again.

More than any other approach, "if you were" separates real estate pros who really care about their prospects from those who regard prospects only as potential commission checks.

>   Agent: *Mrs. Frankel, if you were my own mother, I'd*
>   *say to you what I'm saying now. There is no bet-*
>   *ter investment for anyone today than owning*
>   *their own home.*

If you take this approach with absolute sincerity and your prospect doesn't do an immediate about-face, you know at least you've given them something serious to think about. This approach also helps build a prospect's trust in you.

"In Many Cases"

The phrase "in many cases" is not a personal favorite — but it can work. The trick is to use it with the right tone of voice.

>   Prospect: *It's impossible for me to get a decent house with*
>   *monthly payments as low as my rent.*

Agent: *In many cases, I'd have to agree with you. But there is a new program, offered by the state, only for first-time home buyers . . .*

Using the transition "in many cases" softens the agent's response to the objection and makes it easier for the prospect to agree. The agent could have responded with:

Agent: *But didn't you know that the state offers special rates to first-time home buyers?*

Although the prospect may be interested, irritation at being told they're stupid undoubtedly will outweigh whatever interest a prospect might have in the program.

In both cases, the same information is offered. The first, though, comes in a more attractive package.

Using phrases such as "in many cases" or "under different circumstances" or "normally" increases receptivity to what you say next. These phrases validate the prospect's feelings and take the harsh edges off your words.

Other Important Phrases

A transition allows you to respond to the prospect's objection then move on to an another benefit of the offer.

"In many cases" deserved a heading of its own. But like the phrases that follow, it's a transition used to respond to an objection sympathetically and then move to another benefit of your offer.

Transitions help a conversation flow more naturally by building bridges between thoughts. Use them often and you'll find your calls a lot easier. It feels good to treat people nicely and words like these help you do it:

"You are right, of course, but have you ever thought that . . . ?"

"Naturally, you have a choice . . ."

"What you're really saying is that you are interested, just not right now. Is that right?"

"I know that you only want to do what's best for yourself and your family. Have you ever considered . . . ?"

"The Jones family was in a situation similar to yours. But they realized that . . ."

Language like this encourages empathy between you and your prospect and makes them believe that you see things from their point of view.

Responses to Keep You on Track

In this section, we'll cover a number of objections and provide suggestions on how to handle them.

The words themselves aren't as important as the thinking patterns they reflect. It won't take you long to catch on to how to turn a negative into a positive and move smoothly to the next thought.

"I Can't Afford It"

When you hear these four words, get ready. Prospects are telling you they want it and either they aren't sure it's worth the cost or they doubt that they can pay for it.

If a prospect questions the cost, you can talk about the value of the offer, compare it to other offers, and situate it in the context of current circumstances or market trends. You also may want to mention special incentives such as limited quantity or availability. The goal is to demonstrate that the offer is worth its cost.

You could also throw in comments such as:

"Doesn't your family deserve this? Don't you, too?"

"You get what you pay for" (a lesson we've all learned at some time in our lives).

"This isn't for everybody."

"Think of it as an investment that will increase in value over the next few years."

If money is the problem, break the price down. If a prospect's upper limit for a home is $150,000 and his wife is captivated by a $160,000 home, break down the $10,000 into how much more they'd pay each month.

Ask something like,

"Isn't it worth $50 a month to keep your family really happy?"

Or multiply it out to a year,

"Couldn't you afford $600 a year for a home twice as large as the one you have now?"

Make it easy for the prospect to agree.

When you start throwing around numbers, it's a good idea to let prospects figure it out for themselves. Even over the phone, you can ask a prospect to grab a pencil and paper and do the math. This type of participation increases the prospect's involvement in the conversation.

Before starting prospecting calls, make up index cards for each expected objection. Then write transitions and responses, as the example illustrates.

I Can't Afford It

Transition	Response
I can understand that.	But have you thought about how much this can save you?
Times are tough.	This isn't right for everyone, but if you . . .
I know what that's like.	But think of this as an investment that will increase in value over the next few years.

"I Need to Think It Over"

How many times have you heard this? Sadly, many agents reply with something like, "That's fine, Ms. Emery. If you change your mind, you have my number."

With this response, the agent loses control. At the very least, the agent should keep the initiative and arrange to call back a few days later.

Sometimes prospects really do want to think it over, but often this is just a polite way to try to end the call. If you think that's what's happening, probe for their real objections.

Or you could agree with them that deciding to take the offer requires a lot of thought. Then review the main benefits of the offer. When you go over the same ground, you may find them more willing to tell you what they really think.

A third option is to offer to help the prospect think it through. You might say something like this:

"Mr. Galloway, I understand that. Selling your home is a big step. But wouldn't it help to know current market values, particularly for similar houses right in your own neighborhood? I'd be happy to bring that information to your home tonight. What time is better for you, seven or eight o'clock?"

A fourth response to a prospect who wants to think it over is to add urgency by emphasizing that the quantity is limited or the offer is available only for a certain time. For example, if you're offering a vacation kit, remind them that they only have two more weeks to get it. If you're offering a free home evaluation, emphasize how quickly the market is changing, and how no one knows when mortgage rates will go up.

"I'm Not in the Market Right Now"

As you can probably guess, this objection demands another "timing is critical" response.

Focus on the current market and why it's to the prospect's advantage to act quickly. It may be useful to get records on the real estate market over the past ten years and trace the cycles. Put your own spin on what you find.

"There's no better time than now" is a good line. If mortgage rates are high, they can always refinance later. But the longer they wait, the more it will cost them to buy.

When the market goes up, they'll make more on their home sale. But they'll pay more for their new home, too.

There are many different spins on any argument.

"I Have to Talk It Over with Someone"

When responding to objections like this, keep your voice casual, friendly, and wanting only to help. Don't make them feel that you're pushing them into a meeting.

Again emphasize that timing is critical. You also can tentatively set up an appointment or arrange to drop by a kit. That will make it harder for them to back out of the commitment.

Another tack is to offer to meet with both people.

"I Already Have a Real Estate Agent"

You may not hear this line very often, as most people think of relationships with real estate agents as temporary — something which, by the way, you try to overcome in farming.

Most people lose touch with their agents because few agents follow up. Once a deal is over, they forget the client.

However, there are times when you'll call someone who really has a relationship with another agent or company.

When that happens, don't give up right away. And don't criticize their agent. If you praise the other agent, the prospect will be

> *Always assess your actions for integrity. Even the smallest slip-up can come back to haunt you.*

more inclined to trust you. But then point out what you have to offer right at that moment.

Once, when I was looking for a house, I had an agent who specialized in the area where I wanted to live. But I wasn't happy with her. I called other agents, even met with them, and not one followed through with me. If they had, I would gladly have switched. But none of them really listened to me nor tried to understand me. Obviously, they didn't think I was serious about buying a home. But I was. And they missed out.

Emphasize how your offer can benefit the prospect, even if the prospect has another agent. And start building a relationship that one day could easily lead to the prospect becoming a client. Remember — few agents keep clients forever (although you want to!).

One final note: If you make the mistake of calling a prospect who has already listed their home with another agent, back off. Wait to see if the listing expires.

"Send Me Some Information"

This response opens up the conversation for you to ask questions:

"Would you like a brochure on our services?"

"Can I mail you information on recent sales in your neighborhood?"

After offering the information, find out why they want it. If they don't tell you, that's okay. Get the information in the mail right away and call them back two or three days later. Then you'll have another chance to ask.

"You'd Be Wasting Your Time"

The words sound harsh, but you can soften them with a response such as:

"Mr. Gregg, I'd be happy to give up a few minutes of my time if it means helping you make thousands of dollars. Making money is important to you, isn't it?"

"I Don't Need a New Home"

They may not need one, but chances are they'd like one — if they could get it at the right price. When you hear this, try the little "yes"s:

*"But wouldn't you like more room? Or a bigger
kitchen? Perhaps another bedroom? What about a fireplace to keep you warm in the winter?"*

Most prospects won't mind if you keep trying. Personally I've bought tons of cleaning solutions I didn't need simply because the salesperson did such a good job.

For Sale By Owner (FSBO)

The minute a homeowner puts up a For Sale By Owner (FSBO) sign, the phone begins to ring. Most of the calls, however, will not be from prospective buyers, but from Realtors® looking for the listing.

When you make a FSBO call, keep in mind that you won't be the first agent on the line. To stand out, you need to offer something unique (see sample FSBO phone scripts in Chapter 15).

The FSBO Kit

One generally successful approach is to offer a For Sale By Owner kit. You prepare this yourself. You might include tips for preparing an open house, how to write classified ads, sample documents that will be required and pamphlets prepared especially for FSBO's.

Instead of jumping all over the homeowner trying to get the listing, just offer to drop the kit by their home. That way you'll get your foot in the door in a non-threatening manner.

It is a good idea to let the prospect know that the items in the kit are specifically for homeowners and are not the tools you would use to market their home.

The Commission Objection

When a FSBO says they don't want to pay an agent's commission, you might respond with something like this:

*"Mrs. Foster, when someone says that, it's usually
because either they had a bad experience with a real
estate agent or they're trying to save money. Would
you mind telling me which is true for you?"*

If it's the first, be sympathetic. Ask about what happened. Gently remind the prospect that not every agent is like that. If it's the second reason, consider responding with the following:

The classic: The seller doesn't pay the commission, the buyer does.

When you sell your own home, you attract hordes of bargain hunters. These people have many homes to choose from. You have only yours to sell. That doesn't put you in a very good position for negotiating.

It's hard to negotiate a deal for your own home because of your emotional involvement. You may think that your home is worth more because of certain features you love, but buyers in today's market won't pay for those features.

When you sell your own home, people are forever dropping by to see your property. It quickly becomes a great nuisance. Also you have to advertise your phone number to the world.

Real estate transactions are complicated, with many legal requirements and lengthy procedures. It takes someone who knows the field well to properly handle and check all the paperwork. A missed deadline or forgotten bank statement can easily kill a deal.

There are many ways to handle real estate financing. Only an expert knows them all and can decide which is best in a given situation.

The Advantages of Listing with an Agent

1. We screen prospects and bring only qualified buyers to your home.

2. We take a professional picture of your home and prepare a detailed profile that we give to every interested prospect.

3. We handle showing the home, so there is no inconvenience to you. We let you know in advance when someone is coming to see it, and we work within your schedule.

4. We write and place advertisements in newspapers and magazines for you. These don't cost you anything.

5. We sponsor open houses and special showings.

6. We already have in our files a list of people interested in homes in your area.

7. We can handle the entire back-end by helping to arrange financing, making sure escrow is proceeding smoothly, and keeping everything on schedule.

One agent working the floor got a call from a man planning to sell his own home. He wanted to know how much other people were getting for similar homes in his area.

Apparently, he had called a number of different real estate companies and gotten the cold shoulder. However, this agent took the trouble to look up the prices and call the man back. They had a long and pleasant conversation.

The man was so impressed that he became a client of the agent's. No, he didn't give the agent the listing. But the agent helped him find a new home.

And the agent received a fee for helping with the paperwork when the man's home sold.

Dead Ends

Sometimes you have to give up. Not forever, but for awhile. If a prospect offers four or five objections and you can't overcome any of them, drop it. Be quiet and let the prospect talk. Eventually they'll settle on the most important point and you can try to deal with it.

If a prospect persists with a list of excuses and your conversation isn't going anywhere, politely end the call. Call back in a few months with a different offer.

Occasionally, you'll run into someone who's really having a hard time. Maybe it's financial or personal or job-related. Many people will be very honest with you about this right at the beginning of the call. Believe them. And make a note to call back in six months.

> **"**
> *Sometimes you have to give up a battle to win the war.*
> **"**

Final Points

Remember that an objection does not equal rejection. Interpret an objection as a prospect saying, "You haven't persuaded me yet, keep talking."

Although objections come in many shapes and sizes, they revolve around central themes. These are:

- I can't afford it.
- I don't want it.
- I already have an agent.
- I have to talk it over with someone.
- I want to do it myself.
- I'm not interested.

In more than half your calls, the first objection will not be the real one. Pay close attention to the second; usually it's the truth.

Overcoming objections isn't a matter of memorizing responses. It's learning ways of thinking that soften resistance, make prospects feel important, give them credit for their feelings, and gently glide to a close.

To learn how to overcome objections, do the quizzes in the next chapter.

CHAPTER 12

Quizzes on How to Overcome Objections

> *Think like a wise man but communicate in the language of the people.*
>
> —William Butler Yeats

The following quizzes are designed to help you think quickly as objections arise in your prospecting calls. They are organized according to type of offer and focus on the objections you can expect most frequently. Read the responses carefully, as they explain the nuances of language that can make or break a call.

We've organized the quizzes as follows:

HOW TO HANDLE OBJECTIONS

QUIZ 1 — Introductory booklet offer
QUIZ 2 — Home evaluation offer
QUIZ 3 — Information kit/booklet offer
QUIZ 4 — For sale by owner
QUIZ 5 — Renters — financial assistance offer
QUIZ 6 — Expired listing
QUIZ 7 — Absentee owners
QUIZ 8 — Neighbor to a new listing/sale offer
QUIZ 9 — Corporate relocation offer
QUIZ 10 — Find the mistakes

Good Luck!

QUIZ 1

INTRODUCTORY BOOKLET OFFER

For each objection, choose the best response.

1. I'm too busy to talk to you now.

   a) This will only take a minute.

   b) Are you too busy to find out about how to get a free gift?

   c) I'll keep it short.

   d) I'm busy too. I don't call people unless I think they can use what I have to offer.

2. I'm not interested.

   a) Maybe things will change and you will be interested.

   b) You won't find this kind of information anywhere else. And I've got only 50 booklets.

   c) I'm only making this offer for the next 30 days. If you want one, you'll have to say so now.

   d) You should be interested. Your home is one of your largest financial investments.

3. I've lived here for years. I don't need that.

   a) You probably already know everything in here. You could check it for accuracy.

   b) People like you make this a great neighborhood. Maybe you'd like to give this booklet to a friend.

   c) This booklet not only has the most up-to-date information on the Castle Pines real estate market, it also has facts and figures that aren't common knowledge. For example. . .

   d) I'd like to give it to you anyway.

   e) Take one as a favor to me.

4. I won't have time to read it.

   a) That's why I kept it short. All the information is there — but I also wrote summaries that tell you everything you need.

   b) Keep it for reference only. When you need it, you'll have it.

   c) This is important for every Castle Pines homeowner. You should make time to read it.

d) You don't need to read it. Just look at the charts and they'll tell you everything you need to know.

5. I already have a real estate agent.

a) And I'm sure that person does a good job for you. But do they have the kind of background I do?

b) I'm not trying to get a listing or sell you a house. This is a free gift.

c) But if your agent doesn't work out, maybe you could think of me.

d) That's fine. This is a gift I'm offering to all my Castle Pines neighbors. Whether you have a real estate agent doesn't matter.

6. Are you trying to sell me something?

a) All I'm asking is that you consider using my services if you ever decide to sell your home.

b) No. This kind of information is hard to find and put together. When I finished, I realized that anyone who lives in Castle Pines would find it useful.

c) Absolutely not. I'm offering this booklet to my Castle Pines neighbors at no charge because I think all of us can find it useful.

d) No. This booklet is free.

ANSWERS

1. I'm too busy to talk to you now.

a) Good answer. Responds to remark appropriately and allows agent to quickly move on.

b) Presumptive. It takes away control from the prospect by assuming that the prospect would like a free gift.

c) Fine answer. Different from (a) in that it uses "I." Be careful to watch how much you use "I" in your conversations. Your focus should be on the prospect's needs, not your own.

d) Makes you sound very important and the prospect not important at all.

2. I'm not interested.

a) Vague answer. Flimsy reasoning.

b) Good answer. Politely points out why the prospect should be interested (you won't find this kind of information anywhere else) and creates urgency by mentioning limited quantity.

c) Sounds like a father scolding a child.

d) Don't tell your prospects what to think. Listen to what they tell you.

3. I've lived here for years. I don't need that.

a) Your attempt at flattery undercuts the importance of the booklet.

b) Not bad but a little weak. It makes the booklet sound unimportant (you don't need it but maybe your friend will).

c) Good answer. Responds appropriately to prospect's concern.

d) So what? The fact that you want the prospect to have it is meaningless if the prospect doesn't know you.

e) Why should the prospect do you any favors?

4. I won't have time to read it.

a) Good response.

b) All right, but makes booklet sound unimportant.

c) Presumptive. What gives you the right to say that something is important for every homeowner?

d) Too flippant and casual.

5. I already have a real estate agent.

a) Conceited.

b) Too blatant.

c) Weak.

d) Good response.

6. Are you trying to sell me something?

a) Weak response.

b) All right but too many "I"s.

c) Good response.

d) Bad response because it doesn't keep the conversation going.

QUIZ 2

HOME EVALUATION OFFER

For each objection, choose the best response.

1. You're wasting your time with me.

    a) (Name), even if you aren't thinking of selling your home now, knowing its potential value in today's market can be useful to you . . . (home equity line, credit applications)

    b) I appreciate your concern for me. But I don't regard any conversation with a neighbor as a waste of my time.

    c) I appreciate that. Thank you for taking these few minutes to talk to me.

    d) Every homeowner needs to know the potential value of their home.

2. Why don't you just send me something in the mail?

    a) Because if you're like me, you'll never get around to reading it.

    b) Better yet — why don't I just drop it by your house? Will you be home around 7 p.m. tomorrow?

    c) That would be easier for both of us. But without seeing your home, it's impossible for me to give you a fair evaluation. Your home's condition is very important in determining its value.

    d) I can do that for anyone. But for you, I'd like to do something special.

3. I'm not interested in selling my house.

    a) I can understand that. You have a lovely home. But getting an evaluation is a long way away from selling your home. Basically, it's knowledge that you can use in many ways.

    b) Someday you might be.

    c) What about your wife or husband? Would he or she be interested in knowing how much your home could be worth on today's market?

    d) What if I told you that you could make more money than you ever dreamed of if you sold now?

4. Let me think about it and call you back.

    a) Why wait? If I stop by tonight, you can have your evaluation tomorrow.

    b) Why would you want to think about it? After all, the evaluation is free.

    c) What if you think about it and I call you back in a day or two?

    d) I realize that this is an important decision for you. But remember that there's no obligation to you. I stop by, spend a few minutes looking at your home, go away and write up an evaluation. You can do with it as you please.

5. I already know how much my home is worth.

    a) How much do you think it's worth?

    b) The market changes from month to month, sometimes week to week. I can give you the most up-to-date information.

    c) May I ask if you've had another evaluation done lately?

    d) What would it hurt for me to drop by and give you my opinion?

ANSWERS

1. You're wasting your time with me.
    a) Good answer. Responds appropriately and moves on. Uses name.
    b) Not bad. But a little presumptuous. Sounds put-on.
    c) NEVER GIVE UP THIS EASILY. At the first sign of resistance, show a little spirit.
    d) Why?

2. Why don't you just send me something in the mail?
    a) Too blunt. "If you're like me" builds rapport, but the second part of the response is too negative.
    b) This answer could work. Some prospects, however, might see you as pushy. Whether you used this would depend on the tone of your conversation with a particular prospect.
    c) Good answer. Responds to prospect's objection with strong logic.
    d) Presumptuous.

3. I'm not interested in selling my house.
    a) Good answer. Tells prospect that you've paid enough attention to drive by his or her home and look at it. Provides an argument that makes sense and allows you to continue the conversation.

b) Vague and poorly thought out. You have no idea what will happen to the prospect "someday" (for that matter, neither does the prospect!).

c) Totally undercuts any sense of respect or worth the prospect feels from the conversation. "If you're not interested, whom do you know who might be?" cuts the prospect right out of the picture.

d) Don't make pie-in-the-sky promises.

4. Let me think about it and call you back.

a) Too aggressive and arrogant. Underlying tone is, "Why would you want to do that? Are you stupid?"

b) Not as aggressive as (a) but still runs roughshod over the prospect's feelings.

c) This agent is caving in. He or she doesn't even try to respond to the prospect's objection. They simply accept it and try to retain the illusion of control by saying, "I'll call you."

d) Good answer. Sympathetic and respectful of prospect's feelings. Tries to respond to real objection behind the stated objection. Keeps appropriate balance in the relationship.

5. I already know how much my home is worth.

a) This could keep the conversation going. The problem is that it's potentially confrontational. The prospect hears you saying, "Tell me how much you think it's worth so I can tell you that you're wrong."

b) You're telling the prospect that he or she is probably off the mark without even asking how they arrived at a figure for their home's potential value.

c) Good answer. Responds directly to prospect's objection by asking for more information. Keeps the conversation going in the right direction.

d) Your opinion really doesn't matter to the prospect. This answer ignores that fact that a home evaluation will cost the prospect something — namely, time.

QUIZ 3

INFORMATION KIT/BOOKLET OFFER

For each objection, choose the best response.

1. I don't need it.

   a) (Name), do you know Tom Hartman? Let me tell you what happened to him.

   b) You might someday.

   c) That's what Tom Hartman said. Let me tell you what happened to him.

   d) Better be safe than sorry.

2. I don't want it.

   a) Remember that it's free. I'll drop it by your house so you won't even have to pay postage.

   b) What type of kit would be useful to you?

   c) Are you telling me that you don't care about (having a safe home) (protecting your home from intruders) (etc.)?

   d) How can you not want something this important?

   e) That surprises me, especially considering that the kit is free. I'm sure you have a good reason. May I ask what it is?

3. I'm too busy to . . .

   a) Are you too busy to find out about something that will save you time and money?

   b) Are you sure that you realize the value of what I'm offering?

   c) I'm busy, too. I wouldn't have called if I didn't think you'd find this useful.

   d) I can understand that. That's why I prepared this kit/booklet. It not only can save you time, it also can save you money.

4. What good would this do me?

   a) It depends on how you use it.

   b) You never know when you might need it.

   c) For example, what if . . .(tell story appropriate to kit/booklet).

d) Every one of your neighbors has asked for one.

5. I need to talk to my partner (spouse).

   a) If your partner is like mine, I'm sure that he/she would want the (safest home possible) or (the convenience this booklet offers).

   b) Why don't I just drop it by and the two of you can look it over together?

   c) I'll be in the neighborhood tonight. Why don't I just drop one off?

   d) Of course. Why don't I just call you back tomorrow and see what they said? What time would be good for you?

ANSWERS

1. I don't need it.
   a) Good if you have an appropriate story and can tell it well. In general, avoid fear appeals.
   b) Vague. Poor reason to want a kit/booklet.
   c) Slightly different words than (a), but with same thought. This answer demonstrates how changing even one or two words can alter a remark's tone. "That's what Tom Hartman said" is judgmental. "Do you know Tom Hartman?" isn't. The latter also uses one of our favorite words, "you."
   d) Paternalistic and offensive.

2. I don't want it.
   a) Okay response. Gives a valid reason for prospect to want kit.
   b) Use this only if you think the prospect really doesn't want the kit or booklet you're offering. Don't count on a good answer. The benefit of this question is that it makes the prospect feel good because you're asking for his or her opinion.
   c) Never make a remark like this during a call. It's hostile and offensive.
   d) You're the one who thinks it's important, not the prospect.
   e) Good response. Keeps conversation going.

3. I'm too busy to. . .
   a) Hostile and confrontational.
   b) Hostile. Implies that the prospect is stupid and needs the agent to educate him or her.
   c) Arrogant. The fact that you're busy doesn't matter one whit to the prospect.
   d) Good response. Acknowledges and validates prospect's feelings while giving a logical reason to overcome them.

4. What good would this do me?
    a) This answer waffles. Shows your uncertainty and devalues what you're offering.
    b) Vague and confusing response.
    c) Good response. Personalizes the dilemma or problem that the kit/booklet is to help solve.
    d) So what? Peer pressure is a poor argument.

5. I need to talk to my partner/spouse.
    a) A little presumptuous but okay if the overall tone of the conversation has been "you" and "me."
    b) A bit arrogant. Doesn't pause and acknowledge prospect's feelings.
    c) Good because it keeps up the momentum. It doesn't acknowledge the prospect's objection, but puts a new spin on the situation. Could perhaps combine (a) and (c).
    d) This agent gave up too easily.

QUIZ 4

FOR SALE BY OWNER

For each objection, choose the best response.

1. We want to sell it on our own.

    a) I can understand that. May I ask if you're doing it to save the commission?

    b) Then why do you think so many people list their homes with agents?

    c) There's a lot more to selling your home than putting up a sign. Do you know how to fill out a (name a complicated form)?

    d) Are you sure you want to put up with all the bother of trying to sell your own home?

2. We don't want to pay a commission.

    a) But you pay in other ways. You pay for advertising and other expenses and you have a considerable amount of inconvenience.

    b) Have you ever considered that selling your own home may wind up costing you money? People who try to sell their own homes usually run into two major problems: setting the right price and pre-qualifying buyers. I can help you with both.

    c) You don't pay the commission — the buyer does.

    d) Selling a home takes a lot of expertise. I'm a professional.

3. I don't need you to find a buyer. Lots of people are looking at the house.

    a) Have you had any offers in writing?

    b) That's great. Can I come by and look at it too?

    c) How are you pre-qualifying buyers?

    d) How many of those buyers are serious?

4. I have a friend in real estate who's helping me.

    a) Is your friend working on this full-time?

    b) Is your friend a fully qualified real estate agent?

    c) Do you really think that your friend can help you get the most money possible for your home?

d) That's great. All of us need friends to help in situations like this. What I'm interested in, however, is taking the burden of selling your home off you and taking care of it myself.

5. We're not in a hurry to sell.

   a) When you say, "not in a hurry," what do you mean? Are you planning for it to sell in 30 days, 90 days — or are you willing to wait even longer?

   b) That's good. Then you can hold out for the highest offer.

   c) May I ask then why you're selling?

   d) I understand. But right now the market is on an upswing. It's a good time to take advantage of it.

6. We had a bad experience with real estate agents.

   a) I'm sorry to hear that. Would you mind telling me what happened?

   b) Not all agents are alike, you know.

   c) If you like, I can give you references from satisfied clients.

   d) You just got the wrong agent. Now when can I see your home?

ANSWERS

1. We want to sell it on our own.
   a) Good response. Acknowledges stated objection and looks for real objection.
   b) Argumentative and confrontational. The fact that other people list their homes isn't very important.
   c) Arrogant and intimidating.
   d) Of course they do. They've already made their decision.

2. We don't want to pay a commission.
   a) The response sounds trivial. Advertising costs and inconvenience don't add up to thousands of dollars.
   b) Good answer. Lots of detail and responds specifically to objection.
   c) This sounds too pat. Yes, the buyer does pay the commission but it comes out of the selling price.
   d) Arrogant.

3. I don't need you to find a buyer. Lots of people are looking at the house.
   a) Confrontational.

b) Flippant. This response may get you in the house and allow you to meet the owners, but it's awfully casual.

c) Good response. Keeps conversation going. Treats owner seriously. Builds up your credibility as a real estate professional.

d) Too negative.

4. I have a friend in real estate who's helping me.
   a) Hostile and confrontational.
   b) Hostile and confrontational.
   c) Undercuts positive feelings prospect may have about what he or she is doing.
   d) Good response. Clarifies the situation while responding directly to objection.

5. We're not in a hurry to sell.
   a) They probably don't know themselves. Pinning them down is not a good idea.
   b) Bad response. Urges them to take an action that is probably not in their best interests.
   c) Not bad, but a little off. Diverts attention from the lack of time pressure to the motivation for selling. You should ask this question at some point in the conversation — but maybe not right here.
   d) Good response. Links FSBO sale to local real estate market in general.

6. We had a bad experience with real estate agents.
   a) Good response. Acknowledges prospect's objection and moves along conversation.
   b) Trite. Runs right over prospect's feelings.
   c) Not bad to include this thought. But cuts off prospect's feelings about the past experience and toots your own horn.
   d) Way too abrupt.

QUIZ 5

RENTERS — FINANCIAL ASSISTANCE OFFER

For each objection, choose the best response.

1. I can't afford to buy a home.

    a) (Name), if I could show you how you could own a home for about what you're paying now in rent, how would you feel about buying?

    b) That's what Nancy Jamison said, too. But she's now living in a lovely 2-bedroom on Grove Street.

    c) Are you aware of the special programs that many lenders offer for first time buyers like yourself? Some require very little down payment. I'd be happy to describe them to you. When can we meet?

    d) Many people think that. But they're wrong.

2. Let me think it over.

    a) Why wait? I can meet with you tomorrow. What time is good for you?

    b) If you wait too long, you'll miss out on some great opportunities.

    c) Why are you hesitating? Meeting with me won't cost you anything.

    d) I appreciate your taking this seriously. But wouldn't it help to have as much information as possible when you think this through?

3. I've always rented.

    a) That does give you more freedom than when you own a house. After all, you don't have to worry about repairs or selling a property.

    b) Have you considered the financial advantages of home ownership? The building up of equity and the tax deductions?

    c) Have you ever thought about owning your own home?

    d) Do you know anyone else who might be interested in buying a home?

4. I could never find as house as nice as my apartment in the right price range.

    a) How do you know until you look?

    b) You might be surprised at some of the homes we have listed now. For example, there's a wonderful 2-bedroom Victorian on Howard's Road that you might like. What would you look for in a home?

    c) That may not be true. With the market as bad as it has been lately, you can find some real bargains.

    d) Having a nice apartment is important, but owning a home gives you some real financial advantages.

5. I'm not ready to buy.

    a) What will it take to make you ready?

    b) Why not?

    c) This is a great market for first-time buyers. You'll miss some wonderful opportunities.

    d) I understand. But can I ask why you're reluctant to even explore the possibility? Is there a particular reason why you're not ready to buy?

ANSWERS

1. I can't afford to buy a home.
    a) Good response.
    b) OK but takes focus off prospect.
    c) Good response. Gives information that follows up directly on prospect's objection.
    d) Hostile. Unspoken thought is "and so are you."

2. Let me think it over.
    a) Way too abrupt. Be careful with these presumptive closes. They work sometimes. But other times they're offensive.
    b) Intimidating prospects is usually not a good idea.
    c) This response implies the prospect is stupid for hesitating and motivated strictly by financial considerations. But time, too, costs something.
    d) Good, thoughtful response.

3. I've always rented.
    a) You're being too nice. Stay focused on your goal, which is to persuade this person to buy a house.
    b) Good response but could lead to a quick end to the conversation.

c) Probably a better response at this stage. Keeps the conversation going and allows you to probe deeper for the real objection.

d) Don't ever give up this easily.

4. I could never find as house as nice as my apartment in the right price range.

   a) Confrontational.

   b) Good response. Gets into details of specific properties on market and responds to prospect's concern by asking what they define as "nice."

   c) You ignored the prospect's concern about aesthetics and moved right into financial concerns.

   d) Same as (c).

5. I'm not ready to buy.

   a) Too aggressive. Pay attention to the prospect's feelings, don't ignore them.

   b) Abrupt, especially if you and the prospect have never met.

   c) Use fear appeals sparingly.

   d) Good response. You validate the prospect's feelings and ask for an elaboration of them. This allows the conversation to continue.

QUIZ 6

EXPIRED LISTING

For each objection, choose the best response.

1. Why didn't you look at the house when it was on the market?

    a) I didn't hear about it. Obviously your agent wasn't doing a very good job of marketing your home.

    b) With so many homes on the market, it's impossible for one person to see them all.

    c) While I may not have taken any prospective buyers to see your house, I did keep checking for any sales activity. And at the time, the buyers I had were looking for something a little different.

    d) I spend my time marketing homes that I list, which could be of benefit to you.

2. What can you do any different from our previous agent?

    a) I think that I can find you a buyer. That's something your other agent couldn't do, right?

    b) First why don't you tell me a little about how they marketed your home?

    c) Why do you think your home didn't sell? What do you think the agent did wrong?

    d) I have the resources of one of this town's major real estate companies behind me. Our marketing is intense, fast and well-researched. We know what works.

3. I don't want to relist my property now.

    a) I can understand that. Trying to sell a home is a big job. Why don't I call you back in a few weeks?

    b) What motivated you to list your property in the first place and what are some of your concerns about listing it again?

    c) How have your circumstances changed from when you listed the property?

    d) I can do a better job than your previous agent.

4. Why should I list with a big company like yours?

    a) I appreciate your concern. With big companies you can feel like just a number. But at our company, we work hard to give personal attention to each client. We also have extensive resources that simply aren't available to smaller companies. For example, . . .

b) Why not?

c) Because I can almost guarantee that we'll sell your home within the next 60 days. I have buyers interested in a home like yours right now!

d) Because we handle 75% of the listings in Castle Pines already. People know that we specialize in your neighborhood.

5. Why should I list with a small company like yours?

a) Because I'll have the time to give marketing your home the attention it deserves.

b) Because our track record is comparable to any large company and at the same time, we maintain a level of personal service and attention to our clients that larger companies simply can't handle.

c) Because you'll never feel like just a number with us.

d) Because we're the best.

6. Let me think it over.

a) I realize that you've already been through this once before and it didn't work. All I'm asking for is the opportunity to tell you how I could make it work for you. It costs you nothing and it could gain you a lot.

b) I appreciate your wanting to think about this. But remember that every day you delay, I could have the right buyer show up on my doorstep. You could miss a great opportunity.

c) Every day you spend thinking about it is a day that we lose marketing your home. Don't you want to sell your home as soon as possible?

d) Why wait? I could have your home in the multiple listing service tomorrow.

ANSWERS

1. Why didn't you look at the house when it was on the market?

a) Petty and negative. You're putting yourself in a bad light when you start criticizing their previous agent. Be very careful with this type of language.

b) Avoid this type of reply. It makes you sound as if you don't like to work hard and some of the demands of your job are beyond you.

c) Good response. It points out that you did keep tabs on the house and it answers the objection by explaining that you didn't have any appropriate buyers at that time.

d) This sounds selfish.

2. What can you do any different than our previous agent?
   a) Overly critical. Don't attack the other agent so directly.
   b) Good response. Gives you important information and keeps the conversation going in the right direction.
   c) Again, overly negative. It also treats the prospect as though he or she should know how to market a home.
   d) Presumptuous. The other agent may also have had a lot of resources and marketed the home well. Until you know exactly what happened, don't give this type of reply.

3. I don't want to relist my property now.
   a) You gave up too easily.
   b) Good response. Looks for the objection behind the objection. Keeps the conversation going.
   c) Assumes a little too much. Circumstances may not have changed at all — but attitudes towards agents may have.
   d) Don't criticize other agents.

4. Why should I list with a big company like yours?
   a) Good answer. Responds to the objection behind the objection. Offers specific facts on how you handle marketing and ties those into results.
   b) Too flippant. Treats the objection too casually.
   c) Don't make promises you can't keep.
   d) This isn't a bad answer. The problem is that it fails to deal with the objection directly. Fears of big companies usually stem from expectations of impersonal treatment. This reply ignores that fear and instead points to results.

5. Why should I list with a small company like yours?
   a) No. This makes you sound as if you have time on your hands.
   b) Good answer. It addresses the objection behind the objection and points to a record of success.
   c) Too abrupt. Also doesn't deal with success record, which is important.
   d) Too flippant. Simply saying that you're the best isn't going to convince anyone.

6. Let me think it over.
   a) Good answer. Covers all the bases while acknowledging the validity of the prospect's concern.
   b) In most cases, avoid fear appeals. You want to persuade, not threaten, the prospect.
   c) This is a trick reply. The prospect is almost certain to respond "yes" to the last question. But it's unfair because it doesn't acknowledge the validity of the prospect's concern.
   d) Too abrupt.

QUIZ 7

ABSENTEE OWNERS

For each objection, choose the best response.

1. We're not in a hurry to sell.

    a) Is what you're really saying that you want the best possible price? If so, you won't really know the best possible price until we put it on the market.

    b) That's good. We can take our time determining the price and market it only to a select group of potential buyers.

    c) Don't you need the money? Wouldn't you like to have some extra cash in the next few months?

    d) What's the point of waiting? The market is terrific right now.

2. Why don't you just send me something in the mail?

    a) I'd be happy to. But I'd rather drop it off in person so I can explain a few things. It won't take long. Could we meet tomorrow?

    b) I will. And I'll call you in a few days to make sure you received it.

    c) It's too much material to send in the mail. Why don't I just drop it by your house?

    d) That would be fine. I'll pull together some information on sales of comparable properties in the area and get it off to you today.

3. How do I know that I can trust you?

    a) I'm a licensed agent and I've been handling Castle Pines homes for more than six years.

    b) I sold five homes within two square miles of your property within the past three months. Who else can offer that type of success?

    c) You can call my broker, Richard Ramos, at Greenbrier Real Estate. His number is 555-9999. I'll also be happy to give you the names and telephone numbers of previous clients as references. Call a few and see what they say.

    d) I have a wall full of awards and I'm a member of the St. Mary Hospital Board.

4. If I put my home on the market, the renters will leave and I'll lose that income.

   a) That is a risk. But the renters may stay until the home sells. And even if they leave, your short-term loss of rental income is small compared to the large profit you stand to gain by selling the property.

   b) That's taking a pretty short-term view of the situation. What are you getting in rent?

   c) Don't tell your renters that you're marketing the home until you absolutely have to.

   d) Maybe your renters will want to buy the home. Have they ever discussed this with you?

5. How will I know that you're really marketing the property effectively?

   a) Look at my record. How many other agents do you know who have sold as many homes in the neighborhood as I have?

   b) I'll keep you informed every step of the way. You'll receive regular weekly reports and I'll call several times during the week. You'll know how often I show the property, who I show it to, what the ads look like, where and how often I advertise and when I take other Realtors" on caravan through the property.

   c) I'll send you copies of all the ads and other information I produce.

   d) By my results.

ANSWERS

1. We're not in a hurry to sell.
   a) Good answer. Looks for objection behind objection and uses it to make a point.
   b) Bad. While targeted marketing is a good idea, doing it right doesn't necessarily take any additional time. Also why limit the number of potential buyers unless it's a very peculiar property?
   c) This is not a good answer. Don't assume that money is all-important to everyone. It isn't.
   d) The point about it being a strong market is good. The first remark, "What's the point of waiting?," is rude.

2. Why don't you just send me something in the mail?
   a) Good answer. You need to drop it off in person to explain a few things. The remark is appropriate, as prospect will expect the real estate information to be fairly complicated.
   b) Weak answer. Calling to see if the prospect received it is a poor excuse. Be more professional. Say something like, "I'll call to explain the fine print about . . ."
   c) Poor excuse. The Post Office handles pretty heavy packages on a regular basis. It sounds like you don't want to send it because it will cost too much. That tells the prospect that they're not worth the few extra dollars.
   d) The promptness promised in this response is admirable but don't cave in so easily. First at least try for a face-to-face meeting.

3. How do I know that I can trust you?
   a) The fact that you're licensed is good, but it doesn't really address the issue of trust. The fact that you've been handling Castle Pines homes for more than six years is good, but irrelevant.
   b) Your success is not the same thing as someone trusting you. Sometimes successful people are not trustworthy.
   c) Good response. Make sure the prospect knows your credentials, but offer personal references. These get at the issue of trust far better than credentials.
   d) Your wall full of awards and community service don't tell a prospect anything about your trustworthiness as a real estate agent.

4. If I put my home on the market, the renters will leave and I'll lose that income.
   a) Good answer. It doesn't sugarcoat the situation but it also doesn't paint too negative a picture. It's balanced and reasonable.
   b) First sentence is too critical. Asking what they get in rent is good, as it keeps the conversation going.
   c) Bad response and bad advice.
   d) Why even mention this? If the renters want to buy the home, the owner doesn't need your services.

5. How will I know that you're really marketing the property effectively?
   a) Don't use your past record to justify present actions. This response doesn't match the question.
   b) Good, complete response.
   c) This is only a partial answer. Creating materials is just one small part of marketing a home.
   d) Results don't necessarily correspond to how much effort you put into a home sale. The prospect is asking how much effort you plan to dedicate to him or her, not how quickly you'll sell the property.

QUIZ 8

NEIGHBOR TO A NEW LISTING/SALE OFFER

For each objection, choose the best response.

1. I'm not interested in moving.

   a) I can understand that. You have a lovely home. Perhaps you have a friend, relative or someone at work who'd be interested in living in your neighborhood?

   b) What if I told you that you could probably move into a larger home for about the same mortgage as you have right now?

   c) Even if you're not interested in buying the home, it's worth a look. The (Name) did some beautiful decorating and their roses have won prizes.

   d) Thank you very much for your time.

2. The price is too high.

   a) If you look at comparable sales of other homes in the neighborhood, you'll find it's right in line. The landscaping, bay windows, corner lot and mint condition put this property at the top of its price range.

   b) You get what you pay for and the quality of this home is very high.

   c) I have some less expensive homes, if you'd like to consider them. For example, there's a three-bedroom, one-bath on the market for $147,500. It has a backyard gazebo, family room with fireplace and two-car garage with a workshop.

   d) Why do you think so?

3. I don't like the location.

   a) It's very convenient to shopping and the school bus stops only half a block away.

   b) What do you look for in a location?

   c) Why not?

   d) The fact that it's on a cul-de-sac means you'll have a lot less traffic.

ANSWERS

1. I'm not interested in moving.
   a) Good response. Better if you can comment specifically about their home so they know that you've driven by and paid attention to it.
   b) This is speculation on your part. Avoid it.
   c) Good response if you're trying to get them over for an open house or to tour the property.
   d) You gave up too easily.

2. The price is too high.
   a) Good response. Explains why the price may seem high, but isn't.
   b) Okay response. Not as detailed as (a).
   c) You should first try to find out what the real objection is. This response is appropriate only if you know their financial condition. Otherwise, you've given up too easily.
   d) Okay response. Keeps the conversation going but also allows prospect to express a lot of negative feelings about the property. That's not good.

3. I don't like the location.
   a) These may not be important considerations to the prospect.
   b) Good response. Find out what your prospect's needs are.
   c) Ineffective question — asks for same information as (b) but from a negative standpoint. Always try to phrase questions positively.
   d) Again, this may not be important to the prospect.

QUIZ 9

CORPORATE RELOCATION OFFER

For each objection, choose the best response.

1. We always work with XYZ Real Estate.

    a) Working with companies you're comfortable with is important. All I'm asking for is the opportunity to provide you with some information and show you what I can do to make your relocation the most trouble-free possible.

    b) But look at all that I can do for you . . . I can show you everything on the market, help your executives find the right financing, make the home closings as smooth as possible and even give referrals for follow-up home services.

    c) XYZ Real Estate is a pretty small operation here. They don't have nearly the resources that my company does.

    d) Isn't it time for a change? Change is healthy and I have a lot to offer.

2. We're not ready to choose any real estate agents yet.

    a) If you're planning to start the relocation in June, we'd better get going as soon as possible.

    b) Why not?

    c) Before you make a decision, what if I flew out there and made a presentation to you of the relocation services that I offer? That way, you'd have some of the information you need to decide.

    d) Why don't I put some information in the mail to you? You can look it over and I'll call you back next week.

3. We're letting the executives select their own real estate representatives.

    a) Would you pass my name along to them?

    b) How many executives are you relocating?

    c) That's great. If I sent you some Relocation Kits, would you be willing to distribute them to the executives who will be moving here?

    d) Could you send me a list of their names and addresses so I can contact them directly?

ANSWERS

1. We always work with XYZ Real Estate.
    a) Good response. Emphasizes predominant consideration for most corporate relocation people, which is how to reduce complaints by executives. Now ask, "Can we meet on Friday?"
    b) Use a response like this only if you have something unique to offer. Chances are in this situation that you won't.
    c) Don't be negative about your competition. Remember what Mother said, "If you can't say something nice about someone, don't say anything at all!"
    d) This may be your personal philosophy, but it doesn't give you a leg to stand on in this situation.

2. We're not ready to choose any real estate agents yet.
    a) This isn't your call — it's theirs.
    b) Once again, avoid negativity. You could, however, ask something like, "What information do you need to make your decision?"
    c) Good response. Shows that you're willing to take the initiative and act appropriately. Also responds directly to prospect's objection.
    d) Too passive. Would you want someone like this scouring the market for homes for your top executives?

3. We're letting the executives select their own real estate representatives.
    a) Too passive. Don't count on the relocation officer to do you any favors.
    b) Good for keeping the conversation going but it takes the focus off what you have to offer.
    c) Good response. Shows your high degree of initiative. Could follow-up with (b).
    d) This crosses a line of confidential information and should be avoided. However, you could combine (d) and (c) and ask if you could send the kits directly to the executives involved.

QUIZ 10

Find the nine mistakes made by the agent in the following call.

Agent: Hello, is this Bill Edley?

Prospect: Yes, it is.

Agent: Bill, this is Tom Smithson. How are you?

Prospect: Fine, thank you.

Agent: Bill, I'm calling because I want to do you a favor. For the next 30 days, I'm offering free home evaluations to Castle Pines residents. Would you like one?

Prospect: No. I'm not interested in selling my house.

Agent: It's a great market right now. You could probably make a substantial profit. How much did you pay for your house?

Prospect: Like I said, I'm not interested in selling.

Agent: OK. Good-bye. CLICK.

Prospect: CLICK.

ANSWERS

1. "Is this Bill Edley?" allows prospect to respond, "No, it's not."
2. Tom called the prospect by his first name, "Bill," when they'd never even met.
3. Tom failed to identify his company.
4. Tom didn't ask if Bill had time to talk.
5. Tom made the offer right off the top. There was no relationship-building conversation.
6. Tom misrepresented the situation when he said that he wanted to do Bill a favor. In reality, Tom wants Bill to do him a favor. He never gave Bill a reason to want a home evaluation.
7. "Would you like one?" leaves Tom wide open for a "No!" answer.
8. Tom tries to respond to objection but "It's a great market right now" is vague. The follow-up question, "How much did you pay for your house?" comes without any preliminary relationship-building.
9. Tom (AGENT) hangs up on prospect

CHAPTER 13

The Critical Close

> *It is more important that you
> know where you are going than to get there
> quickly. Do not mistake activity for achievement.*
>
> —*Mabel Newcomber*

You're ready to close when you've dealt with the objections, gotten the prospect to agree with your point of view, and stirred interest and desire. What do you do next?

First of all, don't rush. Too many salespeople try to either run prospects down with steamrollers or even worse, never nail anything down.

Basically, you close when you ask the prospect to act. In the sample scripts in this book, that means asking them to answer your survey, attend a seminar, agree to a free home evaluation, accept an information kit or booklet, attend an open house, or meet with you.

Closing isn't a natural ability. It's an acquired skill. When you start closing, all the hours of thinking about your script, writing it, rehearsing it, and using it will pay off.

But remember that even the world's greatest salespeople hardly ever close on their first attempt. More often, it's the fifth.

Leading up to every commission is a series of closings. First it's sending out information. Then arranging an appointment. Then getting the listing. Then showing properties. Then handling an offer. Then handling another offer. Then getting a contract. Then finishing escrow.

Closes are made one step at a time.

One thing to remember from the moment you pick up the phone is to never appear overanxious. That only makes prospects think you care more about yourself than about them.

Convey a Sense of Urgency

Every close needs a sense of urgency.

That means giving prospects a reason to accept your offer *now*.

In direct marketing, more telephone scripts and letters fail from a lack of urgency than anything else.

If prospects believe they can put something off, especially a big decision involving their homes, they will. While it's hard to push prospects into quick action, you can cultivate that skill. Especially when you're offering something such as an information kit or booklet that costs them nothing.

What you use to create a sense of urgency depends on your offer. Often urgent appeals rely on limited time or quantities.

For example, you may be scheduling free home evaluations in a neighborhood only during the next three weeks. Or you may have only 15 Tax Record Keeping kits to distribute.

You also add urgency other ways. For example, interest rates may have just increased — so you urge prospects to act before they climb any higher. Or maybe a bank is offering a financing package only for a limited period of time. Or perhaps Congress is considering changing the deduction for second homes.

Wherever you can emphasize a time factor, do it. Tell prospects, "If you don't act now, you'll miss a great opportunity."

Before using any script, always check it for a sense of urgency.

When to Close

There's no magic formula for determining the best time to close. In some cases, you'll try to close as soon as you've established the reason for the call and given the prospect several arguments for accepting the offer. In other cases, you'll wait and engage the prospect in conversation.

If you try to close too soon, you could seem overeager. On the other hand, letting the prospect know what you want up front can help.

Signs that could indicate you have an opportunity to close include:

- Prospect's voice changes from cool or argumentative to become more relaxed.

- Prospect compares you to another agent.

- Prospect asks to confirm arrangements to take you up on your offer.

- Prospect asks for your opinion, not information.

Some sales whizzes recommend not trying to close until you've dealt with every objection. That could be quite awhile.

Others recommend ignoring objections until you've wrapped up your presentation and asked for the offer. We don't endorse this approach, as we think it's best to deal with objections as they arise.

The route you choose will vary with each call — depending on you, your offer, and the prospect.

Sometimes when you're dealing with curt and to-the-point people, it's best to follow their example and spell things out right away. Other times, you should try to break through that efficiency barrier and find the real person. Deciding which approach to take is a matter of intuition and experience. Over time, you'll get better and better at it.

> *What we call results are beginnings.*
> —*Ralph Waldo Emerson*

Just remember that during any phone call, you'll almost certainly have to try more than one close. So keep in mind a few ways of asking for each offer. You don't want to sound repetitious, even if you are. Actually it's pretty simple to change things around.

For example, you could attempt your first close with, "I'll be in your neighborhood later this week, and I'd love to stop by. Which day would be best for you, Thursday or Friday?"

The second time, try, "If I stop by on Thursday, about 3 p.m., will you have a couple of minutes to go over this?"

The third time, you could say, "I'd be happy to show you comparable homes right in your area. What day is better for you, Thursday or Friday?"

When closing, the first attempt rarely works. Keep trying, changing your language a little each time. Often it takes four or five close attempts to succeed.

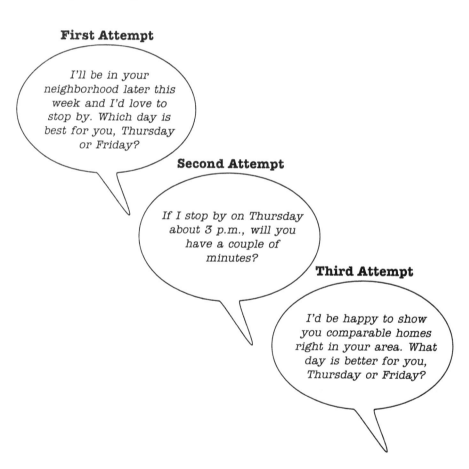

First Attempt

I'll be in your neighborhood later this week and I'd love to stop by. Which day is best for you, Thursday or Friday?

Second Attempt

If I stop by on Thursday about 3 p.m., will you have a couple of minutes?

Third Attempt

I'd be happy to show you comparable homes right in your area. What day is better for you, Thursday or Friday?

Just be careful about getting stuck on one line and always falling back on it. Then you do become repetitious.

How to Close Effectively

I've read 1,001 ways to close. Closes even have names. In sales handbooks, you'll find everything from "The Presidential Close" to "The Puppy Dog Close." Unfortunately, most names don't give you a hint as to how to do them.

While the variations are endless, you can boil closes down to a few techniques.

Although closing is not a natural ability, you can learn the skill through practice.

Direct Close

Most sales pros tell you to stay away from this type of close because it gives prospects too much room to maneuver. Use direct closes only when you're sure the prospect is in your hip pocket and will agree to anything.

Here are a few examples:

"What if I stop by this evening?"

"Why don't I show you what's available?"

"Would you be interested in sitting down and figuring out if this is the best move for you?"

With all three closes, you open yourself to the possibility that the prospect will say no. In fact, you make it easy for the prospect to do so. Many real estate professionals avoid this approach at all costs.

Assumptive Close

With this close, you simply assume that the prospect has agreed to your offer. You talk as if the decision had been made and just finalize details.

This technique is better than the direct close because it assumes the positive. But some people find it offensive.

With an assumptive close, you might say something like this:

"I can meet on Thursday. What time would you like me to stop by?"

"When can I show you what's available?"

"Are you interested in seeing what land is selling for, as well as looking at houses in the area?"

"How soon can we get together?"

If you misread a prospect and use an assumptive close, it's up to the prospect to correct you. Many people find that difficult — so they'll meet with you just to avoid a confrontation.

Forced-Choice Close

Sales experts around the world praise the forced-choice close. This close not only assumes the prospect will agree to your offer — it also gives prospects the chance to make a decision. Since the decision is predicated on the fact that they've agreed to the close, the close itself is taken for granted.

Recognize any of the following?

"I'll be in your neighborhood tonight. What time would you prefer I stop by — seven o'clock? Or is eight o'clock better for you?"

"What area would you like to see — Brookhaven, Ridgeside, or both?"

"Which day is better for you to come to my office, Wednesday or Thursday?"

"Would you like to drop by my office, or is it more convenient if I come to your home?"

Using this type of close, you can be professional, direct, and warm. People won't see you as pushy, but as someone who lets them make their own decisions.

The three approaches just outlined are the standard models. You can dress them up — but when you get right down to it, most closes are variations on these themes.

However, you should be aware of a few other variations that can get you out of a pinch. Many of these have been developed for face-to-face meetings, but they can easily be adapted for use over the phone.

Ben Franklin Approach

Some of us simply can't think unless we write things down. Some of us even make horrendous lists, separated into pros and cons, to help us make decisions.

If you hit a brick wall with a prospect, regroup. Ask the prospect to jot a few things down. Start off with all the reasons why they *shouldn't* meet with you. You've already heard all of these in their objections.

Now have the prospect draw a line down the middle of the page. On the other half, have them write all the reasons why they *should* meet with you.

Make sure the plus reasons are more numerous and substantial than the negative ones.

By the time the prospect is done, the decision has been made. Of course, the primary drawback to this approach is that many prospects will refuse to take the time to write the pros and cons.

Another "Yes"

This is something to think about. I've had people use it on me and it works. Basically, it's a variation of the assumptive close.

It goes like this:

"I can stop by your house Monday afternoon, about three o'clock. You will be home Monday, won't you?"

Before they know what's happening, they've said yes. Why? Because you diverted their attention from the fact that you're assuming they agreed to meet with you. Instead you asked a harmless little question sure to generate a "yes." Afterwards, it's hard for them to backtrack.

Last Ditch

Here you throw caution to the wind. You know you've lost. You're giving up. But the prospect has been friendly and you still have a slim hope. So with a note of sadness and self-incrimination in your voice, you plaintively ask,

"Mr. Elkhart, what did I do wrong?"

Now the prospect wants to help you. And chances are they'll open up and be honest with you.

Once this happens, you're on your way.

What About Your Friends?

Once again, you're ready to throw in the towel. You know you won't get anywhere with this prospect. But it has been a pleasant conversation. Before writing them off entirely, ask if they have any friends or relatives who'd like to live in the area. Or any neighbors thinking of selling their homes.

Talk a little bit about how you specialize in the prospect's area, how you're always on the lookout for new listings or prospective buyers, and how you'd appreciate whatever help they could give you.

You never know what kind of response you'll get. Maybe they are the president of the local country club, with lots of contacts. Or the head of a nearby union with many members who live in your farm. Or a schoolteacher who knows hundreds of families.

Following up a few friendly tips from a "written off" prospect could easily lead to some hefty commissions.

The Finishing Touch

Each time you attempt to close, you're at a crossroad. A prospect can choose either to take up your offer or to refuse it. How you close can affect the prospect's decision.

You should be aware that as the prospect weighs the decision, they consider three things:

- Whether it's okay for them to do it
- Whether the decision is sound
- Whether others will think it's okay, too

Even if the conversation has gone so well that you've closed without a problem, it's still important to give the prospect a psychological pat on the back.

Phrases like these will do it:

"You'll find that knowing what houses are selling for right in your own neighborhood will really help you determine the value of your home."

"With the market as strong as it is today, you're considering a move at just the right time."

"You'll be pleasantly surprised when you see how much your home has appreciated over the past five years."

Too many salespeople drop the ball at the end. As soon as they hear a "yes," they give a mental sigh of relief and drop the courtesies. Now they're just anxious to finalize the offer and move on. That shows in their voices.

Top salespeople know the secret of success is genuine concern for clients. That concern isn't predicated on clients performing as the salespeople desire — it grows out of watching clients take steps to their own benefit.

If you ruin the last 15 seconds of your call by taking off the cloak of courtesy, the prospect may meet with you — once. Or they may call and cancel.

Remember, the close of a call is just as important as its beginning. If you're consistent in your approach, you'll see consistent results.

A Word of Caution

During a call, be careful not to misinterpret prospects.

If someone asks, "Could we have our home in the Multiple Listing Book by Friday?" don't assume that's what they want. Ask, "Why is it important that you have your home in the Multiple Listing Book by Friday?"

Final Points

Closes, the decisive moments when you ask prospects to take up your offers, are the bottom line of farming by phone.

You can try to close at the beginning, middle, or end of a call. Wherever you do it, though, make sure you add a sense of urgency. If you don't give people a reason to act now, they'll delay indefinitely — especially when it comes to a major decision like buying or selling a home.

More people in sales fail because they don't know how to close than for any other reason. Closing is not a natural ability. It's a skill you learn through practice. If you think of it as trying to force people to do something, you'll never make it. Instead think of closing as asking them to take the first step along a path that will make their lives better.

Essentially, there are three ways for you to close:

Direct Close — The least favorite, this makes it easy for prospects to turn you down. You ask something like, "Do you want to meet with me?" It's rather like starting off the conversation with "Do you want to sell your house?" You should banish both phrases from your vocabulary.

Assumptive Close — A bit better than the direct close, assumptive closes assume the prospect has said yes. You just nail down the details as though everything had been resolved. Although you run the risk of a prospect correcting you with, "But I never said I wanted to meet with you. Where did you get that idea?" few people will do that.

Forced-Choice Close — The best of all. Now prospects feel that they're making the decision. But you structure it so that whatever they choose, they still have to take up your offer. You just let them pick the time or place or date. This approach drastically reduces the chances of a "no," while giving prospects the feeling that they have a say in things.

If you're really stuck at the end of a call, there are ways to try to salvage the conversation before the final close.

You can try the Ben Franklin approach, where the prospect writes down all the pros and cons of taking up your offer; the last ditch approach, where you sadly ask, "What did I do wrong?"; the "another yes," where you set up the offer, then quickly follow with a question to which they have to answer "yes"; or you can ask if they know someone in the market to buy or sell a home.

After closing, always reassure prospects that they're doing the right thing.

PRACTICE EXERCISE THIRTEEN

1. Pick three offers. List three ways you can increase the urgency of each one.
2. Identify the type of close used in the following:
    - Would you like to meet with me?
    - When would you like to meet?
    - Which day is better to meet — Thursday or Tuesday?

    Under what circumstances would you use each type?
3. Choose three offers. Write a "psychological pat on the back" for each.

CHAPTER 14

Wrapping It Up

> *There aren't any rules to success that will work unless you do.*
>
> — *Anonymous*

After you close, be quiet. Sometimes when tension disappears, we relax and let words spill out of our mouths. But now it's more important than ever for you to stay professional.

As soon as you finish closing — whether successfully or not — move smoothly into the wrap-up. This stage of the call is as critical as any other.

Good-Bye Is Not Forever

You'll probably never end a prospecting call and think, "Thank heavens; that's the last time I'll have to deal with them."

Never knowing what the future will bring, you can't afford to offend anyone. Someone who moves away from your farm could move back a year later.

If you just don't like someone, work at liking them. You may be surprised at how your feelings can change.

Now let's get into the specific steps of finalizing a call.

If the prospect has agreed to meet with you, you need to:

1. Set up the specifics of the appointment (date, time, and place).

2. Repeat the specifics.

3. Give the prospect your name and phone number.

4. Thank them for their time and patience.

5. Be the last to hang up.

More often, of course, you'll have established the beginnings of a relationship, but the stage isn't set yet for a meeting. Then the wrap up might go like this:

1. Summarize the outcome of the call.

2. Tell them you'll be calling again and give an approximate date.

3. Thank them for their time and patience.

4. Be the last to hang up.

Setting Up the Appointment

When setting up appointments, it's best to schedule them as soon as possible. That way the positive feelings from your call will carry over. Some real estate professionals, though, prefer to schedule all their appointments for the next week, so they can start off

Monday morning with maximum efficiency. Do whatever feels best for you.

Sometimes you may want to meet prospects at your office, where you can feel more in charge and more professional. But most often, you should meet prospects in their homes.

Being willing to drive to prospect's homes demonstrates that they're important to you and that you're willing to give them personal attention.

It also will be useful because you'll see how your prospects live. That should tell you a lot about the kind of people they are.

Once I heard a building contractor talking about how he could walk into someone's house and, in a few minutes, tell you what kind of music they listened to, what kind of car they drove, how often they did their laundry, and whether they watched a lot of TV. Our homes are windows through which others see us.

Use the wrap up to end your call professionally and courteously.

Ultimately, the decision on where to meet should belong to the prospect. Whatever they choose, let them know you'll do everything you can to make the meeting happen.

Not long ago, I met a former top Cadillac salesman. His secret? Whenever he sold a car, he'd call the new owners three months later and remind them it was time for a checkup. The next morning, he'd be at their house, drop off his Cadillac, and drive theirs to the dealership. That night he'd bring it back, all tuned up and ready to go.

After a few months, he had so many referrals that he had trouble handling them. By then, people were calling up, and he was selling cars over the phone. He'd ask what they wanted, they'd work out a deal and that night, he'd be on their doorstep, keys in hand.

Sounds incredible, doesn't it? But people liked how far he went to make them happy.

So let prospects know that you value them and they'll value you in return.

Write It Down, Please

In normal conversation, most people only pay attention to one out of every ten words. That means that prospects are likely to miss important details of your offers.

When giving instructions over the phone, be careful. Repeat everything and if you feel it's appropriate, ask the prospect to write down the details. That way you minimize the chance of a missed appointment or forgotten phone call.

You do the same. Whenever you make a promise to meet someone or send some materials, write it down immediately.

If you arrange to drop something off at a prospect's home, verify the address — even though it's in your prospect file. Chances are it could be a number or two off. This will save you the embarrassment of walking up to the wrong house.

When you note the appointment in your schedule book, write directions next to it. Then you don't have to worry about finding the little scrap of paper with your notes when you walk out the door.

Also remember to give prospects your name and phone number so they can reach you if something comes up.

If the meeting is at your office, ask if they know how to get there. If there's any doubt, go through the directions step-by-step. When prospects get lost, it costs both of you in time.

Say It Again

A cardinal rule for any sales or direct marketing effort is this sequence:

- Tell them what you're going to tell them.
- Tell them.
- Tell them what you've just told them.

Repetition (to a point!) in sales is good. It helps get your points across so people remember them.

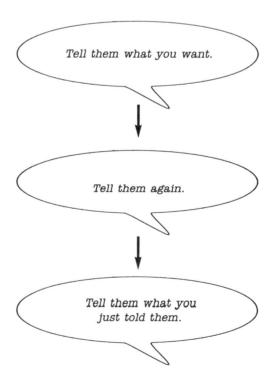

Repetition may seem to be the mother of boredom, but it's actually great for sales. People don't always remember what they hear. As a conversation continues, they think about it. After they've heard it enough times, they begin to believe it.

Post-Close, Follow-up Questions

Once you've closed, it's a good time to ask a few more questions. If you haven't asked how many people are in the family, do it now. Or inquire about what they do for a living. Don't go overboard with your questions or they'll get annoyed. Just ask about the basics so you have a more complete file.

If it has been a pleasant conversation but they're not ready to take up your offer, let them know that you'll stay in touch. That's a signal that you're serious about your work and your commitment to the neighborhood. Don't worry about giving them a specific time frame. Just say something like, "Well, I'll call back in a few months or so, just to see if anything's changed." Hardly anyone will tell you not to bother. Remember, in this business, good-bye is never forever.

Showing Your Gratitude

After the offer is accepted, the instructions given, the psychological pat on the back awarded, is it time to hang up?

Not yet.

You need to say thank-you.

Whether or not a prospect has agreed to your offer, they've given up their time to listen and talk to you. They're entitled to a "thank you."

If you've run into a desperately lonely person who has poured out their heart, or if someone has shared information with you that could be considered confidential, thank them for their confidence. Let them know they can trust you.

Always thank a prospect for their time.

However, on every call, thank the prospect for their time and patience. Then add, "I look forward to meeting you." Or "I look forward to talking to you again."

Thank-you's carry a lot of weight. Prospects remember them. Overlook common courtesy, and people will overlook you.

Always be the last to hang up. Wait for the click that tells you the call is over. If a prospect has a last-minute thought, there's nothing more frustrating than talking into a dead phone line. And how many prospects will go to the trouble of looking up your number and calling you back?

Filing a Reminder

As you place the phone back in its cradle, decide when you'll call the prospect again. Make a note on the prospect's file.

If the prospect falls into your regular farming schedule, you may want to set up a system using small, colored adhesive circles. If you call each home four times a year, you could organize it like this:

Blue stickers	Winter
Green stickers	Spring
Red stickers	Summer
Orange stickers	Fall

If you bump someone from your winter to your spring session, just stick a green circle on their card.

If you decide to call back in a few weeks, pick a specific date and write it in your appointment book or put it on your computerized schedule.

Do this before moving on to the next call.

During the entire conversation, you should take brief notes, describing what objections a prospect raises and your impressions of them. Make sure you can read what you write. It won't be any easier a few months later.

Occasionally, you'll run into a prospect that you hit it off with immediately. Or a call was so positive, even if they didn't agree to your offer, you want to follow up.

It is important to reassure your prospect that they have made the right decision by accepting your offer.

For calls like those, sending a short thank-you note or writing a special handwritten message on your next direct-mail letter might be appropriate.

If you decide a thank-you note is in order, write it as soon as you finish your phone session. Be sure it gets in the mail that day.

If you opt for a handwritten message, make a note and put it in a file you keep just for that purpose. That way, every time you're ready to mail a bunch of letters, you can check the file for which ones need special attention.

Finally, if you promise to send some information, do it as soon as your phone session is over. Enclose a little note. Then write in your schedule book to call them in two or three days to see if they've gotten your material and what they think of it.

If you don't remember anything else, remember to always write everything down. You may think you have the memory of an elephant, but even elephants forget.

Moving On

When the call is over and the notes finished, what's next?

Whatever you do, don't take a coffee break. Don't rush to tell someone about the great appointment you just set up or your fantastic new lead on a half-million-dollar listing.

Keep in mind that after you score an interview, there's no better time to score another than right away. You want to keep that lilt of enthusiasm in your voice. So start dialing.

On the other hand, if the last call was a downer, don't let it get to you. Remind yourself that not everyone will say yes. You only need one . . . or two . . . or three . . . or whatever your goal is for that session.

Sometimes taking a deep breath helps clear your head and brush away unpleasant feelings.

Move through your farm directory systematically. Don't skip people because you dislike their names or you remember a previous unpleasant call. Stay positive, warm, and take each prospect in order. Do the best job you can, and you'll finish your last call of the day with a sense of satisfaction.

Do the best you can, the best way you know how, experiment with doing it better, and, most important of all, keep trying.

Only real estate agents who don't give up succeed.

> *Always finish what you start. Unfinished business tends to pile up.*

Final Points

Down to the last click of the receiver, there are right and wrong ways to handle calls. For the wrap-up, the proper procedure is this:

1. Set up follow-through for the offer.

2. Repeat important information such as time, place, and date.

3. Give the prospect your name and number.

4. Thank the prospect.

5. Be the last to hang up.

If the call ends without the prospect agreeing to your offer, be courteous and kind. Let the prospect know that you'll call again.

Right after a call ends, jot down notes on how you need to follow up and when you plan to call again. Whatever type of follow-up you choose, be prompt and be efficient.

Plunge into your next call without a break. Let the momentum work for you. Right after you've had one good call, your enthusiasm gives you a great edge for the next.

Always remember to end every call on a warm and personal note, echoing the way you started the call. Hold that note until the prospect's final click signals the call is over. Then start again.

PRACTICE EXERCISE FOURTEEN

1. Think about how you react to clients.
   Do you like some better than others?
   Do you act differently around those you like better?
   How can you change these behaviors?
2. The next time you're on a call, take notes.
   When you hang up, go back over the notes.
   Are they legible? Comprehensive?
   How can you improve your on-the-phone note taking?
3. Write three offers.
   Select a major benefit for each.
   Now write each benefit three ways, changing the words but not the substance each time.
4. Analyze your follow-up with clients.
   If you promise a client information, do you put it in the mail that day?
   How can you improve your follow-up?

SECTION FOUR

Sample Scripts

NOTE: These scripts are intended only as general guidelines. They will give you ideas about offers and how to handle objections. Change them so that you're comfortable and you can speak naturally during the calls.

CHAPTER 15

Sample Farm Call Scripts

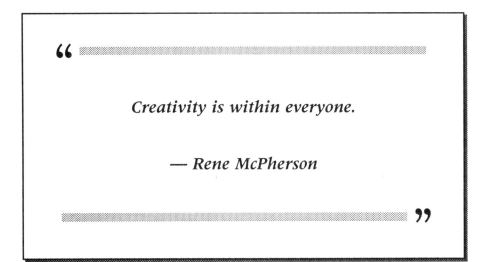

Creativity is within everyone.

— *Rene McPherson*

The following scripts are organized by offer. The first five sections — introductory scripts, general offers, home evaluation offers, information kit offers, and booklet offers — are for general prospecting.

The next five sections — announcement scripts, invitation offers, special circumstances offers, follow-up referrals — are situation specific.

The last section, client farm, will help you keep in touch with former clients.

Before using any script, read it and change it so that you're comfortable with it.

CONTENTS

INTRODUCTORY SCRIPTS

The purpose of introductory phone calls is not to generate leads, but to pave the way for later, more direct solicitations. It's a means of allowing you and prospects to get to know each other and to start building that all-important trust.

"Introductory script with a premium" introduces you and at the same time, offers a free gift. It immediately establishes a positive relationship with prospective clients and demonstrates that meeting their needs is your top priority. This script is primarily for agents who are new to a farm area.

"Seminar invitation" invites prospects to a special real estate seminar you've organized that focuses on your farm. It would be good to follow this up with a short note of confirmation. You could use the "Seminar letter" in *How To Farm Successfully — By Mail* as a model. Organizing a seminar can provide a boost to an agent who's been farming for a while but hasn't seen many results.

"Survey" is a terrific way to position yourself as a real estate professional. It also allows you to collect information that will make later marketing efforts more effective. This script will work both for new agents and those who have been farming an area for a while.

Remember — don't expect any prospect to list a home with you during a telephone call. The purpose of introductory calls is familiarization, not listings. Let the listings come later.

INTRODUCTORY SCRIPT WITH PREMIUM
Geographic or social farm

It's 7 a.m. Joan Lindenhall just wakes up.

Her first thought is, "Oh, no. Today I have to tackle the phone."

When organizing her farm marketing strategy last week, she had decided to introduce herself to the farm by phone. Joan feels more comfortable on the phone and she wants that "personal" contact. Realizing, however, the futility of calling up and saying, "Here I am!," she decided to offer prospective clients a free gift.

Choosing a gift wasn't easy. She thought they would find potholders or kitchen magnets useful, but she didn't like the image they conveyed. She wanted something more professional. Notepads were okay, but not "big" or unusual enough.

Other gifts she considered included:

• a detailed map of the area

• a booklet of discount coupons from local merchants

• note cards with photographs featuring local landmarks

She decided the detailed map was too impersonal; the discount coupons a great idea but a little too commercial; and the note cards hard to create and targeted at the wrong market.

Finally, she decided to write and print up a small booklet detailing the history of the area that included a list of mortgage brokers, title companies, real estate attorneys and other property specialists. If a prospect wanted the book, he or she would probably be interested in the real estate seminar she was planning two months later.

Her next decision was whether to mail the booklet to prospects or drop it by their homes. She decided to play it by ear, depending on how many people wanted the booklet.

If she had the time, she would drop it off and take a chance that they'd be home. If not, she'd keep open the option of mailing it. After all, the primary goal of this call was to introduce herself.

After a long shower, Joan ate a quick bowl of cereal and watched the morning news. About 8:00, she put on a dark wool business suit and did her make-up. She sat down at her desk in her home office. Before starting, she cleared away the stacks of papers, pulled out the phone log she had created the day before, grabbed her prospects' files and glanced over her phone script one more time.

At 9:00, she took five deep breaths and looked at the flowering cherry tree outside the window and made her first call . . .

Joan: *Good morning. Trina Helgman?*

Prospect: *Yes?*

Joan: *Ms. Helgman, my name is Joan Lindenhall and I'm with Greenbrier Realty. Do you have a minute?*

Prospect: *I'm about to leave. But what do you want?*

Joan: *Ms. Helgman, I'm calling because Greenbrier has just put me in charge of Castle Pines real estate. To introduce myself to you and other homeowners, I'm offering a free gift that I'm sure you'll find useful.*

Prospect: *What is it?*

Joan: *It's a unique booklet that describes the history of Castle Pines and more importantly, gives you hard-to-find information about your property. After reading it, you'll have a very good idea of how the value of your house has changed recently and how it's likely to change in the future. Would you be interested in my dropping off a free copy?*

Prospect: *Not really. I have a pretty good idea of how much my house is worth.*

Joan: *Ms. Helgman, this booklet not only describes the neighborhood, it gives you specific numbers. It's a great reference source. Besides, it's free. I can get one to you today. How about it?*

Prospect: *I already have so much clutter around here. I really don't think I need anything else.*

Joan: *I understand. You should see my desk. But remember that this booklet focuses specifically on Castle Pines properties. You won't find it at the local bookstore and frankly, there's no other place that has this type of information. I really would like for you to have it. Can I drop one off today?*

Prospect: *Okay. Do you have my address?*

Joan: *5110 Windy Point Road. Is that right?*

Prospect: *Yes.*

Phrases such as "I understand. You should see my desk." build rapport.

Asking what manner of address she prefers is polite.

> Joan: *How should I address it? Do you prefer Miss, Ms. or Mrs.?*
>
> Prospect: *Ms. is fine.*
>
> Joan: *Ms. Helgman, you'll have your booklet this evening. Would it be all right if I stopped by about 6:30?*
>
> Prospect: *Yes.*
>
> Joan: *If you read it and have any questions, just call me. My number is on the front of the booklet. Call anytime. I'll be happy to help however I can. And Ms. Helgman, thank you so much.*
>
> Prospect: *Thank you. Good-bye. CLICK.*
>
> Joan: *CLICK.*

NOTES:

1. If the prospect had said "No" again, Joan would've dropped it and closed the conversation with, "Ms. Helgman, I appreciate your time. If you ever have any questions about real estate, I'm always here for you. Over the next few months, you'll be hearing more from me as I get to know the needs of Castle Pines homeowners better. Again, thank you for your time."

2. For a social farm, create a booklet that covers real estate trends in the city or county — not just a neighborhood. Use an introduction like, "Ms. Helgman, I'm calling because I'm interested in giving members of St. John's Church top-quality real estate services. To introduce myself to you and other St. John's members, I'm offering . . ."

SEMINAR INVITATION
Geographic or social farm

It's 3 p.m. Barbara can hear the grade school students running out of the classrooms across the street. It has been a good day. She got a call from a couple in her farm interested in selling their home and made an appointment to see them tomorrow evening. The rest of the day, she fielded phone calls, got some paperwork done, and even had the time to drive around her farm looking for new "For Sale" signs. The fact that she'd seen only one, a new For Sale By Owner, made her feel good. She jotted down the address and made a note to call them later.

Now, though, it was time to get ready to call farm residents and invite them to a seminar two weeks away. She could have sent out letters, but she got caught up in escrow problems and hadn't finished them in time. Now she either had to call or change the date. Changing the date would be difficult — the community hall was booked two months ahead.

Besides, she'd already invited Mort Flagler, a local mortgage broker, and Rhonda Chen, the head of city planning, to speak at the seminar. She expected, though, the audience would be most interested in the charts she had prepared of changes in property values over the past ten years. Barbara herself had been surprised at the slow but amazingly steady growth. Every homeowner in the room will probably make money when he or she sells, Barbara thought.

She wanted 30 to 40 people at the seminar. That meant she had to call 150 to 200. She would stop as soon as she reached her goal. She had her best luck calling around dinnertime.

In a soft voice, she read through her script again. If a caller came up with some unanticipated objections, she thought she could handle them.

Barbara used individualized information — the number of years he had owned the house. She didn't play dumb and ask him. Instead she showed that she had done her homework.

Barbara: *Good afternoon. Mr. Brown?*

Prospect: *Yes, this is Mr. Brown.*

Barbara: *Mr. Brown, my name is Barbara Kozlowski. I'm with Greenbrier Realty here in Castle Pines. Do you have a minute?*

Prospect: *Just a minute.*

Barbara: *Mr. Brown, if you invested $100,000 in the stock market, how often would you check the Dow Jones industrial average?*

Prospect: *Probably every day.*

Barbara: *Me, too. And your investment in your home is like a stock investment. I'm calling to offer you an opportunity to check on how your investment is doing. You've owned your house for seven years. Is that right?*

Prospect: *Yes.*

Barbara: *How much do you think your home has appreciated?*

Prospect: *I'd guess about $15,000.*

Barbara: *I've pulled together some figures that show the average seven year appreciation of a Castle Pines home is 25%. Mr. Brown, you could have made about $25,000 on your home. How'd you like to make that much — or more — over the next seven years?*

Prospect: *What are you getting at?*

Barbara: *I'm calling to invite you, together with a small group of other Castle Pines homeowners, to a special seminar on Thursday, October 7th. I've organized it so we can talk about what's happening to our home values and maybe discuss some simple ways to improve our properties. We'll also talk about how changes in the neighborhood affect property values. Can I count on you to show up Thursday night?*

Prospect: *I think I'm busy.*

Barbara: *Mr. Brown, I'm inviting all our neighbors. It's great opportunity for us to get together and talk about what really is our most important financial asset. It could make a difference, too, in what happens to the neighborhood over the next few years. It's right at the community center and I'll have free coffee and cakes for everyone. Will you join us?*

Prospect: *What can I learn that I don't already know?*

Barbara: *For one thing, all the information focuses on the Castle Pines real estate market. You won't find it in the local paper or even the local library. Second, you'll hear Mort Flagler, a local mortgage broker, discuss how to get the most out of your home investment and Rhonda Chen, the head of city planning, talk about proposed changes to Rocky Road. That could affect the value of a number of Castle Pines properties. I really think this seminar would be worthwhile for you. Can I add your name to the list of those who will join us?*

Prospect: *Well, I guess I can make it.*

Barbara: *Great. By the way, I'll have free child care in case anyone else in the family would like to come. Do you think any other family members would be interested?*

If he didn't want to attend, Barbara could offer to send a summary report of the meeting.

Prospect: *My wife, Mary, will probably want to go.*

Barbara: *Does that mean you'll need child care?*

Prospect: *No, that's okay.*

If he did want child care, Barbara would have gotten the number and ages of the children.

Barbara: *Mr. Brown, I'll plan on seeing you and your wife, Mary, at our seminar at the community center on Thursday, October 7th. It starts at 7 p.m. and remember to skip dessert that night — I'll have plenty of cakes and coffee.*

Prospect: *Okay.*

Barbara: *I look forward to seeing you.*

Prospect: *Good-bye.* CLICK.

Barbara: CLICK.

NOTES:

1. For a social farm, emphasize the uniqueness of the group. For example, "I'm calling to invite you, together with a small number of other members of St. John's Congregation . . ."

2. Send a thank-you note to all those who attend the seminar. On the following pages, you will find a sample note along with tips for presenting and organizing a seminar.

THANK YOU NOTE (Handwritten or typed)

Only use first names if you're comfortable with them

Get these in the mail the next day

> March 31, 1996
>
> Les and Mary Brown
> 8993 Butterfield Drive
> Castle Pines, NC 60056
>
> Dear Les and Mary,
>
> Thank you very much for attending the real estate seminar last night.
>
> I hope that you found the seminar informative and worthwhile. If you have any questions about your property specifically, I'd be glad to stop by. Just give me a call at my office (555-8900) during the day or at home (555-8897) or on my pager (555-7703) evenings and weekends.
>
> People like you make working in Castle Pines a real pleasure.
>
> Sincerely,
>
> Barbara Kozlowski
> Realtor-Associate®

(NOTE: IF POSSIBLE, ADD A COMMENT DIRECTED SPECIFICALLY TO THE PERSON. FOR EXAMPLE, "I thought your questions about property taxes were excellent." or "It was interesting to see how many neighbors agreed with you about road problems.")

TIPS FOR PRESENTATION:

Prepare a 20-minute presentation with lots of colorful figures and tables. For pointers, watch talk shows such as "Oprah" or "Donahue" to see how to get your audience involved in the discussion.

Before you begin, make sure everyone fills out and puts on a name tag. Pass around a sign-up sheet asking for names, addresses, phone numbers and specific areas of concern.

Have pictures, graphs and figures prominently displayed.

1. Create large, easy-to-see tables and graphs that...

    a. trace the value of homes in your farm area over the past five years,

    b. list five factors that have significantly affected property values,

    c. list number of homes on market last year and average selling price compared to number of homes on market this year. Compare upper and lower end selling prices.

2. Have a local real estate finance expert talk briefly about new types of mortgages, refinancing, home equity lines of credit, etc. You also may want a property insurance representative or an investment counselor to make a brief presentation. Select speakers who'd address issues of concern to the community. For example, if a new development is planned nearby, you may want to invite a developer or city official who can discuss its impact on the surrounding area.

3. Project future property value trends for the next few years.

4. Prepare one-page summary sheet that they can take home. Distribute at end of presentation so they're not reading it as you're talking.

5. Allow time for questions and answers at end of presentations.

6. Be sure to provide child care and food.

TIPS FOR ORGANIZING DISCUSSION

1. Prepare 15-20 questions. Avoid yes/no questions; ask open-ended ones.

2. Select three or four people that you know will attend and prepare them with questions to ask you.

3. Allow audience members to raise issues of concern but keep discussion focused on those related to property values. Don't be afraid to step in and change topics.

4. Have a colleague in the audience take extensive notes on the discussion (or if possible, tape record it). This will give you a record of important homeowner concerns towards which you can direct future marketing efforts.

SURVEY

Geographic or social farm

Raoul throws his keys on the desk and stretches. It has been a long day. He had taken two sets of clients out to look at homes. Nary a nibble. Nothing seemed right. But he had gotten a better idea of what they'd like. He thought he'd call them the next day about two smaller properties.

He looked at the pile of papers on his desk and groaned. He'd promised himself that he would spend the last two hours that day beginning the telephone survey of his farm. Then he thought about what he could gain by it. Get to know lots of prospects. Potential sales. Great recommendations. He compared prospecting to throwing out a big ball of yarn and watching it unravel. He didn't know exactly where it would end up — but he was pretty sure it would be good.

He got a fresh cup of coffee, glanced at the motivational calendar his girlfriend had given him and began rehearsing his script. He felt pretty good about it. After all, he wasn't giving anyone a hard sell — all he was after was information. And people did like to talk.

Raoul:	*Mrs. Goldman, please.*
Prospect:	*This is she.*
Raoul:	*Mrs. Goldman, this is Raoul Ramirez. I'm with Greenbrier Real Estate. Perhaps you've seen our signs around Castle Pines?*
Prospect:	*I think so.*
Raoul:	*Mrs. Goldman, I was wondering if you could do me a favor.*
Prospect:	*Yes.*
Raoul:	*As a real estate agent specializing in Castle Pines, it's important for me to know as much as I can about our neighborhood and the people who live here. I have a few questions that I'm asking all Castle Pines homeowners. Would you take three to four minutes to answer them?*
Prospect:	*Sure.*
Raoul:	*Thank you so much, Mrs. Goldman. First, can you tell me the year you bought your home?*
Prospect:	*1992.*
Raoul:	*Why did you decide to buy in Castle Pines?*
Prospect:	*It's close to my office and it has excellent schools.*
Raoul:	*Great. How many people live in your home?*
Prospect:	*Let's see. My husband, myself and three children. Five of us.*
Raoul:	*Do you own or rent?*
Prospect:	*We own our home.*
Raoul:	*What do you think are the top three advantages to living in Castle Pines?*
Prospect:	*I like the way the neighborhood is maintained. We also like the convenience. It's close to restaurants and shopping.*
Raoul:	*What do you think are the top three drawbacks to living in Castle Pines?*

Prospect: *I have the impression that crime is on the rise. I worry about that. I also am unhappy about the new development on Noble Street. I can't think of a third one.*

Raoul: *I know a lot of other homeowners feel the same way you do about the new development. Just a few more questions. Would you mind telling me your favorite features of your home?*

Prospect: *The screened porch and the garden.*

Raoul: *How much longer do you expect to live in it?*

Prospect: *I don't know. Sometimes we talk about moving, but I'd guess we'll be here another three or four years.*

Raoul: *Could you please tell me your occupation and the occupation of other adults in your home?*

Prospect: *I'm an attorney and my husband is an engineer.*

Raoul: *Is there anything you'd like to add?*

Prospect: *Just that overall, we've been very happy in Castle Pines.*

Raoul: *That's terrific. Mrs. Goldman, I want to thank you for taking the time to help me. Would you like a copy of the survey results when I'm finished?*

Prospect: *Sure.*

Raoul: *Your address is 4897 Evergreen Road, right?*

Prospect: *Right.*

Raoul: *Great. You'll probably receive these in the next two to three weeks. And Mrs. Goldman, thanks again for your time.*

Prospect: *You're welcome. CLICK.*

Raoul: *CLICK.*

When possible, comment on what the prospect says. Be supportive, not critical.

If a prospect doesn't want a copy of the results, don't push it.

Always hang up last.

NOTES:

1. Take extensive notes during these interviews. You should glean valuable information that you can use later to create very targeted marketing appeals. For example, if a prospect expresses concern about crime, make sure that you send him or her an offer for a "Crime-Stoppers" kit or a "Neighborhood Watch" kit.

2. For a social farm, change the introduction of yourself to read, "As an agent interested in giving St. John's members top quality real estate services, it's important for me to know as much as I can about your real estate needs and desires. I have a few questions . . ."

3. Summary of results would include:

   • average length of time families have been in homes
   • percentages of owners and renters
   • average number of people per household
   • average length of time people expect to be in homes
   • top five advantages to living in Castle Pines
   • top five drawbacks to living in Castle Pines
   • breakdown of occupations

GENERAL OFFERS

General offers discuss the status of the real estate market in general and link it to a specific neighborhood or in the case of a social farm, group of homeowners. In other words, these provide a local angle to national trends. This interests homeowners who read national statistics but aren't sure how the numbers apply to their own neighborhoods and circumstances.

These offers also enhance your standing as a real estate professional, as they allow you to demonstrate your understanding of the national real estate market and your knowledge of the local market. What's very important, however, is that you develop the links between national and local trends carefully. You have to use strong logic.

Look for that in the phone scripts that follow.

"Good times" and "Bad times" are examples of phone scripts that give reasons to sell when a market is heading up or down. They work because they make sense.

"Annual Report" offers a premium — a one-of-a-kind document with real estate information specific to your farm neighborhood. It should be of interest to anyone who takes their investment in their home seriously. While you can use this phone script any time of the year, most "Annual Reports" appear in June, September or January.

"General offers" are good for either new agents or those who have been working a farm for a while. They should be a staple of your marketing plan which you pull out at least once a year. They're economically driven and most homeowners are interested in economics.

GOOD TIMES

Geographic or social farm

Rumbles of an upswing in domestic home construction dominated the real estate section. After a seven-year slump, it looked like things finally might be improving.

As Pat read the story in the local newspaper, she noticed its AP dateline. As usual, it was oriented to the entire U.S. Not Castle Pines, North Carolina, USA. If the reporter had asked her, she could have told him that things were looking up. Sales for the past six months had been climbing beyond the office's expectations. Prices were inching up, too.

Pat put down the paper to think. Everyone in her farm who even glanced at the business page would see this story. With such a large headline, who could miss it? How many of my farm residents, she mused, would wonder how it applied to them? Do they have any idea what all this means?

Letting them know might not be a bad idea, she speculated. After all, at least four or five people in the farm were probably thinking of selling their homes. This could be the incentive that pushed them into doing it.

The next day, Pat began working on a script for calling prospects. It took her several days to polish it, then she pulled out her list, organized her files, and sat down to make the calls.

Child:	*Hello?*
Pat:	*Hello. Could I please speak to Mr. Tushkent?*
Child:	*Just a minute. I'll get him.*
Prospect:	*Hello?*
Pat:	*Mr. Tushkent, this is Pat Reilly with Greenbrier Realty. Do you have a minute?*
Prospect:	*Just a minute.*
Pat:	*I'm calling about something in the local paper the other day. Did you see the story about how the national real estate market is booming?*
Prospect:	*Yes, I did.*
Pat:	*Well, what's true nationally is also true locally. As the story pointed out, interest rates have dropped substantially. In fact, today they hit 8-1/2%. You've owned your home five years, right? So you bought when rates were about 12%?*
Prospect:	*I'm paying 11-1/4%.*
Pat:	*Mr. Tushkent, have you considered that you and your family could be living in a larger, more comfortable home for the same monthly payments that you're making now? May I ask how many children you have?*
Prospect:	*Two.*
Pat:	*How old are they?*
Prospect:	*Rob is seven and Elaine is 11.*
Pat:	*As your children become teenagers, a little more room couldn't hurt, could it? If you've ever wanted an extra bathroom, guest room, or den, now's a great time to do it. Tell me, what do you look for in a home?*
Prospect:	*Well, my wife likes to cook so we need a big kitchen. I do a lot of work in the garage.*
Pat:	*What kind of work?*
Prospect:	*Mostly woodwork. I'm a manager, but I like to work with my hands.*

Pat works at engaging the prospect in conversation through a series of open-ended questions.

Pat gives the prospect a number of choices — weekday or weekend, day on which to meet, whether they go out and see the homes or look at pictures.

Pat:	*If you'd like a home with a big, roomy kitchen and a garage with a workshop, I know of two or three homes on the market right in your neighborhood. (Pause) Would you like to have a look at them this weekend? Or I could bring photographs and descriptions over to your home in the next day or two. What would you prefer?*
Prospect:	*I have to talk to my wife about this.*
Pat:	*Of course. I'd be happy to sit down with both of you and go over the facts and figures. In just a few minutes, you'd clearly see why now is such a good time to move up. And just think . . . it probably won't cost you any more than what you're paying right now. Now what is better for you — a weekday or the weekend?*
Prospect:	*Weekend, I guess.*
Pat:	*Let me see. I have Saturday at 1 p.m. or Sunday at 4:30. Which is better for you?*
Prospect:	*Saturday.*
Pat:	*All right. I'll meet you at your home Saturday at 1 p.m.*
Prospect:	*Fine.*
Pat:	*Thank you very much, Mr. Tushkent. If you need to reach me before Saturday, my number is 555-8876. Or you can call me at home, 555-9987. I look forward to meeting you and your wife.*
Prospect:	*Good-bye.*
Pat:	*Good-bye.*
Prospect:	*CLICK.*
Pat:	*CLICK.*

Pat gives the prospect a way to reach her if he changes his mind. This is common courtesy.

NOTES:

1. Pat had done her homework and knew when the prospect had bought his home and what rates were that year. It's easy to have this information in front of you — just pull out the prospect's farm file and make a table of average mortgage rates for the past 15 years. You'll impress them with your knowledge and it will take very little time to prepare.

2. If the prospect doesn't want to look at properties, Pat should suggest that he consider refinancing and ask if he'd like referrals to some excellent mortgage brokers in the area.

BAD TIMES

Geographic or social farm

Larry stared out the window, reflecting on the sagging sales at the real estate office. He'd read all the sales books that talked about turning a downside into an opportunity. But how could he do it? Every time he picked up the paper, headlines wailed about the abysmal real estate market. Everyone in the country thought they'd plunged into a hole from which it would take a long time to recover.

The truth is, he'd closed on a house four days earlier. And he was working on five other listings. Sure, that was fewer than before. But these were good, solid properties. The momentum might have slowed, but there was still action.

He also had established a great relationship with a mortgage banker and was learning about all the creative ways to finance home buying. He laughed as he thought that when the economy slows down, lenders' creativity speeds up. They'd never have allowed so much flexibility on the buyers' part if the market had stayed strong.

Now he had to take this bad news and turn it into something good. He didn't want his prospects thinking that it was a bad time to sell — it really wasn't. At least not for sellers in certain circumstances. But could he communicate this to his farm?

They'd never know if he didn't tell them.

He sat down, pulled out a piece of paper and started working on his "Bad Times" phone script.

Larry: *Good morning. Mr. Poussaint?*

Prospect: *Yes?*

Larry: *Mr. Poussaint, this is Larry Kelly with Greenbrier Realty. Do you have a minute?*

Prospect: *Sure.*

Larry: *Mr. Poussaint, how would you describe today's real estate market?*

Prospect: *Pretty bad.*

Larry: *That's what I was afraid of. You see, Mr. Poussaint, things aren't as bad as you might think. In fact, in Castle Pines, Greenbrier has sold five houses in the past month. Does that surprise you?*

Prospect: *A little.*

Larry: *Well, the moral of the story is that you can't always believe what you read. The truth is that good, well-marketed homes sell every day. But people still think we're in a slump. That's one reason why I have some terrific bargains available in Castle Pines. (Pause) Mr. Poussaint, you live in a three-bedroom, two bath ranch, don't you?*

Prospect: *Yes.*

Larry: *What would you say if I told you that there's a house very similar to yours but with more square footage just two miles away? It has just been repossessed by the bank. It's worth about $240,000 and right now, it's listed at $180,000. How would you like to take a look at this house?*

Prospect: *I'm not planning to move.*

Larry: *I can understand that. But now's a great time to pick up a real bargain. The house I mentioned has a beautifully landscaped garden and a gourmet kitchen. I also have a house on Potter Street that's priced well below market value. The seller has just been transferred and he's willing to do some financing. Tell me, Mr. Poussaint, what do you look for in a house?*

Prospect: *Bedrooms. I have four teenagers.*

The script has two major appeals: security (the market isn't as bad as you think) and fear (don't miss this opportunity).

> Larry: *Wouldn't it be great to move to a home with more than enough room for everyone? And if you can find a house priced below its appraised value . . . Opportunities like this don't come along every day. What would it hurt to look?*
>
> Prospect: *It wouldn't, I guess.*
>
> Larry: *Great. Would you like to meet Thursday or Friday or would Saturday or Sunday be better for you?*
>
> Prospect: *Thursday would be fine. Remember — I just want to look. I'm not really interested in buying.*
>
> Larry: *That's fine. How about I pick you up at 7?*
>
> Prospect: *Seven's all right.*
>
> Larry: *Perfect. I'll pick you up Thursday at your home at 7 p.m. If you need to reach me before then, you can call me at 555-9980 during the day or at 555-9978 during the evening.*
>
> Prospect: *Great.*
>
> Larry: *Mr. Poussaint, thank you very much. I look forward to seeing you.*
>
> Prospect: *Thank you. CLICK.*
>
> Larry: *CLICK.*

NOTES:

1. This phone script works because Larry had some great bargains ready to describe and he had checked to make sure the bargains were comparable to (or better than) the prospect's current home.

2. If the prospect had turned him down again, Larry could have made one last try. He could have asked, "Mr. Poussaint, if you could design your home any way you wanted, what kind of home would you have?." The prospect would have given a general description and Larry would have promised that if a house like that came along, he would let the prospect know. This gives him the room to continue the relationship, despite the prospect's unwillingness to agree to this particular request.

3. For a social farm, change the emphasis from "In Castle Pines, Greenbrier has sold five houses . . . " to "In (city or county), Greenbrier has sold . . ."

ANNUAL REPORT

Geographic or social farm

Reggie crumpled up his last phone message and tossed it into the wastebasket. His calls for the day returned, it was time to start on his next major project. For the past few weeks, he'd been collecting real estate statistics on the local area. Unlike the broad national numbers that dominated the newspaper, these figures reflected the everyday reality in which he lived and worked.

With his printer's help, he'd put the figures in an attractive Annual Report. Only three pages long, it summarized the average selling price of homes in the area, the percentage of homes that sold either at the full listing price or within $10,000 of it, how long the average home stayed on the market, the total number of listed homes, how many listed homes were taken off the market unsold, and the number of homeowners who chose to list with Greenbrier Real Estate. It also listed specific homes which sold, came under contract or were put on the market, together with the listing and actual selling prices. Finally, he included a page describing current listings and their prices.

He knew that as a homeowner, he'd appreciate having a copy of a report like this. So he decided to offer it to everyone in his farm.

Calling seemed to make sense. It would give him more personal contact and he'd avoid the hassle of mailing. Getting the report done had been a big enough chore.

Confident that he had something valuable to offer, Reggie drafted a script, broke his prospect list into manageable segments for daily calling and got psyched.

Reggie did his homework and let the prospect know that he was aware of when she bought the home.

Reggie: *Good afternoon. Is this Anne Anderson?*

Prospect: *This is she.*

Reggie: *This is Reggie Philipps from Greenbrier Real Estate. Can you give me a minute?*

Prospect: *Maybe.*

Reggie: *Ms. Anderson, did you know that your home has probably appreciated at least 7% over the past 12 months?*

Prospect: *I thought the value had gone up but I wasn't sure how much.*

Reggie: *Well, I'm calling to offer you something that every Castle Pines owner should have. And it won't cost you a penny.*

Prospect: *What is it?*

Reggie: *It's the Castle Pines Annual Real Estate Report. It details all real estate activity in Castle Pines over the past 12 months. Now if you haven't bought or sold your home during that time (and I see that you haven't), you may think that this doesn't apply to you. But it does. This report will give you a good idea of your home's current market value. Ms. Anderson, have you ever thought about taking out a home equity line of credit?*

Prospect: *I've thought about it.*

Reggie: *Well, this report can help you estimate how much cash you can get. You'll also find it helpful when you have to report the current value of your home on credit applications. Besides, it's just good to know. Every year the market changes. Could I drop off a copy at your home?*

Prospect: *I really don't think I'll have time to read it.*

Reggie: *Ms. Anderson, I understand. Like you, many people don't have time for a lot of reading. That's why I kept this report short. If you want details, they're there. But the main facts are highlighted in a brief summary. I can stop by your house today. Remember — it's free.*

Prospect: *Well, all right.*

Reggie: *You made a good decision, Ms. Anderson. You won't find this information anywhere else. And if after reading it, you want to know specifically how much your home is worth, give me a call. I'll be happy to figure it out for you. My number will be on the cover. (Pause) Thank you, Ms. Anderson. I'll see you later.*

Prospect: *Thank you. CLICK.*

Reggie: *CLICK.*

NOTES:

1. For a social farm, Reggie would simply use statistics based on a larger geographic area, such as the city or county.

2. A sample Annual Report follows these notes. You can also find an Annual Report direct mail package in *How To Farm Successfully — By Mail.*

3. Reggie should drop off the Report with a large post-it note reading, "Thanks! Let me know if you want a specific estimate of your home's value. Reggie." His numbers should be below in big print.

1995 CASTLE PINES REAL ESTATE REPORT

Photo

Prepared by: GREENBRIER REAL ESTATE
Reggie Philipps, Realtor-Associate®
90067 Carbondale Road * Campbell, NC 60056
(w) 704/555-8900 (h) 704/555-8897
(fax) 704/555-8901 (pager) 704/555-7703

REAL ESTATE ACTIVITY IN GENERAL
(January, 1995-December, 1995)

Average selling price:

Percentage of homes sold at
full listing price or within 10%:

Number of weeks average home on market:

Total number of listed homes:

Number of listed homes
taken off market unsold:

Number of Greenbrier real estate
listings in Castle Pines:

REAL ESTATE ACTIVITY BY SPECIFIC HOMES

SETTLED

Address	Bedrooms/ Baths	List Price	Actual Days on Market	Mo. Sold	Style

UNDER CONTRACT

Address	Bedrooms/ Baths	List Price	Actual Days on Market	Mo. Sold	Style

LISTED

Address	Bedrooms/ Baths	List Price	Actual Days on Market	Mo. Sold	Style

(Create key for style abbreviations and place at end)

Keep these figures monthly and preparing the report will be a snap!

HOME EVALUATION OFFER

Perhaps the most common offer in real estate direct marketing is for a free home evaluation. While a type of back-end premium, this really is a very directed appeal. It stops just short of asking for a listing.

Many real estate agents say they have the most success with this kind of offer. The reason is simple: it's a great way to pre-qualify prospects. While you can expect a high rejection rate, those who do respond will be excellent prospects. After all, anyone interested in a free home evaluation will at least consider selling.

FREE HOME EVALUATION

Geographic or social farm

Francine twisted a long strand of brown hair around her second finger. Lost in thought, she stared at the print of a sailboat on Chesapeake Bay on the wall across from her. This month she didn't have the prep time to pull together a direct mail package. She had several in the works, but none of them was ready to go. Calling farm prospects seemed like a good alternative. She knew the importance of constant, regular contact.

But what could she offer them?

Starting off the call by saying, "I'm Francine Logan. Do you want to sell your home?," seemed ludicrous. Yet she'd read plenty of sales books that advocated just that type of pitch. No, she'd rather have something to offer. Something just one step short of asking for a listing.

What about free home evaluations? With the current up-and-down market, homeowners might want this. At least they'd get an idea of what their properties were worth. And even if the prospect hotly denied she or he was interested in selling, anyone who asked for an evaluation could be counted on to at least think it over.

Francine flipped on the computer and started working. Three hours later, she had a script she felt comfortable with.

Francine: *Good morning. Ron Winston?*

Prospect: *This is Ron.*

Francine: *Ron, my name is Francine Logan. I'm with Greenbrier Real Estate. Perhaps you've seen our signs around town?*

Prospect: *Yes, I'm familiar with your company.*

Francine: *Good. Ron, I see that you bought your home seven years ago. Do you remember what happened to the real estate market two years later?*

Prospect: *Not really.*

Francine: *We had a short time when home prices shot up rapidly. A lot of homeowners didn't realize how much their homes had appreciated. As a result, many were caught off guard and missed an ideal opportunity to sell. It looks like that opportunity is coming around again. Have you thought at all about selling?*

Prospect: *Not really.*

Francine: *That's understandable. I've driven by your home and it looks lovely. But if you've ever been interested in moving up to a larger, more expensive home, now is a great time. You bought your home for $124,500, didn't you?*

Prospect: *That's right.*

Francine: *Do you realize that with appreciation, your home could be worth at least $175,000 . . . and that equity means you can move up . . . for about the same monthly mortgage you have now?*

Prospect: *I've thought about it. But we're happy here.*

Francine: *What do you like so much about your home?*

Prospect: *The location. We like the corner lot. We also like the space. I cook and there's a gourmet kitchen.*

Francine: *Even if you aren't planning to move, knowing the value of one of your primary financial assets is important. For the next 30 days, I'm scheduling free market evaluations for Castle Pines homeowners. Can I pencil you in?*

Using the prospect's first name is fine in this situation since the prospect identified himself that way. If he had replied "This is Mr. Winston," then using his first name would have been inappropriate.

Prospect: *I don't think so.*

Francine: *Ron, you'd be under absolutely no obligation. I'll drop by, see your home and leave. In about three days, you'll receive a written evaluation that includes prices of comparable homes which have sold recently. Then you can do whatever you like. Call me or don't call me — the decision is yours. All I ask for is about 15 minutes of your time. Would Wednesday evening work for you?*

Prospect: *Okay.*

Francine: *Is 7 p.m. okay?*

Prospect: *That's fine.*

Francine: *Ron, I'll see you Wednesday at 7 p.m. at your home at 667 Windy Way. Thank you very much for your time.*

Prospect: *Good-bye.* CLICK.

Francine: CLICK.

NOTES:

1. If prospect had declined again, Francine could have talked about the importance of knowing your home's value when applying for home equity credit line or general credit applications (see previous phone script). If that line of argument didn't work, she should have finished by complimenting him again on his lovely home and saying that she understands why he's reluctant to leave it. She also could have reminded him that he'll be receiving a newsletter and other information from her in the future.

2. Francine knew when he had bought his home and how much he paid for it. She kept his prospect file on the computer in front of her the whole time she was talking. When the conversation ended, she typed notes in the file.

3. The direct mail version of this offer uses a personal client's story. While stories almost always engage prospects' attention, they can be difficult to tell. Use a story in this script only if you're very comfortable with it and if you keep it short.

INFORMATION KIT OFFERS

These offers emphasize back-end premiums which, hopefully, will attract hard-to-reach prospects. Unlike free home evaluations which target potential sellers, these kits are more "relationship-building." In other words, they provide an excellent way for you to initiate a conversation with a prospect and begin getting to know her or him.

If a prospect requests a kit, drop it off at his or her home. If this is impossible, then mail it. Call in a few days to see whether they received it and if they have any questions. Short follow-up calls are a great way to keep a relationship going.

Creating the kits, however, does take some advance preparation. To make them seem important, most kits should have five or six elements. This would include several brochures and, when possible, discount coupons or small free gifts. For many of these kits, you can work out "cooperative" arrangements with other local groups such as the police or fire departments, hardware stores, airport shuttle services, insurance agents, etc. Developing these ties will strengthen your connections to the community and increase your credibility.

In some cases, you'll have to write the brochure or handout yourself. For example, you may have to type up a list of emergency phone numbers. With a computer, this will be easy. You can find most of the information you'll need in the yellow pages of your phone directory or from the reference department of your library.

When you finish, package the kits attractively and inexpensively. Be sure to have your name, address and phone numbers prominently displayed.

HOME FIRE PROTECTION KIT OFFER

Geographic or social farm

Randy sorted through the morning mail. Valu-paks from local stores, title company documents, insurance ads and the monthly rent bill made up the pile. He smiled when he came across a postcard from Rosa Martinez. He had helped sell her small home on River Street a few months ago. She had moved into an apartment complex designed for "older adults" and was on a cruise in the Caribbean. "Just wanted to keep in touch," she wrote.

He paused when he picked up a reminder card from the local fire department. He'd forgotten that it was fire season. Time again for home inspections. What a hassle! Two firemen walked around town dropping off notices for a few hours and his phone rang off the hook. Homeowners called him to find out who could shovel the leaves off their roofs, pull out the waist high weeds, and check their fireplaces.

Maybe he could save himself some time if he notified homeowners in advance of hazardous conditions. It'd be easy enough. The fire department had lots of brochures — the trouble was, they only distributed them after a homeowner had been cited. He could call the department and see if they'd give him a stack of their materials. He could also call Fred at the hardware store and ask if he was interested in offering a discount coupon on home smoke detectors or fire extinguishers. Ted, the chimney sweep, might also want to have a coupon.

Randy picked up the phone. He called the fire chief, hardware store and chimney sweep. Within an hour, he knew what he'd put in the package. Then he sat down to write out the phone script.

Randy: *Good afternoon. Could I please speak to John Plumb?*

Woman: *Just a minute, I'll get him. Who may I say is calling?*

Randy: *This is Randy Littner, with Greenbrier Real Estate.*

(PHONE DROPS. Randy hears woman call out, "John, some real estate guy is on the phone.")

Prospect: *Hello?*

Randy: *Mr. Plumb? My name is Randy Littner. I'm with Greenbrier Real Estate here in town. Do you have a minute?*

Prospect: *I'm pretty busy.*

Randy: *This won't take long. I'm working on a project with the Castle Pines Fire Department that I'd like to talk to you about.*

Prospect: *What is it?*

Randy: *Every year fires damage about ____ homes in Castle Pines. To help protect homeowners like yourself, the Castle Pines Fire Department has helped me put together a Home Fire Protection Kit. I'm offering it free to you and other homeowners.*

Prospect: *I'm not interested.*

Randy: *I can understand that. No one ever thinks a fire will break out in their home. But things happen. And the tragedy is that most fires can be prevented. This kit, for example, includes a brochure with 99 ways to "fire-proof" your home, a comic-style booklet for kids, a directory of emergency phone numbers and discount coupons from a local chimney sweep and Fred's True-Value Hardware for fire extinguishers and smoke alarms. Mr. Plumb, do you have smoke alarms in all your bedrooms?*

Prospect: *No.*

Randy: *Then this would be perfect. It also has tips about clearing up your lawn, checking electrical appli-*

The kit is introduced as a creation of the Castle Pines Fire Department, with the real estate agent assisting. This is important for establishing credibility.

ances and getting rid of flammable chemicals. Can I put you down for one?

Prospect: *I don't think so.*

Randy: *Mr. Plumb, did you know the Johnson family on Harvard Street?*

Prospect: *No.*

Randy: *Their home burned last October when a dryer overheated. They didn't have a fire extinguisher and they lost everything. Mr. Plumb, it's better to be safe than sorry. What I'm offering won't cost you anything but it could give you tremendous peace of mind. Can I drop by your Fire Protection Kit today?*

Prospect: *Okay.*

Randy: *Thank you very much. Your address is 7788 Cripple Creek Way, right?*

Prospect: *Right.*

Randy: *What time is best for you?*

Prospect: *Any time after 7.*

Randy: *Mr. Plumb, thank you very much and I'll see you later this evening. Good-bye.*

Prospect: *Good-bye. CLICK.*

Randy: *CLICK.*

NOTES:

1. Randy's first response to the prospect's objections was to argue with logic: look what's in the kit, wouldn't this be good to know? When the prospect rejected him twice, Randy switched to an emotional appeal with personal stories about people who had experienced home fires. If you want to make this a dynamite appeal, gather some stories about fires in your area (ask your local fire department for the most heart-tugging ones they can remember). If they're good enough, you may want to skip the logical appeals and move right to the emotional.

2. This offer would work terrifically a week or two after a home fire in the neighborhood.

VACATION KIT

Bethany doodled on the notepad in front of her. It was 3 p.m. on Wednesday. Outside sun streamed through the thick leaves of the magnolia tree. She looked up and saw a robin perched on a branch, watching her.

Summer was coming and she was glad. Soon she'd start water skiing at the lake and throwing weekend barbecues for her friends. She'd pack away her wool sweaters and pull out her shorts and T-shirts. She should think about a vacation. Where should she go this year? The Caribbean? A dude ranch in Colorado? A California spa?

Suddenly she sat up with a jolt. Here she was, thinking about her own vacation, when everyone in her farm would probably be making vacation plans, too.

"What a great opportunity for more contacts," she thought. "I could put together a vacation package that covers everything someone needs to do before going away!"

She picked up the phone to call a friendly local detective for brochures on how to make a home look "lived in." She also called a local kennel and airport shuttle service to see if they were interested in having coupons in her direct mail package. On the way home that afternoon, she stopped by the post office to pick up a handful of "vacation hold" forms and a discount store to buy several dozen travel size shampoos, deodorants and toothpastes.

A few days later, she started calling.

Bethany: *Good afternoon. Mary McCarthy, please.*

Prospect: *This is she.*

Bethany: *Hi, my name is Bethany Ramos. I'm with Greenbrier Realty here in town. Do you have a minute?*

Prospect: *Just a minute.*

Bethany: *Mrs. McCarthy, are you planning to take a vacation this summer?*

Prospect: *Why?*

Bethany: *About this time of year, I like to do something special for my neighbors in Castle Pines. Something to make your life a little easier and your summer a little more relaxing. This year I've put together a special Vacation Kit. Where do you usually vacation?*

Prospect: *I usually visit my mother in Minneapolis. Sometimes I go to Chicago or Louisville.*

Bethany: *Do you have other relatives there?*

Prospect: *A few.*

Bethany: *Well, I'm sure that you could use this kit. It lets you leave home knowing that everything has been taken care of. Inside you'll find a vacation "To Do" list covering everything from picking up extra prescription medicine to turning off the air conditioning. It also has a tip sheet on how to keep your home looking "lived in" . . . a vacation hold request for the post office . . . and phone numbers for kennels, pet care services, newspaper circulation departments and airport shuttle services. It took quite a bit of work to pull it together . . . but I'm offering the kit free . . . as a thank you for all the support I've gotten from Castle Pines homeowners over the year. Can I put you down for one?*

Prospect: *Uh... I don't know.*

Bethany: *There's one more thing, Ms. McCarthy. For each person, I include a special personal gift. I really would like for you to have one. Do you usually*

If the prospect had said, "I don't think so," Bethany could have responded, "Why not?" and tried to engage in a deeper level of conversation.

> *take your vacation at the beginning or at the end of summer?*
>
> Prospect: *Usually at the end.*
>
> Bethany: *Then there's plenty of time to get one to you. Your address is 678 Stone Hill Road, right?*
>
> Prospect: *Yes, it is.*
>
> Bethany: *Great. I'll drop off your free Vacation Kit next week. What day is better — Tuesday or Thursday?*
>
> Prospect: *Tuesday. We bowl in a league on Thursday.*
>
> Bethany: *That's fine. I'll stop by Tuesday about 7 p.m. And Ms. McCarthy, can I ask a favor?*
>
> Prospect: *What is it?*
>
> Bethany: *If you think of anything I should add to the kit, will you please let me know? I really want this kit to be useful to you and my other Castle Pines neighbors. I've put in everything I can think of, but you might have some more ideas.*
>
> Prospect: *Okay.*
>
> Bethany: *Ms. McCarthy, it's been a pleasure talking to you. You'll have your Vacation Kit on Tuesday. Thank you very much.*
>
> Prospect: *Thank you. Good-bye. CLICK.*
>
> Bethany: *CLICK.*

NOTES:

1. This script is an example of a presumptive close. The prospect never agrees to take the kit, but keeps answering questions. There is really no reason for the prospect not to take the kit — so this type of close is appropriate.

2. If the prospect had been willing, Bethany could have asked more questions about her vacation plans and what her favorite vacations have been. However, Bethany should have avoided any questions about specific dates as this could have raised the prospect's suspicions.

HOME TAX RECORD KIT

For the 100th time, Leslie caught herself biting her nails. Across the desk, her accountant shuffled through her receipts, pay stubs, bills and lists of figures. She had a sinking feeling in the pit of her stomach. She knew that the papers were out of order. But how could she keep track of everything? Every year, she did the same thing. She grabbed a file folder full of bills . . . made a small attempt at sorting them out . . . and wound up bringing the stacks to her accountant. Maybe she should change. But could she change?

In the car driving home, Leslie thought about her filing system. It wasn't working. She hated the way her accountant sighed each time she sorted through the stack. Her friend, Sally, had mentioned a new tax sorter. Leslie hadn't thought about it twice. But now she did. She pulled over at the office supply store and went in.

Three days later, Leslie had the year's bills neatly sorted into all the appropriate file envelopes. This tax sorter was great! She liked it so much she thought about offering it to her farm. Probably a lot of people had the same problems getting organized as she did. How much would 50 cost?

The next week, Leslie was on the phone, offering free tax sorters to farm residents.

Leslie: *Good afternoon. John Harrison, please.*

Prospect: *This is he.*

Leslie: *Mr. Harrison, this is Leslie Telliam with Greenbrier Real Estate. Do you have a minute?*

Prospect: *Maybe.*

Leslie: *Mr. Harrison, I'm calling because I'd like to help make this tax season a little easier for you.*

Prospect: *How?*

Leslie: *I've found a great Home Tax Record Kit. I like it so much that I'm handing out free ones to my friends and neighbors in Castle Pines. I'd like for you to have one, too.*

Prospect: *I don't need one.*

Leslie: *Mr. Harrison, I've never seen a kit like this. It has special compartments for pay stubs, mortgage receipts, loan payments, travel receipts and a lot more. Do you do your own taxes?*

Prospect: *Yes, I do.*

Leslie: *Then I'm sure you'll find this a big time saver. I not only use it myself, my mother and boss have them, too. They're a great way to keep organized. Can I give you one?*

Kit's credibility is enhanced by fact that "Mom" and "boss" use it.

Prospect: *I already have something like that.*

Leslie: *Since this tax record kit is free, you could see how it compares to the one you already have. Maybe you'd like this one better. I picked up 50. Only 20 are left. Can I put you down for one?*

This script differs from the others in that it uses a limited quantity ("only 20 are left") appeal to overcome an objection.

Prospect: *Well, all right.*

Leslie: *Let's see. That's John Harrison, 4523 Knob Hill Road, right?*

Prospect: *That's right.*

Leslie: *Mr. Harrison, I'll drop off your free Home Tax Record Kit tomorrow. Would around 7 p.m. work for you?*

Prospect: *That would be fine.*

Leslie:	*Thank you very much, Mr. Harrison. And let me know how you like it, Okay?*
Prospect:	*Okay. Good-bye. CLICK.*
Leslie:	*Good-bye. CLICK.*

NOTES:

   1. This script could be used at end of year or during tax time.

GARAGE SALE KIT

Shyam drove slowly down the streets of his farm. Every week, he had the habit of taking a few hours to drive through his territory looking for changes. How much he saw surprised him. He knew that the Ferrars were painting their garage — the Robinsons were adding on — the Taylors had their driveway repaved — the Lincolns had finally bitten the bullet and paid for a landscaper.

That night, as he read the evening paper, his eye caught an address in his farm: "6778 Rocky Point Road — Garage Sale Saturday and Sunday." He immediately went over to his computer and looked up the address. George and Stacy Franklin lived at that address for four years — the house had four bedrooms and two baths. The Franklins had never responded to any of his direct mail campaigns. But they'd received them.

Five minutes later, he was on the phone.

Prospect: *Hello?*

Shyam: *Stacy Franklin?*

Prospect: *Yes.*

Shyam: *Mrs. Franklin, my name is Shyam Sithuram. I'm with Greenbrier Real Estate here in Castle Pines. You may remember some of the letters and newsletters I've sent you.*

Prospect: *I vaguely remember some sort of letter.*

Shyam: *I'm calling because I saw your ad for a garage sale in the* Tribune. *And I was wondering if I could help.*

Prospect: *How?*

Shyam: *I've put together a Garage Sale kit that includes large signs to put up around the neighborhood . . . colorful flags for your driveway . . . price stickers . . . a thick black magic marker . . . and tips on how to organize and manage your garage sale most effectively. Could I drop one off at your house?*

Prospect: *I don't think so. How much does it cost?*

Shyam: *It's absolutely free. I make kits like this for my Castle Pines neighbors like yourself. I started doing it because so many of the people who asked me to sell their homes wanted to hold garage sales before they moved. This kit makes the whole process a lot simpler. By the way, you're not planning to sell your home, are you?*

Prospect: *We've thought about it. But we still haven't made a decision.*

Shyam: *Maybe we could talk about that when I drop off this kit. I just sold two homes similar to yours. One was a 4-bedroom, 2-bath on Windy Road. The other was a 3-bedroom, 2-bath on Bluff Drive. Would tomorrow afternoon be a good time or would the evening be better?*

Prospect: *The afternoon would be fine. Could you come by about 2?*

> Shyam: *Sure. I'll see you about 2. I'll bring the kit and some other material for you to look over.*
>
> Prospect: *Thank you. Good-bye.*
>
> Shyam: *Good-bye.*
>
> Prospect: *CLICK.*
>
> Shyam: *CLICK.*

NOTES:

1. This script emphasizes the level of service that Shyam provides for his clients. It doesn't focus on the extra money they can make from garage sales.

2. It's very important that you call as soon in the week as you see a notice for a garage sale and that you get the kit to them promptly.

3. For materials to put in the kit, check with your local office supply store or ads in real estate magazines. Garage Sale Promotions offers *The Garage Sale Book* which you can also use (1-800-663-7054).

LEAD INS FOR OTHER INFORMATION KITS

HOME CRIME-STOPPERS KIT

Lyle: *Hello. Ron Roberts?*

Prospect: *This is Ron Roberts.*

Lyle: *Mr. Roberts, this is Lyle Brummer at Greenbrier Real Estate. Do you have minute?*

Prospect: *Why?*

Lyle: *Mr. Roberts, you live on Pine Crest Drive, don't you? Did you know that two months ago, a home on Sea Ridge Road — just a few blocks from you — was burglarized?*

Prospect: *No, I didn't.*

Lyle: *It's unfortunate but here in Castle Pines, more than five homes have been robbed in the past six months. I'm concerned about that and that's why I'm calling.*

Prospect: *Yes?*

Lyle: *Working with the Castle Pines Police, I've put together a Home Crime-Stoppers Kit. I'm offering it free to homeowners like you.*

Prospect: *What's in it?*

Lyle: *. . .*

NOTES:

1. Cooperative opportunities for this offer could be with the local police, alarm companies and insurance companies.

2. This kit could contain:
   - booklet on how to burglar-proof your home
   - booklet on how to inventory and protect possessions
   - identification labels for valuable articles
   - identification labels to post on windows and doors
   - emergency stickers for telephone
   - directory of emergency phone numbers and procedures.

NEIGHBORHOOD WATCH KIT

Lyle: *Hello. Could I please speak to Ron Roberts?*

Prospect: *This is Ron Roberts.*

Lyle: *Mr. Roberts, this is Lyle Brummer at Greenbrier Real Estate. Do you have a minute?*

Prospect: *Why?*

Lyle: *Mr. Roberts, a group of neighbors are concerned about rising crime rates in the area. Did you know that half a dozen Castle Pines homes have been robbed in the past six months?*

Prospect: *No, I didn't.*

Lyle: *One of the homes was only a few blocks from yours. Anyway, with the help of the Castle Pines Police, I've put together a special Neighborhood Watch Kit. It's absolutely free and I'm offering it to all my neighbors. By looking out for each other, we can protect our homes and families.*

Prospect: *What does it involve?*

Lyle: *The kit includes window stickers for your home, a handy card to put by the phone for emergencies, a booklet on how to stop neighborhood crime and information on how to set up a Neighborhood Watch program. In a few weeks, we'll have a meeting and go into the program in more detail. Right now, our concern is to get this material to homeowners like you. Can I drop off this Neighborhood Watch Kit later today?*

Prospect: *I'm not sure I want one.*

Lyle: *At this stage, you don't have to do anything. All Neighborhood Watch programs involve is posting some signs and looking for anything unusual at a neighbor's house. It really won't take any of your time. And besides, your neighbors will be watching your house, too. Can I drop off your kit today or would tomorrow be better?*

NOTES:

1. Cooperative opportunities for this offer could be with the local police, alarm companies and insurance companies.

2. This kit could contain:
   - booklet on how to prevent crime in your neighborhood
   - window and door stickers for the home
   - emergency card to put by telephone
   - information from local police on how to set up Neighborhood Watch Group.

HOME SAFETY KIT

Lyle: *Hello. Could I please speak to Ron Roberts?*

Prospect: *This is Ron Roberts.*

Lyle: *Mr. Roberts, this is Lyle Brummer at Greenbrier Real Estate. Do you have a minute?*

Prospect: *Why?*

Lyle: *Mr. Roberts, how safe do you think your home is?*

Prospect: *Pretty safe.*

Lyle: *Most of us think that. But the truth is that home accidents are far more common than we realize. That's why, together with the Castle Pines Fire Department, I created this free Home Safety Kit. Do you have any children at home, Mr. Roberts?*

Prospect: *Not now.*

Lyle: *Well, if children ever come to visit, it's important that they can't get into medicine cabinets or stuff under the kitchen sink. For the next 30 days, I'm offering free Home Safety Kits to my Castle Pines neighbors like yourself. (Pause)*

            Each kit includes a checklist so you can determine how safe your home is — a detailed booklet telling you how to "accident-proof" your home — a brochure on special precautions to take when small children are around — a guide to basic first aid — a handy card with emergency numbers to put by your phone — and, best of all, free "tamper-proof" locks for your cabinets and plugs for your electrical sockets. That's quite a bit, don't you think?

Prospect: *Sounds like it.*

Lyle: *For the 30 days, it's yours — free. All you have to do is say that you'd like a kit. How about it?*

NOTES:

1. Cooperative opportunities for this offer could be with the fire department and local hardware store.

2. This kit could contain:

   - checklist to determine how safe your home is

   - booklet describing how to "accident-proof" your home

   - brochure on safety measures to take when small children are in the home

   - guide to basic first-aid

   - card to put by telephone with emergency numbers and services

   - "tamper-proof" locks for cabinets and plugs for electrical outlets

ENVIRONMENTAL ACTION KIT

> Lyle: *Hello. Ron Roberts, please.*
>
> Prospect: *This is Ron Roberts.*
>
> Lyle: *Mr. Roberts, this is Lyle Brummer at Greenbrier Real Estate. Do you have a minute?*
>
> Prospect: *Why?*
>
> Lyle: *Mr. Roberts, I'm calling you about a neighborhood clean-up program. Do you ever take your disposable plastic bottles over to Sav-on? (Name recycling center nearest prospect's home.)*
>
> Prospect: *No.*
>
> Lyle: *If you're like me, you probably weren't even aware it was there. What about toxic chemicals — do you know where to drop off things like used motor oil?*
>
> Prospect: *I just put it in cans and stick them in the trash.*
>
> Lyle: *Mr. Roberts, I've prepared an Environmental Action Kit with information specifically for Castle Pines homeowners. In it, you'll find out how to get rid of toxic materials, when recycling trucks will pick up your old newspapers, where to drop off metal and plastic containers and hours at the local landfill. It's packed with facts that you won't find anywhere else and it's absolutely free. Could I put you down for one?*

NOTES:

1. Cooperative opportunities for this offer could be with utility companies, recycling centers, waste disposal companies, and water companies.

2. This kit could contain:

   * booklet with tips on how to protect the environment in your everyday life
   * information on how to prepare old newspapers, plastics and glass materials for pick-up
   * list of convenient recycling centers and landfills, together with their hours and acceptance policies
   * tips on how to dispose safely of things such as paint, toxic cleaners, insect pesticides and motor oil
   * names and telephone numbers of agencies to contact with more specific questions.

BOOKLET OFFERS

Like information kit offers, booklet offers are back-end premiums. They do, however, take a little more work to pull together. But once you've finished them, all you need to do is update them every six or twelve months. The booklets also make great gifts for new homeowners moving into your farm or corporate human resource personnel handling relocations into your area.

The "Home Reference Booklet" should contain names and telephone numbers for home-related services in your farm area. Add as many as you can think of — from house cleaners to garage door repair services. Try to eliminate anyone with a bad reputation. To check the reputations, call a few long-time farm residents first. If they can't help, ask them to recommend a friend or neighbor who can advise you.

The "Home Investment Services Booklet" should list services such as insurance agents, bank officers, appraisers, attorneys — again, check with people who live in your farm for recommendations. This premium could well appeal to a different audience than the "Home Reference Booklet." You can test this by offering half your farm the "Home Reference Booklet" and the other half the "Home Investment Services Booklet."

As with the information kits, the most time-consuming part is pulling the information together. Once you've done that, you have a great premium to use year after year.

HOME REFERENCE BOOKLET OFFER

Geographic farm

Tom's phone rang for the fifth time in an hour. The sewer back-up on Main Street had resulted in flooding along Canyon Drive. Homeowners were calling him for repair referrals. It was good to know that so many people remembered him in times of trouble — he just wished they'd keep him in mind the next time they decided to sell their homes.

When he hung up, Tom started thinking about all the calls like this that he got every year. Scribbling on his neat white desk pad, he figured that he got maybe five calls a week for repair referrals — each call took about five minutes — that added up to 25 minutes a week or 1250 minutes a year (based on 50 weeks). That 1250 minutes a year amounted to almost 21 hours.

In 21 hours, he could write a newsletter . . . prepare a direct mailing . . . take 10 prospective buyers on home tours or do 10 listing presentations. All of these activities could pay off handsomely. Still . . . he didn't want clients to feel that he was closed to questions.

Tom decided to try an offer he'd read about. He'd take the names and addresses of repair and other home-related services out of his Rolodex and put them in a booklet. Then he'd offer the booklet free to farm residents. Every year he could update it. It would be a great way to build a sense of community within the farm, provide a valuable service and enhance his own reputation.

One and a half weeks later, Tom made his first "Handy Home Reference Booklet" offer.

Tom: *Hello. Ruth Portage?*

Prospect: *This is Dr. Portage.*

Tom: *Dr. Portage, this is Tom Huddleston with Greenbrier Real Estate. Do you have a minute?*

Prospect: *Sure.*

Tom: *Dr. Portage, as a homeowner, I'm sure that you've turned to the Yellow Pages a number of times. Maybe you've had a leaky roof — or a plugged up toilet. Tell me, when was the last time you had to call a repair service?*

Prospect: *Last month. A circuit breaker overloaded and I had to get an electrician in here to fix it.*

Tom: *I know that your time is valuable. And I want to help you make the most of your time. That's why I've prepared a wonderful booklet, the "Handy Home Reference Booklet." In it, you'll find telephone numbers and addresses for every type of home-related service in the Castle Pines area. Think of it as a mini-Yellow Pages. But there is one important difference — the people listed in the booklet have been screened by myself or my clients. You can count on them to be trustworthy and dependable. I'm offering this booklet free to my Castle Pines neighbors. Can I put you down for one?*

Prospect: *Well, I already have most of the repair people I need.*

Tom: *Dr. Portage, what happens if your electrician is on vacation the next time you have a problem? Or your favorite plumber is on a job when you need immediate help? Having this booklet certainly wouldn't hurt. And I'll bet that you'd find it a tremendous help. Would you like one?*

Prospect: *How can I be sure the people are dependable?*

Tom: *I've used many of them myself. Others were referred by clients whom I trust. Services that are particular favorites are marked with stars. Why don't you just take a look at it? Remember — it's free.*

Prospect: *All right.*

Tom: *Dr. Portage, is your address still 887 Ridge Road?*

Prospect: *Yes, it is.*

Tom: *Great. It turns out that I'm going to be right by your house later today. Will you be home around 6:30?*

Prospect: *I think so.*

Tom: *I'll see you then. And Dr. Portage, if you come across anyone you'd like to add to the booklet, call me, okay?*

Prospect: *Sure. Bye. CLICK.*

Tom: *CLICK.*

Saying "I'll be right by your house later" gives you a reason to stop by.

NOTES:

1. Another approach would have been to start asking the prospect in more detail about their home repair needs and mentioning specific services in their area.

2. To reduce your expenses, you could sell advertising space in the booklet to local home-related services as well as list their numbers and addresses.

HOME INVESTMENT SERVICE BOOKLET OFFER

Geographic farm

Steve hung up the phone. Almost an hour of conversation with the title company had finally straightened out a problem in a escrow set to close tomorrow. It was frustrating dealing with the paperwork of these transactions, but he was grateful for Irma's intelligence and thoroughness. He'd never dealt with a better title officer.

He remembered what it had been like to work with the ABC title company. At the time, just starting out, he didn't realize how incompetent they were. Now he knew. If he could help it, he'd never work with anyone but Irma again.

The phone rang. Jeff, another agent across town, was on the line. He wanted a recommendation for a title company. Steve told him about Irma.

When they finished, Steve started counting the number of competent people he dealt with at title companies, law offices, mortgage brokers, and inspection services. It was more than he realized. He wondered how many other people had such an extensive network of contacts. Probably not many, he said to himself.

He got an idea. He'd put together a booklet of all these people and offer it to homeowners in his farm. They didn't have to be selling or buying a home to find it useful — real estate problems came up all the time.

Five days later, he made his first call.

Steve:	Good afternoon. Edward Wilson?
Prospect:	Yes.
Steve:	Mr. Wilson, my name is Steve Rosen. I'm with Greenbrier Real Estate. Perhaps you've seen "For Sale" signs with my name on them in Castle Pines?
Prospect:	Maybe.
Steve:	Well, I'm not calling because I want to sell your home. In fact, I'm calling because I want to give you something. As a Castle Pines homeowner, you should find it very useful.
Prospect:	What is it?
Steve:	Almost every day, someone calls me for a referral for an insurance agent, mortgage broker, attorney or appraiser. I thought to myself, "Why don't I put all the names of the people I use in a booklet and give it to my neighbors here in Castle Pines?" So I created the Home Investment Services Booklet and I'd like for you to have one.
Prospect:	I'm not a real estate agent. Why would I need it?
Steve:	The next time your property insurance bill is due, you'll have a ready-made list of agents who handle Castle Pines homes. You can easily call around for estimates. Or if you want to refinance, the booklet has some great referrals for mortgage brokers experienced in our area.
Prospect:	I don't know.
Steve:	There's one more major advantage that I haven't mentioned. Everyone in the booklet is someone you can trust. They're people I know and have worked with for years. You'll also find all the numbers you need for county offices such as the tax assessor's. Mr. Wilson, how would you like to have your Home Investment Services Booklet tomorrow?
Prospect:	That would be fine.
Steve:	Just let me double-check the address — 7756 Coral Ridge Road, right?

Gave specific examples that elaborate on personal benefits of having the booklet.

Quasi-assumptive close, "How would you like to have your booklet tomorrow?"

Closed by asking for feedback, which is an indirect way of telling a client that he or she is important to you.

Prospect:	*That's right.*
Steve:	*Mr. Wilson, would it be all right if I dropped off your Home Investment Services Booklet about 4?*
Prospect:	*Sure.*
Steve:	*And if you have anyone you'd like to add or feedback on anyone listed, give me a call. Your opinion is important to me.*
Prospect:	*Be happy to.*
Steve:	*Mr. Wilson, thank you very much for your time. I'll see you tomorrow.*
Prospect:	*Good-bye.* Click.
Steve:	Click.

NOTES:

1. Cooperative opportunities exist with home-related investment services throughout your area.

ANNOUNCEMENT SCRIPTS

Announcement offers apply only in certain circumstances and only to selected individuals. While still considered "mass marketing," you make them to a separate group within your farm.

For example, when you have a new listing, you might want to call all the homeowners within a one-mile radius of the home. This enables you to use the "Neighbor to a new listing" script. It also lets your farm know that you're successful. The next time someone decides to list their home, you have a greater chance that they'll turn to you.

You can reinforce this impression when you call using the "New sale" script. Now you not only had a listing, you sold the home. And your positive reputation skyrockets.

You have to be careful, however, of tooting your own horn too loudly. Arrogance turns people off. Quiet confidence impresses them.

NEIGHBOR TO A NEW LISTING

Elizabeth opened her car door smiling. In her briefcase, the ink was still fresh on the listing contract. She'd wanted to sell this home for years. A stately, white-pillared colonial in a sea of natural wood contemporary homes, it had tremendous curb appeal. She loved how the owners would put electric candles surrounded by wreathes in the windows during the holidays.

As she drove off, she wondered how many of the neighbors had dreamed about owning a home like this. Classic. Elegant. Maybe a little worn at the edges, but nothing some elbow grease and a few dollars couldn't fix in a flash.

She looked at the streamlined contemporaries lining the street. Everyone had their own taste, but sometimes people liked a change. If she lived nearby, she'd at least check into the colonial. Or she'd try to find some friends who'd be interested. For a second, she saw herself sitting on the back verandah, sipping a drink under the tall trees.

This is going to be fun, she thought. And even before reaching the office, she began composing what she would say when she started her "Neighbors to a new listing" calls the next day.

Elizabeth: *Hello, Penny Nelson?*

Prospect: *Yes, this is Penny Nelson.*

Elizabeth: *Ms. Nelson, this is Elizabeth Gideon. I'm with Greenbrier Real Estate here in town. You may have seen my signs around Castle Pines.*

Prospect: *Yes?*

Elizabeth: *Well, soon you're going to see one more sign. And it's very near your home. I'm calling to ask you a favor.*

Prospect: *What is it?*

Elizabeth: *The Thomases have asked me to help them find a new owner for their home at the corner of White Rock and Crestview. I'm sure you're familiar with it — it's the lovely white colonial with the sloping yard and brick sidewalks in front. Anyway, Joy Thomas has just been transferred to Boston and they have to move quickly.*

If you've ever been in the home, you know how elegant it is. With four bedrooms, everyone has their own room. In the back, French doors open to an enormous patio.

I'm calling to see if you have any friends or relatives who might be interested in the home — or if you yourself might be interested.

Prospect: *How much is it?*

Elizabeth: *It's listed for $215,000 and the Thomases are willing to help with financing. I don't know what you're paying now, but chances are this could be less.*

Conversation focused on the home itself and ease of financing it.

Prospect: *It sounds interesting. Let me think it over and get back to you.*

Elizabeth: *Ms. Nelson, if you'd like to see the home, I'd be happy to take you through it. It's a wonderful home and as beautiful on the inside as it is on the outside. You can see for yourself how lovely it is and you'd have absolutely no obligation. Would tomorrow be good or is Wednesday better?*

Elizabeth reassured prospect that looking carries no obligation.

> Prospect: *I guess it wouldn't hurt. What about Wednesday at 2 p.m.?*
>
> Elizabeth: *Perfect. You live at 556 River Ridge Road, don't you?*
>
> Prospect: *Yes.*
>
> Elizabeth: *Fine. I'll pick you up Wednesday at 2 p.m. If you need to reach me before then, my number is 555-0989. Ms. Nelson, thank you very much for your time. I look forward to seeing you.*
>
> Prospect: *Thank you. Good-bye. CLICK.*
>
> Elizabeth: *CLICK.*

NOTES:

1. This script could have been adapted to invite the prospect to an open house.

2. Elizabeth avoids jargon. She says, "The Thomases have asked me . . . " not "I'm listing the home." She keeps it personal by giving a short explanation of why the Thomases have to move.

NEW SALE SCRIPT

Two months later, Elizabeth is sitting in the Thomas' living room explaining two offers. After a bit of discussion, they decide to counter offer the first one.

Elizabeth leaves, fairly confident that the offer will be accepted.

One week later, the deal is done. Six weeks later, escrow closes.

Elizabeth celebrates with a day at a health spa where she's buffed, massaged, catered to and perfumed.

The next day, back in the office, she picks up the phone and begins calling the Thomases' neighbors.

Woman: *Hello?*

Elizabeth: *Hello. Could I please speak to Roger Rossi?*

Woman: *Roger, it's for you.*

Prospect: *Hello?*

Elizabeth: *Mr. Rossi, this is Elizabeth Gideon. I'm with Greenbrier Real Estate here in town. Do you have a minute?*

Prospect: *That's it.*

Elizabeth: *I don't know if you've heard yet — but the Thomas home — that lovely white colonial at the corner of White Rock and Crestview — has sold. Your new neighbors will be Tom and Theresa Young. Tom owns the Chrysler dealership in Chapel Hill. Theresa teaches at Putnam College. While I hope that you'll welcome them to our neighborhood, I also was wondering if you could help me.*

Prospect: *How?*

Elizabeth: *When selling the Thomas home, a number of people approached me about living in Castle Pines. Now that the Thomas home is off the market, I have very few homes to show them. I'm calling to see if you — or perhaps a friend or neighbor — have ever thought about selling. Now's a great time.*

Prospect: *I've thought about it, but I'm not really interested.*

Elizabeth: *What about any of your friends or neighbors?*

Prospect: *No one I know of.*

Elizabeth: *Mr. Rossi, I really appreciate your taking the time to talk to me. If you ever have the slightest thought about selling your home, I'd appreciate it if you'd call me. Can I send you my number and some information about the current real estate market?*

Prospect: *Sure.*

Elizabeth: *Your address is 4357 Coal Track Road, isn't it?*

Prospect:	*Yes.*
Elizabeth:	*Mr. Rossi, it has been a pleasure to speak to you. And don't forget to welcome the Youngs to the neighborhood! Good-bye.*
Prospect:	*Bye. CLICK.*
Elizabeth:	*CLICK.*

NOTES:

1. If the prospect knew of some friends or neighbors who had talked about moving, Elizabeth would have gotten their names and numbers. She would have called them right away. She also would have sent the prospect a thank you note for the referral the next day.

2. It would have been good if Elizabeth had added specifics about potential buyers. For example, she could have said something like, "When selling the Thomas home, I met a young couple named Perry. They're looking for a three-bedroom, two-bath home like yours. I know your home is not on the market, but I thought I'd call and see if you've ever thought about selling. Or perhaps you have some friends or neighbors who might have mentioned it . . ." You should only use this approach, however, if you really do have clients looking for a house like the prospect's.

INVITATION OFFERS

Open house invitations appeal to neighbors' curiosity. They are made in hopes of drawing them into face-to-face meetings with you.

These are warmed up by highly personal writing and "urgent" notices, such as "this is priced well below . . ."

While you can't expect everyone to respond positively to an open house invitation, those who do may be good prospects. People may not be interested in moving right away, but if they're willing to look . . . there's a possibility down the road . . .

OPEN HOUSE INVITATION

Bridget marked the date on her calendar. March 30th — the first showing of the Robinson home. She enjoyed holding open houses, especially when a home had just gone on the market. She liked fixing the place up — putting bread to bake in the oven — and meeting the people who trooped through. It reminded her of the parties she used to throw.

There was one problem, though. Getting people to turn up. Not everyone combed the weekly open house notices in the paper. And neighbors didn't always see the sign. This time, she wanted the open house to be different. For one thing, the house was different. It was a stunning contemporary set far back into a hillside. The interior had been designed by an architect and this showed in its tasteful lines. No picture in the Sunday paper could capture the beauty and integrity of this particular home.

Bridget decided to try a new approach. Before this open house, she would call a list of prospects and invite them. Maybe it wouldn't work. But maybe it would. All she had to lose was time. Time was valuable, she admitted. But if she didn't keep experimenting with new marketing approaches, pretty soon her sales would slacken. She didn't want that to happen. She liked the nice upward curve in her income.

The next day, Bridget called the first prospect and invited her to the open house.

This script emphasized the house's selling features. What you emphasize depends on the circumstances. For example, if a house has great owner financing, build the phone script around that.

If Bridget planned to serve refreshments at the open house, she could have added something like, "I'll have coffee and cakes, too."

Bridget:	*Hello, Emily Redfeather?*
Prospect:	*This is she.*
Bridget:	*My name is Bridget Smith. I'm with Greenbrier Real Estate here in town. Do you have a minute?*
Prospect:	*Yes?*
Bridget:	*Your neighbors, Tom and Sally Trinidad, asked me to call. They live at 433 Marigold Drive, just about five blocks from you.*
Prospect:	*I don't know them.*
Bridget:	*They're wonderful people and they've asked me to help them sell their home. It's a white house with green shutters. Do you know it?*
Prospect:	*Not really. I'm not interested in moving.*
Bridget:	*Even if you're not interested in moving, you might enjoy dropping by a small open house I've having at the Trinidads' Sunday at 2 p.m. They have a delightful English garden and have done some wonderful decorating. You might even get a few ideas for your own home.*
Prospect:	*I don't think I have the time.*
Bridget:	*Ms. Redfeather, even if you could stop by for a few minutes, it might be worth your while. The Trinidad's is one of the nicest homes in Castle Pines. If you're not interested yourself, perhaps one of your friends or relatives might be. Can you think of anyone?*
Prospect:	*Not offhand.*
Bridget:	*Well, if you happen to drive by this Sunday, please stop in. And if you ever have any questions about your home or its value, call me. I specialize in the Castle Pines market and I'd be delighted to help you.*
Prospect:	*Okay.*
Bridget:	*Ms. Redfeather, it has been a pleasure talking to you. I hope to see you Sunday.*
Prospect:	*Good-bye. CLICK.*
Bridget:	*Good-bye. CLICK.*

NOTES:

1. This phone call ended unsuccessfully but Bridget did a good job of meeting the prospect's objections. Not every call will work out the way you want it to (in fact, most won't) . . . but every call is a step in building a relationship. Just because someone doesn't accept your invitation this weekend means little. They could easily accept one of your other offers next month. Remember — not everyone is at the same place or needs the same things. You could always follow up this type of call with a card with your name and phone number.

2. If you have an assistant, you may want to ask them to make the preliminary calls inviting neighbors to the open house. If anyone seems very interested, you can call them back. Start the call with, "My assistant, _____ _____, told me that you planned to drop by our open house at 433 Marigold Drive this Sunday. I'm just calling to let you know that I'm looking forward to meeting you. He also mentioned that you were interested in . . ."

SPECIAL CIRCUMSTANCES OFFERS

If you visit any real estate office in the country, chances are you'll overhear a conversation about how to handle For Sale By Owners. Often when a new agent starts, the broker passes over the classified ads and tells him or her to start calling all property owners trying to sell their own homes.

As any FSBO will tell you, more agents than prospects call on a For Sale By Owner sign. For FSBOs, consider a two-step approach, using both mail and the phone. It might work better, for example, to send a letter and then follow it up with a phone call. Or you might want to call first and follow up the call with a letter.

According to a recent survey by the National Association of Realtors", 54% of the FSBOs in the hot market of 1993 would go it alone again. In the slow housing markets of 1989 and 1991, only 36% and 41%, respectively, said they would try it again. That means if the market in your area has been dragging, FSBOs might be an excellent source to tap for listings.

Offering a FSBO Kit is an effective introduction for many agents. If this kit doesn't work, however, the owner may wonder whether you could sell it any better.

For this reason, it's best to keep materials in the kit pretty generic — use magazine and newspaper reprints, directories and how-to material from third-party sources. Make sure that the prospect knows this material is designed for FSBOs and is not what you would use to sell the home.

Expired listings can also be a gold mine — just keep your ethics on the up and up and don't get involved if another agent is still in the picture.

Relocations are proving a growing revenue source. We have two phone scripts, one for corporate human resource departments and the other for individuals.

Renters are another good source of prospects. With them, assistance in financial planning is useful. For example, "After taxes, your monthly house payment would probably be only $200 more than what you're paying in rent." Since many agents overlook renters in their farms, you may be able to tap into something big.

As for absentee owners, one Orange County, California Realtor" told me that his farm had only 10% absentee owners but they made up 50% of his farm business.

Like renters, absentee owners are often ignored by agents. But unlike renters, absentee owners have listings to give — often more than one. This group also buys and sells properties more frequently than owner-occupants.

FOR SALE BY OWNER

Gregg slowed down as he hit Canyon Road. Someone in the office had mentioned seeing a new "For Sale By Owner" sign that morning. It should be somewhere along here.

"So many people try to do this on their own," he shook his head. "We could take away so many of the headaches." The worst part, he knew, were the unrealistic prices that many owners set. He was surprised, though, that he hadn't done many home evaluations that led to For Sale By Owners.

FSBOs think they know what the house is worth just by reading the paper, he said to himself. No wonder it takes so long for most of them to sell.

There was the sign. Neatly printed. Stuck on a post in the front part of the large yard. Two phone numbers. Gregg jotted them both down. He also noted the address. He'd look it up as soon as he got back to the office. The home looked well cared for. A tricycle was in the driveway — that meant kids. It also had a basketball hoop above the garage. Teenagers?

At the office, Gregg typed in the address on his computer. His farming software program displayed the information: John and Irene Hotchkins were the owners. The house had three bedrooms, two baths. They had bought it five years earlier for $155,000. Special features included a spa in the backyard, stone fireplace in the family room and a workshop in the garage. It had about 2,700 square feet.

John and Irene had not responded to any of his direct mail letters.

Gregg pulled out the MLS books and looked at recent selling prices of comparable homes in the neighborhood. If the Hotchkins home was in good condition, they could probably get about $205,000. He wondered what they were asking.

Before calling, he thought about the approach. If the Hotchkins had children, the move was probably job-related. Otherwise they wouldn't be taking their kids out of school in the middle of the year. Kids also meant that they probably didn't have as much time to show the house and keeping it neat might be a bother. He had a choice of four strategies:

- Offer a For Sale By Owner Kit. These had been very popular and helped get his foot in the door. When FSBOs got tired of trying to do it themselves, they often called him.

- Opt for a co-op arrangement where the owners agreed to let him preview the house and bring through potential buyers.

- Wait a few weeks and let them know about his success in selling other neighborhood homes.

- Ask them to allow him to present a marketing plan for their home.

FSBO KIT OFFER

Gregg:	*Hello, Mr. Hotchkins?*
Prospect:	*Yes.*
Gregg:	*Mr. Hotchkins, this is Gregg Mulvaney with Greenbrier Real Estate here in town. Do you have a minute?*
Prospect:	*Not really.*
Gregg:	*Mr. Hotchkins, I'll be quick. I'll calling to offer you something to help you sell your home. It's free and there's no obligation to me.*
Prospect:	*What is it?*
Gregg:	*It's a For Sale By Owner Kit that I put together especially for independent-minded homeowners like yourself. In it, you'll find information about how to advertise your home in the local paper, tips on showing your home and hosting an open house, a complete directory of local lenders, appraisers and escrow firms and most important of all — samples of documents you'll need to finalize your sale.*

Gregg listed everything in the kit. This makes it sound large and impressive.

You're probably wondering why I'm doing this. Well, I've been selling homes in Castle Pines for six years. I know how hard it is. It's a frustrating, time-consuming process. And to be honest, if you eventually decide that you want someone to help, I hope you'll think of me.

Gregg was straightforward about why he was doing this.

Now — when can I drop off your free For Sale By Owner Kit?

Prospect:	*I think I already have something like that.*
Gregg:	*You may. But I doubt that it has information specifically for Castle Pines. For example, I list title companies and agents that I know you can trust. They're local and they're dependable. The kit doesn't cost you anything — why not give it a try?*
Prospect:	*All right. Send it to my home.*

Gregg emphasized that the kit is free. You know this is important to a FSBO since they're selling their own home to save the broker's fee.

Gregg: *I could do that. But I'm showing properties near your home tomorrow. It would be easier just to drop it off. Will you be home around 3?*

Prospect: *Maybe. If I'm not here, my wife will be.*

Gregg: *That's fine. I'll see one of you tomorrow afternoon around 3. And Mr. Hotchkins, if you have any questions after reading through the kit, give me a call. My number is on the cover. I'll be happy to help however I can.*

Prospect: *Okay.*

Gregg: *Mr. Hotchkins, thank you very much for your time.*

Prospect: *You're welcome. Good-bye.*

Gregg: *Good-bye.*

Prospect: *CLICK.*

Gregg: *CLICK.*

NOTES:

1. The prospect's "Not really" response when Gregg asked for a minute of his time led to Gregg getting into the offer quickly. Gregg also could have started the conversation with something like, "I'm sure that you think I'm calling because I saw the For Sale sign in front of your house. You're right. But what I'm calling about is to offer you something that will help you sell your own home."

PREVIEW SCRIPT

Gregg: *Hello. Is this Irene Hotchkins?*

Prospect: *Yes, it is.*

Gregg: *Good afternoon, Mrs. Hotchkins. This is Gregg Mulvaney with Greenbrier Real Estate here in town. Do you have a minute?*

Prospect: *Yes.*

Gregg: *Yesterday when I was showing the Clancy home on Forest Street, I noticed your "For Sale" sign. Your home looks very attractive and it's in an excellent location.*

I'm calling to ask if you'd be interested in allowing me to show your home to some potential buyers.

Prospect: *I don't know. We really wanted to sell it ourselves.*

Gregg: *I realize this isn't exactly what you had in mind, but it could help you sell your home a lot faster. Buyers know that I specialize in Castle Pines properties — that's why I have a list of people eager to buy in your neighborhood. For example, there's a couple looking for a three-bedroom home in the $200,000 range. How much are you asking for your home?*

Prospect: *$225,000.*

Gregg: *That may be a little high for them, but I'm sure they'd be interested in seeing the home. Would it be possible to give me a preview?*

Prospect: *I'm not sure. What would this mean in terms of commission?*

Gregg: *Mrs. Hotchkins, if this couple or anyone else I take to your home decides to buy it and you accept their offer, there would be a commission. I'd be more than happy to sit down and talk to you about how the commission would work. Are you and Mr. Hotchkins free on Saturday afternoon?*

After mentioning that you saw the "For Sale" sign, compliment the home. Use specific references so they know you took the trouble to go out and look at it.

> Prospect: *No, we have a Little League game.*
>
> Gregg: *What about Sunday after 12?*
>
> Prospect: *That would work.*
>
> Gregg: *Shall we say 1 p.m.?*
>
> Prospect: *That's fine.*
>
> Gregg: *Mrs. Hotchkins, I appreciate your willingness to meet with me. I do have a number of buyers for Castle Pines homes. I'll see you Sunday . . . and thank you for your time.*
>
> Prospect: *Sunday it is. Good-bye.*
>
> Gregg: *Good-bye.* CLICK.
>
> Prospect: *CLICK.*

NOTES:

1. Gregg's strongest argument is that he has buyers already interested in owning Castle Pines homes. The fact that he mentions one particular couple strengthens his argument even further. If you don't have prospective buyers, don't say that you do. Just note that you specialize in Castle Pines homes and buyers who want to live there come to you specifically for that reason. If you do have a list of buyers, try to add some details about them to this conversation.

2. Don't say that you saw the sign when you were out with prospective buyers if it's not true. But if you were, dropping the address of the house you were showing increases your credibility. Details in general increase credibility — but guard against bogging listeners down with them.

FOUR WEEKS AFTER FSBO ON MARKET SCRIPT

Gregg: *Good morning. Mr. Hotchkins?*

Prospect: *This is John Hotchkins.*

Gregg: *Mr. Hotchkins, my name is Gregg Mulvaney. I'm with Greenbrier Real Estate. You may have seen my name on signs in your neighborhood.*

Prospect: *What do you want?*

Gregg: *I drove by your house recently and noticed that your "For Sale By Owner" sign is still up. May I ask if you've accepted any offers?*

Prospect: *Not yet.*

Gregg: *Mr. Hotchkins, in the past three months, I've sold three homes in Castle Pines. The Ramirez home at 556 Lone Pine Road for $176,500. The Smithson home at 667 Trail Star Drive for $245,000. And the Sanchez home at 435 Rocky Road for $247,500. Are you selling your home yourself because you want to save the commission?*

Prospect: *That's part of it.*

Gregg: *If I was in your situation, I might do the same thing myself. But if you're getting tired of all the effort involved, I think there's a good chance that I could sell your home relatively quickly. I have a number of people interested in living in Castle Pines. How much are you asking?*

Prospect: *$225,000.*

Gregg: *What kind of shape is your home in?*

Prospect: *Pretty good. We did some painting before putting it on the market and I replaced the water heater.*

Gregg: *May I ask why you're selling it?*

Prospect: *We're just outgrowing it. We need a larger place and we wanted to see if we could make some money on this one.*

Gregg: *How long ago did you put the house on the market?*

The mention of bringing descriptions of larger houses at the end shows the prospect that Gregg was listening and paying attention to everything that he said.

Prospect: *Six weeks ago.*

Gregg: *Look, Mr. Hotchkins. By now, I'm sure you have some questions about selling your home. I'd be happy to meet with you and your wife and help however I can. I also have some sample forms that you'll need when you accept an offer. Of course, there's absolutely no obligation. I know that you want to sell your home yourself and I respect that. But I think that I can help. Would tomorrow evening be a good time?*

Prospect: *I work until 7.*

Gregg: *Could we meet at 7:30 or 8?*

Prospect: *7:30 should be fine.*

Gregg: *Mr. Hotchkins, I'll plan on meeting with you and your wife tomorrow evening at 7:30. In case you're interested, I'll bring some photographs and descriptions of larger houses on the market.*

Prospect: *Thank you.*

Gregg: *Good-bye.*

Prospect: *Good-bye.* CLICK.

Gregg: *CLICK.*

NOTES:

1. Gregg didn't give the prospect his phone number because it would have made it too easy for him to change his mind and cancel. If something did come up, the prospect would have to go to the trouble of looking up Greenbrier Real Estate in the phone book.

2. If the prospect had "closed up," Gregg would have stopped asking questions about the house. Notice, too, that he didn't start asking them until he had explained why he was calling. If he had started the list right off the bat, the prospect would have only been half-listening, thinking, "What does this guy want?" It comes across as arrogant. You're asking them to respond to very personal questions without giving them a reason to do so.

FSBO MARKETING PLAN SCRIPT

Gregg: *Hello, Irene Hotchkins?*

Prospect: *Yes?*

Gregg: *Mrs. Hotchkins, this is Gregg Mulvaney with Greenbrier Real Estate here in town. Do you have a minute?*

Prospect: *Just a minute. I have to go pick up my son from soccer practice.*

Gregg: *Mrs. Hotchkins, I drove by your house today and noticed your "For Sale" sign. Would you mind telling me how much you're asking for your house?*

Prospect: *We put the price at $225,000. That's what some friends across the street sold their house for.*

Gregg: *Yes, I know. I looked up the selling prices of houses in your neighborhood before calling. Did you know that setting a realistic price is the biggest difficulty that most people have when trying to sell their own homes?*

Prospect: *I've heard that. But we sold our house once before and it worked out fine.*

Gregg: *You were fortunate. Not many people who sell their own homes find it that easy. Anyway, I'm calling to make you an offer. Based on what you've said, I think that I could help you and your husband. What I'd like to do is develop a complete proposal for marketing your home. I've specialized in Castle Pines real estate for several years and I think that you'd be interested in hearing some of what I've learned. I know that you intend to sell your own home. I'm just asking you to listen. Would Saturday afternoon be a good time?*

Prospect: *I have to talk to John about this.*

Gregg: *Of course. Why don't we just set up a time and then if you need to change it, you can call me back? Would 1 o'clock Saturday be all right?*

Gregg's remarks hinted that the price is not realistic. But he didn't come right out and criticize their decision. He just planted a seed — that could make them worry later.

The logic behind Gregg's offer is that he really knows the market and they could benefit from listening to him.

> Prospect: *Usually the kids are out playing by then. That should be fine.*
>
> Gregg: *Mrs. Hotchkins, if for some reason you need to change the time, call me. My number is 555-9890. In the meantime, I'll start working on the marketing plan so it's ready when we meet on Saturday. Do you have any other questions?*
>
> Prospect: *I don't think so.*
>
> Gregg: *Great. I'll see you and Mr. Hotchkins on Saturday.*
>
> Prospect: *Good-bye. CLICK.*
>
> Gregg: *CLICK.*

NOTES:

1. Gregg will carefully prepare for the presentation and if they don't list with him, he'll offer them a For Sale By Owner Kit that he brought along — just in case.

2. Be careful in assuming that a couple is married or that the woman has taken the man's last name. In this case, however, property records showed a legal tie. Often it's better to discretely ask the status of a relationship or avoid referring to it. "Partner" is a good word.

EXPIRED LISTING SCRIPT

Tamar searched through the MLS one more time. She just wanted to double-check that the house at 3131 River Road hadn't sold. Nothing. It had disappeared from the listings and there was no hint of a sale.

She'd first noticed the "For Sale" sign in front of the house about five months ago. She remembered the irritation she felt whenever someone in "her" farm chose to list with another agent. As usual, she rushed right back to the office and looked them up in her farm files. The house was owned by Jerry and Jennifer Rosen. They'd lived there for 15 years, which meant they probably had built up substantial equity. They'd remodeled the basement seven years ago. The house had a large lot, backyard screened porch and hot tub.

They'd never responded to any of her direct mail letters.

Two days ago, the sign in front of their house vanished. That could mean the listing had expired. Maybe they were negotiating with another agent. Maybe they had decided not to sell the house. Maybe they just wanted a break from the constant showings and hassle.

Well, she'd never know unless she called them.

Calling people she'd never met was hard for her. Even though she realized that her fears were groundless, she couldn't kick that sinking feeling in the pit of her stomach every time she had to make one of these calls. She found that it was mostly the anticipation that was difficult. Once she had them on the line, her fears melted away. She knew that overcoming this type of fear was the only way she would ever succeed at her work.

She read over the script. Then she picked up the phone and dialed with a steady hand.

If the prospect was still listed with an agent, Tamar would've said, "Mrs. Rosen, thank you so much for your time. I enjoyed talking to you and I hope that you sell your home soon."

Tamar emphasized that listening to her imposes no obligation on the prospect.

Tamar:	*Hi. Jennifer Rosen?*
Prospect:	*This is Jennifer Rosen.*
Tamar:	*This is Tamar Sitwell. I'm with Greenbrier Real Estate here in town. Do you have a minute?*
Prospect:	*Barely.*
Tamar:	*I'll be quick. I specialize in selling Castle Pines homes, so I drive around the neighborhood a lot. About five months ago, I saw the "For Sign" in front of your house. Then, last Tuesday, I noticed that it had disappeared. I checked the computer and can't find your house listed. May I ask if you're still listed with Broadmoor Realty?*
Prospect:	*No.*
Tamar:	*Have you listed with any other real estate company?*
Prospect:	*We're thinking about it. But we haven't made a decision yet.*
Tamar:	*I'm glad that I called today. Ms. Rosen, in the past six months, I've sold three homes in Castle Pines. One was the Ramirez home at 556 Lone Pine Road, which I believe is very similar to your home. The others were at 667 Trail Star Drive and at 435 Rocky Road. Each home was on the market an average of five weeks and each sold for within 90% of its listing price.*
	Ms. Rosen, if you can set aside 30 minutes, I can give you a detailed proposal of how I would market your home.
Prospect:	*We're pretty busy in the next few days.*
Tamar:	*I can understand that. But last year I sold ____ homes in Castle Pines. I'm only asking you for the opportunity to present my ideas.*
Prospect:	*Yes. But there's another agent who's been calling and we're thinking of going with her.*
Tamar:	*You should go with whomever makes you feel most comfortable. All I'm asking for is a half hour of your time. You listen to me and I walk*

out the door. You're under absolutely no obliga-
tion to me. The decision is yours.

Prospect: *I have to ask Jerry about this.*

Tamar: *That's understandable. But would it be possible
to set up a time now? My schedule fills up pretty rapidly and I'd like to do this within the next
three days. How does Thursday evening sound?*

Prospect: *I have a yoga class that night. What about
Saturday morning?*

Tamar: *That's fine. Is 10 o'clock all right?*

Prospect: *I think that will work.*

Tamar: *10 o'clock it is. I'll deliver my presentation . . .
you listen . . . and then I leave. Ms. Rosen, thank
you for your time. I look forward to meeting you
on Saturday.*

Prospect: *See you then. Good-bye.*

Tamar: *Good-bye. CLICK.*

Prospect: *CLICK.*

NOTES:

1. The logic behind this appeal is Tamar's success in selling other homes in the neighborhood. She points out how long they stayed on the market and how well the selling prices matched the listing prices. This is important information to a prospect with an expired listing.

2. If the prospect had not listed with anyone and seemed willing to talk, Tamar could've asked her if she was unhappy with the process and why. That would've helped Tamar tailor her appeal. For example, if the prospect said that she didn't think the previous agent had adver-tised the house well enough, Tamar could've point out that her list-ings appear every night in the local paper as well as in the Home Listings Book. She also would bring other agents there on caravan and hold weekly open houses.

3. If the prospect had said that they had changed their mind about sell-ing the house, Tamar could've asked, "May I ask why? Is because you really don't want to move or because you don't think that you can get the right price for your house in today's market?" The prospect would respond and Tamar would ask, "If you really believed your home would sell for a reasonable price within the next two months, would you be willing to list it again?"

RENTERS TO BUYERS SCRIPT

Bob sighed as he read the classifieds. Imagine a two-bedroom apartment for $1,200. If he didn't work in local real estate, he'd probably think the apartment must be pretty nice. But he knew better. It could be anything from a dive to a luxury penthouse. The rental market had gone crazy.

When driving through his farm area the other day, he'd counted the number of blocks with apartment houses. Five long, windy blocks with door-to-door apartments. The renters paid a pretty penny for them, too, with the average one bedroom starting at $650 a month.

He'd just sold a house where the owners would pay that much. But they'd get tax deductions, credit lines, equity build-up . . . the renters, on the other hand, got no tax breaks and no equity. They left their apartments with nothing but a stack of canceled checks.

Bob started trying to figure out how many people lived in those five blocks of apartments. If each building had 10 units . . . there were about 25 buildings . . . that added up to 250 residents or families.

Right now, Bob had an unusually large number of "starter" homes in the listings. This would be a great time to call and try to interest some of the renters in buying.

The next day, he got on the phone.

Bob: *Good afternoon. Henry Davidson, please.*

Prospect: *This is he.*

Bob: *Mr. Davidson, this is Bob Turnbull with Greenbrier Real Estate here in town. Do you have a minute?*

Prospect: *What for?*

Bob: *Mr. Davidson, I'm calling to give you some information about rent increases. I've been doing a little study and I've found that the average rent in our area has been going up 15% a year. Can I ask when was the last time you had a rent increase?*

Prospect: *Last year.*

Bob: *Was it in the neighborhood of 15%?*

Prospect: *About that.*

Bob: *How many rent increases have you had in the last five years?*

Prospect: *Three.*

Bob: *Mr. Davidson, there is a way that you can stop worrying about rent increases. For about what you're paying now in rent — or maybe even less — you could probably own your own home. That would mean lower taxes, equity build-up and no more aggravation from noisy neighbors. Have you ever considered owning a home?*

Prospect: *Yes. But don't you need a down payment?*

Bob: *In some cases. Not always. With the market as up and down as it has been over the past few years, a number of lenders have developed special programs for first-time buyers. I'd be happy to explain some of these programs to you. Could we meet tomorrow night?*

Prospect: *I don't know.*

Bob: *Mr. Davidson, we have a number of charming and unique homes that would be great for first-buyers — available right now. I'd be happy to sit down and help you work out the numbers . . .*

Bob had done a small survey before making these "prospecting" calls. That information became his "hook" for getting into the call.

Bob investigated first-time buyer financing programs and had the information in front of him as he made the calls.

> *then we could drive around and look at some of the properties. What if we meet tomorrow around 6:30? Will you be home from work by then?*
>
> Prospect: *That sounds all right.*
>
> Bob: *Mr. Davidson, I'll be at your apartment tomorrow at 6:30. I'll bring descriptions of some of these financing plans and we'll see what we can work out. Thank you very much for your time. I'll see you tomorrow.*
>
> Prospect: *Thank you. Good-bye.*
>
> Bob: *Good-bye.*
>
> Prospect: *CLICK.*
>
> Bob: *CLICK.*

NOTES:

1. If the renters had been older people who had already sold a home and weren't interested in another or people who obviously weren't interested in buying, Bob could've asked if they thought any of their neighbors might be ready to buy.

RELOCATION SCRIPT — CORPORATE HUMAN RESOURCES

Denise set the phone softly down in the cradle. Her friend, Carolyn, had just told her that the Trend Corporation planned to move its corporate headquarters to Castle Pines. That meant probably at least 25 executives would be shopping for homes in the area. In upper price ranges, too.

The move was scheduled for next fall. It was April. She'd better get busy. What would be the best approach? A letter? A call? Both?

Denise decided to call first, then send follow-up information. She was afraid that if she didn't, the information would wind up in the "dead letter" file. At least if she called, they would have a voice to associate with the letter. And she'd have a good excuse to call again. The more contact she had with the corporate resource office, the better.

First, though, Denise called Trend's corporate headquarters in suburban New York. She asked the operator for the name and title of the person in charge of corporate relocations. She also did a search through a business data base for information on the Trend Corporation.

Trend was a pretty high end corporation with a fairly conservative mentality. Executives with children would want to know all about the local school system and private schools. Proximity to golf courses would be a selling point. So would lakefront property. In many cases, travel time to the airport would make a difference. Denise listed all possible considerations she could think of. Then she began writing her phone script.

The offer to fly there and meet with the relocation officer is a big plus. It demonstrates the depth of your interest.

Denise:	*Could I please speak with Tom Young, please?*
Operator:	*Just a minute, please.*
Prospect:	*Hello?*
Denise:	*Is this Tom Young?*
Prospect:	*Yes, it is.*
Denise:	*Mr. Young, my name is Denise Wilson. I'm with Greenbrier Real Estate in Castle Pines, North Carolina. I understand that your company has decided to relocate its headquarters to this area. It's also my understanding that you're the human resources executive in charge of the relocation. Is that correct?*
Prospect:	*Yes it is.*
Denise:	*Could I ask when you're planning to start the move?*
Prospect:	*We'll start at the end of July and finish by September 1.*
Denise:	*Mr. Young, I'm sure that you're interested in minimizing the headaches of moving. Especially for your executives. How many executives do you expect to relocate to this area?*
Prospect:	*About 30.*
Denise:	*Mr. Young, I've prepared special Relocation Kits for executives like yours. These kits include sample MLS listings, maps, local public and private school ratings, recreational opportunities, a restaurant guide and a Chamber of Commerce booklet. They're a great way to introduce executives to this area. Would you like me to put some kits in the mail?*
Prospect:	*That might be a good idea.*
Denise:	*About how many would you like?*
Prospect:	*25, I think.*
Denise:	*Mr. Young, what if I deliver them in person? I have some time next week when I could fly up at my own expense. Then we could discuss in detail exactly what you're looking for in this*

relocation. At Greenbrier, we've handled a number of successful corporate relocations. I'd be happy to give you references.

Prospect: *I don't know that a personal meeting at this stage is necessary.*

Denise: *It might be a little early, but it could really help smooth the process. The more I know about your company, the easier it will be to provide the level and type of service you need. How does next Wednesday afternoon look?*

Prospect: *I'm not sure.*

Denise: *I'll not only bring the kits, I'll bring some pictures of Castle Pines neighborhoods and real estate statistics. Even if you decide not to use my services, I think that you'll find the meeting very valuable in terms of learning about Castle Pines in general. Is 1:30 next Wednesday afternoon open?*

Prospect: *Okat. I'll meet you in my office next Wednesday afternoon.*

Denise: *Thank you very much, Mr. Young. If you think of anything else you'd like me to bring, give me a call. My number is 704/555-9898. Otherwise, I'll see you on Wednesday.*

Prospect: *See you then.*

Denise: *Good-bye.*

Prospect: *CLICK.*

Denise: *CLICK.*

NOTES:

1. Relocation Kits are an excellent way to begin building a relationship with a corporate relocation officer. Pack them with information and present them attractively. Most of this information is free — it just takes a little time to assemble.

2. Another approach might have been to describe the extent of services you're willing to provide — from picking up executives on house hunting trips at the airport to setting up weekly housecleaning services after the move-in.

RELOCATION SCRIPT — INDIVIDUAL

Jeff was surprised when he read in the paper that Alan Briggs was moving back to town. Alan had left Castle Pines 15 years ago when he joined the Air Force. Now he was retiring and coming home.

Alan had never seemed to like small towns. Chicago, New York, even Los Angeles were more his style. Maybe traveling around the world for so many years had mellowed him. The newspaper story said Alan was married and had two small children. That meant he'd need a house with three bedrooms and a yard.

Alan lived in Newark, New Jersey. Jeff called information and got the phone number. Jeff didn't think Alan would remember him. After all, he'd been several years behind Alan in high school.

Woman: *Hello?*

Jeff: *Hi, could I please speak to Alan Briggs?*

Woman: *Alan, it's for you.*

Prospect: *This is Alan Briggs.*

Jeff: *Alan, this is Jeff Madison from Castle Pines. You probably don't remember me — I was a couple of years behind you in high school. Anyway, I read in the local paper that you were leaving the Air Force and moving back here to Castle Pines. When are you thinking of doing that?*

Prospect: *I don't remember your face but your name is familiar. My wife and I are planning to come back as soon as school is out for the kids. So it'll be sometime in June.*

Jeff: *That's great. I know a lot of people are looking forward to seeing you again. I'm calling because I work with Greenbrier Real Estate. I was wondering what you were planning for housing arrangements. Are you interested in buying down here?*

Prospect: *If I can afford it.*

Jeff: *The market's pretty good right now. Especially for buyers. You said you had children. What kind of house are you looking for?*

Prospect: *Probably three bedrooms and two baths.*

Jeff: *I'd say the average price for a nice-sized home like that in Castle Pines is $175,000. And there's a lot of favorable financing available. Do you own a home now?*

Prospect: *Yeah. It just went on the market.*

Jeff: *May I ask the listing price?*

Prospect: *$155,000.*

Jeff: *Alan, off the top of my head I can think of about three properties that might interest you. Would you like me to send you information on them?*

Prospect: *Sure.*

Jeff: *What's your address?*

Notice how Jeff keeps his comments brief and asks a lot of questions. Asking questions increases the prospect's involvement.

Jeff does not assume that the prospect is interested in buying right away. Jeff asks about his plans.

Prospect:	*345 Lincoln Drive, Newark, New Jersey 45506.*
Jeff:	*Alan, have you and your wife thought about taking a trip down here to look at homes?*
Prospect:	*We thought about it, but we haven't made any arrangements yet.*
Jeff:	*If you're planning to move in June, it'd probably be good for you to come down in the next two weeks. Is that possible?*
Prospect:	*Maybe. I'll have to see.*
Jeff:	*Why don't I send you the MLS listings I mentioned? I'll also include a special relocation kit I've prepared for people moving to this area. In it, you'll find a map, statistics on the local schools and a Chamber of Commerce booklet.*
Prospect:	*That sounds good.*
Jeff:	*I'll call you next Monday to see if you have any questions and to find out if you've set a date for a trip down here. I'll also check on some other properties, so I should have a number to show you when you arrive.*
Prospect:	*That would be fine.*
Jeff:	*Alan, thank you very much. I'll put this material in the mail today.*
Prospect:	*Good-bye.*
Jeff:	*Good-bye.*
Prospect:	Cʟɪᴄᴋ.
Jeff:	Cʟɪᴄᴋ.

NOTES:

1. If the prospect had been unfamiliar with the area, Jeff could have spent more time describing things like neighborhoods, price ranges, schools, sports, etc.

2. When calling because you heard someone was moving to the area, it's important to let them know how you heard about their move. Otherwise they'll be trying to figure it out while you talk.

ABSENTEE OWNER/LANDLORD SCRIPT

Tom drove past the corner house with gray shutters on a pie-shaped lot for the tenth time that day. He noticed that it looked vacant. The tricycle that usually stayed in the driveway had disappeared and the living room drapes were closed. He knew that the house had been a rental for the past 10 years — he wondered if the owner was ready to sell. By now, the maintenance costs should be adding up.

Back at the office, Tom looked up the address in his farm files and checked the record. The owner, Mary Satterwaite, lived in upstate New York. She had had the house 15 years. If he called soon, there was a chance he could catch her between tenants. Looking for new renters was always a pain. Maybe she would be interested in selling.

Five hours later, Tom picked up the phone.

Tom mentioned that he has driven by the house. It's good to add specific details and let them know that you're really interested.

Tom: *Hello, Mary Satterwaite?*

Prospect: *Yes, this is she.*

Tom: *Ms. Satterwaite, my name is Tom Reynolds. I'm with Greenbrier Real Estate in Castle Pines. You own a house at 545 Pine Grove Road, don't you?*

Prospect: *Yes.*

Tom: *May I ask how large the house is?*

Prospect: *Three bedrooms and one bath.*

Tom: *How many years have you owned it?*

Prospect: *Sixteen.*

Tom: *I'm calling because I have a problem and you have an opportunity. Over the past few months, the real estate market in Castle Pines has been extremely active. In fact, we've run out of inventory. I drove by your house earlier today and noticed that it looks vacant. Homes like yours are quite marketable. Have you ever considered selling?*

Prospect: *A long time ago. But I decided against it.*

Tom: *Well, if you were waiting for the right time, this is it. The market has never been better than it is right now. How much did you pay for the house?*

Prospect: *I inherited it from my parents. It was paid off.*

Tom: *After all these years, I'm sure that your repair and maintenance bills are adding up. With the equity in your Pine Grove house, you could buy a newer property that would be much easier to keep up. Have you looked at any other investment properties in this area?*

Prospect: *No, I haven't.*

Tom: *It's something you might want to consider, especially now that the market is so strong. I specialize in Castle Pines real estate and I'm fairly confident you could get a good price for the house. Last month, for example, I sold a three bedroom on Lone Pine Road for $213,000. I also sold properties on Trail Star Drive and Rocky*

Tom made a point of describing his recent sales in the area. This bolsters the impression that he is competent.

Road. I'm sure that your house would be in that range. I have some time available tomorrow. I could stop by your house and then call you with an evaluation based on these other sales. Would that be useful to you?

Prospect: *I don't know.*

Tom: *I can understand your hesitation. Selling a property is a big decision. But if you're looking for a profit, now is the right time. When I call with the evaluation, I also could describe an intensive marketing plan. All you have to do is listen. You'd have no obligation to me at all. Could I get in to look at the property tomorrow?*

Keep emphasizing why now is a good time to sell.

Prospect: *Yes. I keep a key outside the house. But if I decide to list the property, I'd have trouble renting it. Then I'd lose the rental income. If it doesn't sell quickly, that could hurt.*

Tom: *Well, you could rent it with the understanding that you'd give a 90-day notice if the property sold. Or you could leave it unrented and take the chance that it would sell quickly. Our average turnaround is six weeks — which is only one to two months' rent. Your profit should more than compensate for that loss. In decisions like these, I've found that it's good to have as much information as possible. I could have the evaluation ready for you in two days. Would that be sufficient?*

Prospect: *That would be fine.*

Tom: *Now where is the key?*

Prospect: *Under the back door mat.*

Tom: *Ms. Satterwaite, I'll stop by your house tomorrow. By the end of the next day, I'll have a written evaluation based on recent sales of comparable homes in the neighborhood. Can I fax it to you or should I put it in the mail?*

Prospect: *You can drop it in the mail.*

Tom: *Your address is 667 Sutter Point, Rockville, New York, 10110, right?*

Prospect:	*That's right.*
Tom:	*Great. I'll call you when it's complete. I can tell you in general what to expect and then we can talk again when you receive it.*
Prospect:	*Good.*
Tom:	*Ms. Satterwaite, I'll talk to you in a few days.*
Prospect:	*Okay. Good-bye.*
Tom:	*Good-bye.*
Prospect:	CLICK.
Tom:	CLICK.

NOTES:

1. If Mary had been adamant about not wanting an evaluation, Tom would've offered to send her descriptions of comparable properties that recently sold. See *How To Farm Successfully — By Mail* for a sample cover letter. He also could have offered information (e.g. local newspaper stories) about recent upswings in the housing market.

ABSENTEE OWNER VACANT LAND SCRIPT

Tammy left Martin's drug store carrying a cold drink. It was the hottest summer she could remember. Since she was in the neighborhood, she decided to stroll down Greenville Street. A short block of neatly kept two- and three-bedroom homes, it was lined by tall oaks with leaves that hung limply in the heat.

The Ramos family had painted their house. It looked nice — a light brown with evergreen trim. They were sprucing up the yard, too. Next door the Smiths needed to clean up their driveway. Oil stains glistened in the sun. Tammy tripped on a crack in the sidewalk and spilled a little of her drink. She hoped no one saw her stumble.

At the end of the block, new weeds were sprouting up on the Anderson's vacant lot. They'd owned the lot for years. Maybe at one time they planned to build here. She doubted that they ever would. It was a nice lot. A big elm stood in the back. A house would get the morning sun. She wondered if they'd ever thought about selling the lot. They could get a good price now, she thought. She decided to call and find out.

Later that afternoon, she dialed their number.

Tammy:	*Hello, Ruth Anderson?*
Prospect:	*Yes.*
Tammy:	*Mrs. Anderson, this is Tammy Beiderman. I'm with Greenbrier Real Estate in Castle Pines. I'm calling because I know you own the lot on Greenville Street. There have been some changes recently in the real estate market that I think you should know about.*
Prospect:	*What kind of changes?*
Tammy:	*Lately we've had a rush of buyers. Right now, we don't have enough homes on the market to meet their demands. So they're buying lots and building. That has driven land prices up quite a bit in the past few weeks. What are your plans for your lot?*
Prospect:	*At one time, we had planned to build. Now we're not sure.*
Tammy:	*Well, you were smart to choose a lot in an area with high buyer demand. Right now, I'm sure that you'd pocket a nice profit if you sold. You bought the lot seven years ago. Is that right?*
Prospect:	*Yes.*
Tammy:	*Have you ever thought about how much you could make if you decided to sell?*
Prospect:	*Sometimes.*
Tammy:	*You know, if you wanted to see if it would sell, it wouldn't cost you a penny. I'd pick up all the marketing costs — you'd just pocket the profit. With the low inventory of houses around here, you're in a great position. What do you think?*
Prospect:	*It sounds good. But I have to talk to my husband.*
Tammy:	*Of course. Why don't I put an agreement in the mail for both of you to look over? All it does is allow me to market your property. You can read it — talk about it — and make a decision. But if you're going to sell, now's a great time.*
Prospect:	*All right. We'll talk about it.*

> Tammy: *Are you still living at 7604 Porter Way, Chesterton, Indiana, 47696?*
>
> Prospect: *We're still here.*
>
> Tammy: *Great. I'll put this in the mail today and I'll call you next Wednesday. Will that give you enough time to discuss this?*
>
> Prospect: *It should.*
>
> Tammy: *Would 7 p.m. be a good time to call or would 8 be better?*
>
> Prospect: *Seven should be fine.*
>
> Tammy: *All right. I'll call you next Wednesday at 7. I'll put this agreement in the mail today. Mrs. Anderson, thank you very much for your time.*
>
> Prospect: *Thank you. Good-bye.*
>
> Tammy: *Good-bye.*
>
> Prospect: *CLICK.*
>
> Tammy: *CLICK.*

NOTES

1. This approach pushes prospects to sign a right of sale contract. Only use it if you really think you can sell the land for a fair value. If the market isn't very good, take another approach. One might be that it doesn't hurt to put the lot on the market and see what happens.

FOLLOW UP REFERRALS

One of your strongest openings in prospecting is a referral. Referrals give you instant credibility (assuming that the prospect thinks well of the person you mention) and provide a reason for the conversation to continue.

A referral from a friend or business associate of a prospect is better than one from another real estate professional, but both are far better than nothing.

Whenever you can drop a familiar name to a prospect, do it.

CLIENT REFERRAL SCRIPT

Yesterday Brian stopped by the Farmington home just to check on how they were doing. Three weeks ago, they'd moved into a large white colonial he had listed. He'd enjoyed meeting them — Donna Farmington was a pediatrician; Roger Farmington was an investment broker. They flew a small plane — and so did Brian.

He walked up to the front door and saw Roger spraying some pesticides on the flowers on the side of the house. Calling out "Hello," he started to step gingerly across the new grass. Roger looked up with a smile and waved him over.

They chatted a few minutes about the most common garden pests in the area.

Donna came out, wiping her hands on her jeans. She'd been scrubbing out the basement. Like Roger, she gave him a warm greeting. They talked a little about conditions at the local airport. During a severe storm the past week, a couple of planes had some minor damage. And next month, a local resident who wanted the airport shut down was scheduled to make a presentation to the City Council.

After about 10 minutes, conversation waned and Roger got ready to leave. Just before turning away, he had a thought. He said, "One more thing — This past week we've gotten some great new listings — homes that hardly ever come on the market. Know anyone else who might be interested in moving to Castle Pines?"

Roger thought for a minute. "You know, we had a few friends over last weekend to see the place. One guy, Bill Hammerer, really seemed to fall in love with it. He could be interested — I know he has been thinking about moving for quite a while."

Donna chimed in, "That's right. Several months ago, he mentioned something about moving. I wasn't paying much attention — but maybe you should call him. Hold on a minute, I'll get his number."

She was back in a flash with the number written on a blue post-it note. "Bill Hammerer — 555-9985"

"Thanks a lot," Brian said. "I'll let you know what happens."

"Good luck," Roger called out as Brian walked away.

The next morning, Brian called Bill.

Prospect: *Hello?*

Brian: *Bill Hammerer?*

Prospect: *Yes?*

Brian: *Mr. Hammerer, I'm Brian Taylor. I'm with Greenbrier Real Estate. Your friends, Donna and Roger Farmington, suggested that I call you.*

Prospect: *What about?*

Brian: *They mentioned that you'd stopped by their new home last weekend and you seemed to really appreciate the Castle Pines area. I'm calling to see if you'd like me to take you around for a few hours and show you some of the great homes we have available. But first — let me ask — where do you live now?*

Prospect: *In Forest Glen.*

Brian: *Do you own or rent your home?*

Prospect: *Own it.*

Brian: *Were Donna and Roger right in thinking that you really liked Castle Pines?*

Prospect: *I did. I particularly liked their home. I'm not really very happy with where I'm living now but I haven't done any serious looking.*

Brian: *What is it about your home that you don't like?*

Prospect: *It's pretty small — just 2,000 square feet. And it doesn't have much of a yard. But it does have a two-car garage with a workshop area.*

Brian: *I have a few houses right now that might interest you. One is a three-bedroom, two-bath with 3200 square foot. It's on a block similar to the Farmington's. Another is a two-bedroom, two-bath home with a large basement workshop. How many people live in your home?*

Prospect: *Myself, my girlfriend and her little boy.*

Brian: *So a two-bedroom might work for you?*

Prospect: *Maybe.*

Brian: *Bill, what about my taking you and your girl-friend to see some of these homes later this week? You'd find out what kinds of homes we have here in Castle Pines and you'll probably get a better idea as to whether you'd like living here. Which would be best — Thursday or Friday?*

Prospect: *We're both off on Friday.*

Brian: *What about Friday morning at 10? If you can come to my office, we can talk about what's available, pick out some properties and then I'll take you through them. Is 10 okay?*

Prospect: *That's fine.*

Brian: *My office is at 90057 Carbondale Road, right next to Lucky's. The phone number is 555-8900. So I'll count on seeing you Friday.*

Prospect: *Friday it is.*

Brian: *Mr. Hammerer, thank you very much for your time. I'll tell the Farmingtons that I spoke to you.*

Prospect: *Good-bye.*

Brian: *Good-bye.*

Prospect: Cʟɪᴄᴋ.

Tammy: Cʟɪᴄᴋ.

Brian opened and closed the call with references to the Farmingtons.

NOTES:

1. If the prospect had resisted setting up an appointment, Brian would've emphasized that there was no obligation — the visit would just help him get to know Castle Pines better.

2. Brian could have added more urgency by describing properties priced below market value or that just came on the market or whose owners want to sell quickly or houses that for any reason won't stay on the market long.

3. If the prospect refused to see the homes, Brian could have offered to send descriptions of the properties in the mail. (For this, you could adapt the "Client Referral" letter in *How To Farm Successfully — By Mail.)*

BROKER REFERRAL SCRIPT

Allison took the call. A broker in Syracuse, New York, was on the line. She had just listed a $175,000 house — the client was being transferred to Castle Pines — and the broker wanted an agent to help the client find a new home.

They talked a few minutes about how much the client could afford — what kind of home the client wanted — and what neighborhood features were important. For example, the client had no children. So the school district didn't matter. But the client did enjoy excellent restaurants and shopping. Proximity to them would be a priority.

Allison took extensive notes. Then she got the client's number. Before calling, she looked through the listings and picked out about five homes she thought the client might like. She had the descriptions in front of her when she called.

Prospect: *Hello?*

Allison: *Could I speak with Victoria Chen?*

Prospect: *This is she.*

Allison: *Ms. Chen, my name is Allison Barnes. I'm with Greenbrier Real Estate in Castle Pines, North Carolina. Your broker in Syracuse, Barbara Brown, called me this afternoon. She told me that you're selling a home there and moving down here. May I ask what type of home you'll be looking for?*

Prospect: *I was thinking about a three-bedroom, two-bath contemporary. My home now is a Victorian that I remodeled. I think that I'm ready for something different.*

Allison: *Are you saying that you want a newer home?*

Prospect: *Not necessarily. I'm pretty handy so I could do a minor fix-up. I guess I was talking more about the look. I'd like a lot of windows — maybe a view.*

Allison: *There are some homes on the market that might interest you. Offhand, I can think of a contemporary with a wooded view and large deck. It's listed for $195,000. Then there's a slightly smaller home that's about five years old. It has a great layout and has been very well kept up. What kind of location do you want?*

Prospect: *Something that's quiet — maybe a little isolated — but close to shopping.*

Allison: *Would you like me to send you some information on properties in Castle Pines? I could send you some descriptions that you might find interesting as well as a a magazine review of local restaurants and a calendar for the local symphony.*

Prospect: *That would be terrific.*

Allison: *If I think of anything else, I'll put it in. When are you planning to come down here and look for a house?*

Mention broker who made referral at beginning and end of call.

Prospect: *I'm not sure yet. Probably in about three weeks.*

Allison: *Well, I'd love to help you. After you have a chance to look through the property descriptions, I'll give you a call. We can probably weed out a lot of properties over the phone. Where should I send the information?*

Prospect: *My home. 765 Willow Way, Syracuse, NY 10001.*

Allison: *I'm so glad that Ms. Brown called me. Working with you will be a pleasure. Do you have a pencil and paper?*

Prospect: *Yes.*

Allison: *My number is 704/555-8900. If you have any questions, don't hesitate to call. In the meantime, I'll put together this packet and mail it today. I'll call you Thursday or Friday to see what you think. What day and what time would be best for you?*

Prospect: *Why don't you call me late Friday at work? The number is 315/555-2543.*

Allison: *I'll do that. It was a pleasure to speak to you. I'll call you in a few days.*

Prospect: *Same here. Good-bye.*

Allison: *Good-bye.*

Prospect: *CLICK.*

Allison: *CLICK.*

NOTES:

1. For a letter to send with the material, adapt the "Broker Referral" letter in *How To Farm Successfully — By Mail.*

2. Other points Allison could have made in the call include how excellent the Castle Pines real estate market is and her qualifications as a Castle Pines real estate specialist.

3. If the prospect didn't seem interested in Allison's services, she could have followed up the call by sending a short letter thanking the prospect for her time and enclosing a free map of Castle Pines. This costs very little and it may cause the prospect to have second thoughts about using Allison.

CLIENT FARM

While most of your time should be spent prospecting for new clients, it's vital that you maintain positive and warm relationships with past ones. With the average American moving every five years, it's likely that a client who's happy with your services will turn to you again. Satisfied clients also are more likely to refer you to friends, colleagues and relatives.

You don't have to have frequent contact with former clients — once or twice a year is sufficient. We suggest one call a year and a holiday card in the mail. A sample phone script follows.

It may seem easy to put off making these contacts, especially when you're focusing on increasing your immediate income. Don't give in to the temptation. Remember that long-term, not short-term, payoffs will give you income security.

KEEPING IN TOUCH SCRIPT

Brad pulled out his list of sales for the year. Pretty good, he thought. Then he pulled out lists for the past five years. Except for the third year, the number of sales showed a steady rise. During the year that dipped, he had had marriage problems and one of his children had been quite sick. He had taken a lot of time off and that had hurt his income. Fortunately, he and Marsha had straightened things out and Kevin's medical condition had stabilized.

Looking at the list, he thought about what he could do to show these people how much he appreciated them. Each one had taught him something about real estate . . . and about himself.

The past weekend, he'd been out in the country and noticed that the orange trees were ready to harvest. Why couldn't he offer a small assortment of farm fresh produce? It wouldn't cost that much and a lot of clients would really appreciate it. Ken Knudsen, who owned one of the largest farms in the area, was a good friend. He would probably give Brad a good deal. Then Brad could pick up some inexpensive baskets. He wouldn't have to put much produce in each one — just enough to make a pleasing presentation.

A week later, Brad was on the phone.

Prospect: *Hello?*

Brad: *Hi, Dick?*

Prospect: *Yes.*

Brad: *Dick, this is Brad Crenshaw from Greenbrier Real Estate. I was just calling to see how things are going. How's the new home?*

Prospect: *Pretty good. We're thinking about doing a little remodeling and we need a new living room carpet but overall we're pretty satisfied. The kids love the playground.*

Brad: *That's great. That was a good house for you and you certainly bought at the right time. When you're ready to remodel, let me know. I can recommend two or three contractors who do excellent work.*

Prospect: *That would be great.*

Brad: *And how are the kids doing?*

Prospect: *Ted started Little League and Nancy's gotten involved in soccer. There are a lot of kids around here.*

Brad: *That's a great neighborhood for kids their age. How's your job going?*

Prospect: *Pretty well. I'm off to Thailand next month for a couple of weeks.*

Brad: *Will you be going up to Chaing Mai?*

Prospect: *Not sure yet. If I squeeze out a couple of days, I will.*

Brad: *Dick, I just finished putting together a small gift for you. It's my way of showing appreciation for your business over the years. I've got a basket full of fresh produce from Ken Knudsen's farm sitting on my desk with your name on it. Could you or Judy pick it up later today or tomorrow?*

Prospect: *Sure. Judy could stop by tomorrow. Probably mid-morning.*

Brad: *I should be here from 10 to 5. If I'm out for some reason, I'll have the basket on my desk*

Most of this conversation should be about the client. At the end, bring up the gift.

> *with your names on it. And Dick, thanks again for your business over the years. Remember to call me when you remodel.*
>
> Prospect: *Will do.*
>
> Brad: *See you later. Good-bye.*
>
> Prospect: *Good-bye.*
>
> Brad: *CLICK.*
>
> Prospect: *CLICK.*

NOTES:

1. Consider seasonal gifts. For example, around Halloween you might want to offer free pumpkins.

2. You probably won't have time to drop off the gifts yourself. So ask them to stop by your office. For a personal touch, write their names on cards attached to the gifts.

SECTION FIVE

You Can Do It!

CHAPTER 16

When The Phone Rings

> *Ability will enable a person to get to the top,*
> *but it's character that keeps them from falling off.*
>
> — *Anonymous*

When your phone rings, a top-notch opportunity could lie on the other end.

Sadly, all too often we handle calls simply as requests for information. We ignore sales techniques exactly when they could do the most good — because someone who takes the trouble to call is motivated. Don't let them get away.

Typically someone calls because they spotted your ad in the paper or your number on a "For Sale" sign. Always ask callers where they got your name, as the answers will tell you which of your marketing efforts works best. That enables you to better plan your marketing expenditures.

But even if someone is motivated enough to call, that doesn't mean they know what they want.

Maybe they liked a house's seclusion. Or the redwood trim. Or the front yard shade trees. If you can find their "hot button," you can suggest other homes they might want to see.

Frankly, hardly anyone ever buys the home they circle in the paper or see as they drive along the street. When people buy, it's usually another home with the same feature that first nabbed their attention. Your job on incoming calls is the same as with outgoing calls — you pitch an offer and cross your fingers for a positive response. The difference is — with incoming calls, you have to make up the offer quickly.

Turn a Caller into a Client

Within a few minutes of receiving a call, you should be working on turning that caller into a client.

Whether you get the chance to meet someone calling you depends on your sales skills. There are specific things you can do to intensify the caller's interest.

In a sense, callers are pre-qualified prospects because of the level of their interest. Assume they're ready to buy — even if they say they're just looking. If they're interested enough to look, they can be interested enough to buy. In short, treat every caller as a hot prospect.

The Right Time to Answer

Believe it or not, there is a right time to answer the phone. No, it's not on the first ring. That makes you seem overanxious. It's not on the fifth ring, either. Then you make the caller wait too long.

The right time to answer is on the third or fourth ring.

Letting a phone ring two times gives you the necessary seconds to make a mental break with whatever you're doing. You can take a deep breath, pump up your enthusiasm and answer with an excited lilt in your voice.

The last thing in the world you want to do is to answer sounding rushed, impatient, or in the middle of something else.

Every prospect deserves your full attention. Make sure you give it to them.

Take Charge

From the beginning of the call, take control. All too often real estate agents let the caller lead the way. That doesn't help them or you.

Statistics prove that most callers don't really know what they want in a home. They need someone to interpret what they want, show them what's available, and help them make a good decision.

Remember that real estate is highly complicated. Especially if you're not engrossed in it 40 hours or more a week. Keeping up on the latest market dips, mortgage rate fluctuations, and special types of financing takes an expert — *you*.

When a caller is defensive and tries to take charge, often it's because another agent has refused to share any information unless the caller agrees to a meeting.

Be Helpful

You can be helpful and, at the same time, let a caller know that you could help even more.

You start by having all the information they need at your fingertips.

Whenever you work the floor, make sure you've seen the latest "sold" sheets. Know which properties have offers on them, which are in escrow, and which have closed. Then for every house your office lists, have in mind two or three alternatives. Pick houses in the same type of neighborhood, same price range, or that offer some of the same features. Since most people don't buy the home they call about, always be ready to suggest others.

The Bare Bones of an Incoming Call

Here is a basic outline for handling an incoming call:

Introduction — Identify your company and politely ask how you can help the caller. Don't give your name.

Keep At Your Fingertips:

Descriptions of listed properties	✔
Properties that have offers on them	✔
Properties that are in escrow	✔
Properties that have sold	✔
Two or three alternatives for every home your office lists	✔
Current mortgage rates and financing information	✔

When answering incoming calls, always keep this information at your fingertips.

Ask Qualifying Questions — Sometimes this is necessary, other times the caller offers the information without your asking. Just try to find out what he or she wants to know.

Give Requested Information — Fill in the answers for the caller, giving them the satisfaction that you're taking them seriously and not putting them off.

Ask Probing Questions — Ask questions to find out what the client really wants. At this stage, you begin relationship-building.

Give Alternatives — In some ways, this is a variation of a close. You respond to the caller's request, but you also are ready with alternatives. Begin suggesting them.

Overcome Objections — Even on incoming calls, callers are bound to come up with objections. Handle them the same way you do on farming calls. Be polite, warm, friendly, positive, and intelligent.

Close — Ideally your close on an incoming call resembles that of an outgoing call — you offer additional information, a home evaluation, a meeting or whatever. The goal is to find a reason to continue the relationship.

Wrap-Up — As in farming calls, you confirm the details of the offer. At the very least, you get the caller's name and address and promise to send information later. Remember to double-check the name and address. Stay warm and courteous. Thank them for their time. Reassure them they're taking the right step. And always let them hang up first.

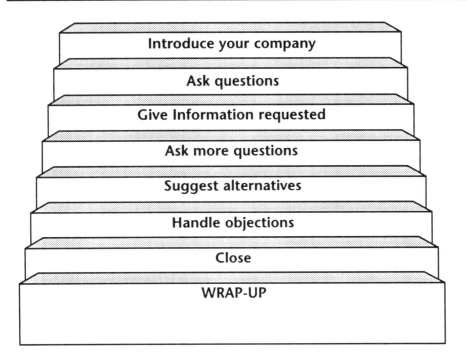

Handle incoming calls in the following steps:

- Introduce your company
- Ask questions
- Give Information requested
- Ask more questions
- Suggest alternatives
- Handle objections
- Close
- WRAP-UP

What to Say When You Answer

Before you take on telephone duty, make sure you've done your homework. Know all about the houses listed and advertised, as well as alternative properties.

Let the phone ring twice. On the third ring, pick it up and say,

"Jenkins Realty. Good morning. How may I help you?"

Remember — you don't give your name when you answer the phone. Why? Because at this point, it's meaningless. It will go in one ear and out the other.

If you hold it back, you can share it later in the call. Once they know you a little, chances are much better that they'll remember who you are.

There's another plus, too. If you wait, then you can give your name and ask for theirs in return.

We all know how reluctant many callers are to identify themselves. Waiting until the two of you have established some rapport is a good way to break down that resistance.

Ask Plenty of Questions

There's no reason why you shouldn't treat every incoming call with the same care you give your farming calls.

After answering the caller's questions, ask a few yourself. Begin building a relationship with the caller.

Most of the tips described in the previous section work equally well for both types. In fact, you should be able to steer an incoming call in exactly the same direction as a farming call.

How? With questions.

Questions are the heartbeat of good sales calls because they draw out prospects and build relationships.

But don't move too quickly. Wait for the caller to ask a question, then feed one back.

This technique works if you also give the caller some information. Refusing to share information will only make the prospect feel frustrated. They could easily wind up in an angry outburst and hang up. This happens more times than you think.

Callers have lots of reasons to be cautious. Maybe they already have an agent. Or they're not ready to commit to anything except conversation. Or they don't really know what they're doing. Respect their caution and try to overcome it with information and questions. Also — be courteous and be kind.

Finally, if the unthinkable happens and a caller asks you a question you can't answer, don't fudge it. Admit that you don't know and promise that you'll check it out and get right back to them. Then do it.

If you're honest and keep your word, people will respect you.

How to Get a Caller's Name

Many callers don't like to give their names because they're afraid you'll start pressuring them. Or they'll feel obligated to you.

Being anonymous has its advantages. You can't call them back. They can ask whatever they like. When they hang up, that's it. The relationship terminates. But for someone who's in the market for a home, not giving a name has definite drawbacks. It's up to you to point them out.

These include:

- You won't be able to provide them with important information about new houses on the market.

- You won't be able to call them back if something happens on the property that interested them.

- You won't be able to invite them to open houses so they can see what comparable homes in the neighborhood are selling for.

- You won't be able to provide them with information on financing packages.

However, there are ways to coax callers into identifying themselves. When someone calls about a property, put them on hold a few seconds. Explain that you're digging out the right property description.

When you return, gently inquire,

"Thank you so much for waiting. May I ask who's calling, please?"

Depending on your tone of voice, this can come across as kind or as pushy. If the caller does respond with their name, start using it right away.

If you have difficulty getting the caller's name, be patient. Wait until you sense the person is at ease with you; then give your name and ask for theirs.

Instead of a blunt

"May I ask your name?"

try this softer approach,

"My name is Gina Jordan. And your name is . . . ?"

If the caller still won't give their name, ask for it again when you offer to drop off some information or put something in the mail. Then they'll be forced to share their name and address with you.

Here's a list of material that might interest incoming callers:

- Map of the area they asked about
- Brochures about your company
- Pictures and descriptions of properties similar to the one they asked about
- Financing information
- Booklets on special services you offer

Always try to drop off information at the caller's home. Since so many callers want only to drive by properties, offering to hand-deliver materials in advance can be very helpful. That way you're able to meet the caller, but in a less pressured situation than when you show a property.

However, if a face-to-face meeting is out of the question, settle for the next best thing — getting something to the prospect in the mail. When you do this, as soon as you hang up, check the telephone directory for the caller's phone number. Make a note to call him or her back in two or three days. Then stuff the information in an

If a caller doesn't want to give you their name, don't give up. Wait until the person is at ease with you then try again.

envelope with a note and your business card, and mail it as soon as you can.

When you call back, the person may be surprised to hear from you. But you can swoop right past the surprise and get to the point by asking if they've seen the property and what they think of it. Don't give the prospect time to wonder about how you got their number.

Every so often, you'll run into someone who has really been burned. Even if you directly ask for their name, they'll refuse to give it. What can you do then?

Something like this might be in order:

"I can appreciate your not wanting to give out your name. But every day new listings come into our office. And the best buys are snapped up right away. Some don't even last 24 hours."

Then stop. Let the caller respond. Don't push any more. You've made your point. If you use this approach and it works, it's very important that you make good on your promise. Don't say you'll check listings every day for someone and then not do it. After a week or two without hearing from you, they'll move on to someone else. And they'll think you were lying just to get their name.

Even if there aren't any listings that meet their needs, call anyway. Let them know you're looking out for them.

Dealing with Specific Questions

When a prospect asks for specific details on a listing, they really want to know something more. What does it mean if a living room is 12' by 13'? If the room is all glass, it will have a very different feeling than a paneled room with rustic beams across the ceiling.

Tell the prospect how the room feels, too. Keep in mind that we think in pictures. Use your words to create enticing images in the prospect's mind.

For example, what if the prospect asks, "How big is the family room?" Your response might go like this:

When a caller asks for specific details on a listing, use your words to create enticing pictures.

"The family room is just the kind of place it's nice to curl up in during the winter. You can sit in front of an enormous fire, watch the afternoon sun filtering down through the trees outside, and see the birds in the backyard. It's a comfortable room, with one entire wall of brick and a floor-to-ceiling bookcase big enough for books

and knickknacks. On paper, the dimensions are 10' by 13'. But the large windows make it seem bigger."

Or they may ask, "How big is the lot?" Instead of giving them the dimensions, try something like,

"The lot will surprise you. From the street, it doesn't seem very large. But the back is breathtaking. When you go out the door, you're on an old brick Spanish patio. Where it ends, the stucco terraces begin — yards and yards of them on a gently sloping lawn. In one garden, you can grow roses. In another, cactus. There's plenty of room. At night, you can sit outside and see all the city lights. It feels like another world."

The Price — To Tell or Not to Tell?

When you answer the phone and someone says, "I'm calling about a house I saw in the paper," or "I just drove by a house and saw your sign," you know there's one thing uppermost in their mind — price.

Some companies feel that giving out the price of a listing is fine. Others caution that it should be held back and that you should push instead to show the property.

When someone asks about price, they really want to know if it's in the right range. And looks can be deceiving.

Once I drove by a slightly run-down redwood cottage on a large lot. Calling the listing agent, I discovered that the price was more than $200,000.

I was shocked. It looked like a small older home. But there was a lot more than I could see from the street. It turns out that it had four bedrooms and a pool.

If a particular property is clearly out of question for the caller, ask what price range they're in. Know the market well enough to have some other houses in mind. Don't write someone off just because the property they called about is beyond their reach. That just shows the caller has good taste.

When a caller asks about the price and you give it, be sure to include other elements. For example, is the owner willing to carry some of the financing? Has the price recently been reduced? Is there a low assumable mortgage? Include some of the specifics, because we all know that what a mortgage really boils down to is the monthly payment, not the asking price.

But don't dwell on the financing specifics. Dwell instead on how wonderful the home is. If they talk price, you talk benefits. People buy things not because they can afford them, but because they want them.

Start stirring up an emotional interest in the home and you'll have a head start.

Incoming Callers' Objections

When a prospect calls you, you'll hear certain types of objections more than others. But remember that for every objection, there's a positive response.

You may want to copy down some of the responses that follow and slip them into your script book. Put them in a special section for incoming calls. The better prepared you are, the more effectively you'll handle each and every call.

"I Just Want to Drive By"

One of the most common objections offered by incoming callers is that they simply want to drive by the property and call you back if they're interested.

This situation is dangerous because a prospect looking on their own cannot be sold. Here's a good response to the "drive by" request:

> *"It is important to see a house from the outside. I'll be more than happy to drive you there. Then if you want to go inside, we can do it on the spot. But first, maybe I can save you some time. Tell me, how many children do you have?"*

"Let Me Think It Over and I'll Call You Back"

"I'll think it over" is another popular objection. Here a good response might be something like this:

> *"I can understand that. You're making an important decision. Unfortunately, in the market today, there isn't a lot of time to decide. Good listings like this one disappear in a few days. You do think that timing is critical, don't you?"*

Adding urgency is one of the most effective ways to deal with indecision.

> ❝
> *Tackle problems as they arise. Delay makes problems snowball.*
> ❞

"I Drove By and It Looks Very Run-down"

When the prospect is calling because of a "for sale" sign — and they've already seen the house's exterior — you're likely to get much more specific objections such as, "It looks so run-down."

Remember, of course, that it can't be that bad in the prospect's mind since they did take the time to call you.

Nonetheless, you need to respond to specific objections with specific responses. To a "run-down" objection, you may respond with,

> *"Yes, but look at its price. You can't touch other four-bedroom homes in King's Ridge for under $150,000. This is a great opportunity."*

MOST COMMON OBJECTIONS FROM INCOMING CALLERS

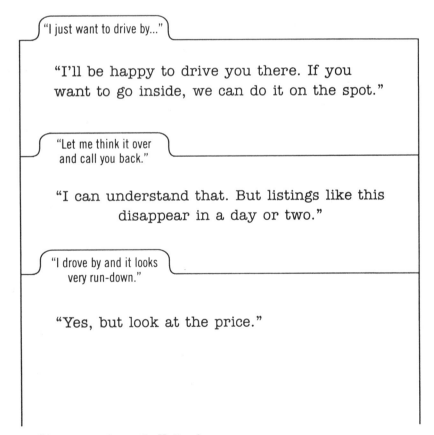

"I just want to drive by..."

"I'll be happy to drive you there. If you want to go inside, we can do it on the spot."

"Let me think it over and call you back."

"I can understand that. But listings like this disappear in a day or two."

"I drove by and it looks very run-down."

"Yes, but look at the price."

Make up objection/response cards for your script book. Put them in a special section for incoming calls.

Sample Incoming Call Script

It's Sunday afternoon and Agent Wilma Wilcox is working the floor. In front of her is the Sunday paper, with her office's listings circled. Also nearby is a sheet on which she has grouped similar houses by neighborhood, price, or features. For every listing, she has two or three alternatives. The Multiple Listing Book is open and waiting. The phone rings.

Introduction

Agent: Homebound Real Estate. May I help you?

Prospect: Yes. I'm calling about a home I saw advertised in today's paper.

Ask Qualifying Questions

Agent: Could you please tell me what the ad said?

Prospect: It says it's a four-bedroom ranch on a half acre in Mundelein.

Agent: Oh, yes. We've had quite a few calls on that home today. It's a beautiful property — the home is charming and there's plenty of land. Let me get the specifics for you. Just a minute, please.

(Pause for brief hold)

Give Requested Information

Agent: Thank you for waiting. The home is listed for $175,000. It's 3,000 square feet, with a kitchen the whole family can eat in, a dining room that's perfect for entertaining, four good-sized bedrooms with closets big enough for clothes and toys, three baths, and from every room you can look through wide windows to the rolling countryside. The workmanship is of a quality you don't very often find anymore. And best of all, there's a wonderful sense of serenity in the home. Tell me, how many are in your family?

Ask Probing Questions

Prospect: Three children, my wife, and myself.

Agent: Do you own your home now?

Prospect: No, we just moved to this area about a year ago. I wanted to rent for awhile first, so we'd have a better idea of where we wanted to live.

Agent: That was a wise decision. Then you've been out to Mundelein and you like it?

Prospect: Yes, I like the country feeling, even though it's close to the city. But I'm not sure I want to pay more than $150,000.

Trial Close 1

Agent: We have a number of listings in Mundelein. I can think of two or three that might interest you. I'd be happy to drive you out there this afternoon. Either five or six o'clock is fine for me. What's best for you?

Prospect: I appreciate the offer, but I'd rather just drive out there myself. Then if I'm interested, I'll call you back.

Overcome Objections

Agent: I can certainly understand your wanting to see the homes first. But sometimes it's hard to tell what a home is really like if you only see it from the street.

Prospect: That's true. But I really would rather do it this way.

> *You cannot antagonize and persuade at the same time.*
>
> *—Anonymous*

Trial Close 2

Agent: Whatever you like. However, I would appreciate it if you'd let me give you some information on available homes in that area.

Prospect: Sure. That's fine.

Wrap-Up

Agent: And your name is?

Prospect: Tom. Tom Pitzer.

Agent: Is that spelled P-I-T-Z-E-R?

Prospect: That's correct.

Agent: And your address, Mr. Pitzer?

Prospect: 11273 East Bay Road, Chesterton, Indiana 46304.

Agent: 11273 East Bay Road, Chesterton, Indiana 46304. Great. I'll drop off the information to you this afternoon. Now if you want to drive by the properties before I get over there, let me give you the addresses. They are: 700 Lincoln Street, 809 Grant Street, and the property you called about is at 912 Johnson Street. Do you have a map of the Mundelein area?

Prospect: Yes, I do.

Agent: Good. You won't have any trouble finding the homes. Just take the first DeKalb exit off the freeway. Then turn right at the first stop light. They're all in the Terrace Acres subdivision.

If you have any more questions, Mr. Pitzer, my name is Wilma Wilcox and I'll be more than happy to help you. The number here, again, is 555-2345.

Prospect: Well, Wilma, thank you. It has been a real pleasure to deal with someone so helpful.

Agent: Thank you, Mr. Pitzer. And I hope you see something you like.

Prospect: Good-bye.

Agent: Good-bye.

Prospect: CLICK (prospect hangs up first).

Agent: CLICK (Wilma hangs up last).

Wilma goes straight to the phone book, looks up the Pitzers' phone number and jots it down. Then she puts together the information he wanted and, on her way home, drops it off at their home. No one is there — so she leaves it by the front door with a note and her business card.

Switching from Information to Conversation

During the previous conversation, Wilma gave the caller everything he asked for. Then she quickly moved into a few questions of her own. Within a minute, the call became more personal and warm. There was give and take. In other words, a real conversation developed.

Knowing the right moment to switch from information to a conversation can be tricky. But here are a few tips:

Prospect: Well, I like that house. But it's out of my price range.

Agent: There are three other homes in the same neighborhood that might meet your needs. But before I tell you about them, would you mind telling me how many there are in your family?

See how easy it is to lead into questions?

Prospect: I'm calling about that cute country cottage you're advertising in today's paper. The one for $80,000.

Agent: Oh, that's a charming home. Lots of character. Tell me, what size home are you looking for?

Prospect: I'd like to know more about the three-bedroom, two-bath home that just went on the market.

Agent: You must mean the house on Elm Street. Is that it?

Prospect: I'd like to know more about the three-bedroom, two-bath home that just went on the market.

Agent: You must mean the house on Elm Street. Is that it?

Prospect: Yes.

Agent: I'm sorry, but the owners just accepted an offer. How long have you been looking for a new home?

Prospect: I'm calling about the "unique contemporary" advertised in yesterday's paper. Can you tell me where it is?

Agent: I'd be happy to. It's in the Canyon Park area. Are you familiar with the neighborhood?

> *Prospect:* I'd like more information on the older home you're advertising, the one with hardwood floors and a fireplace.
>
> *Agent:* Why, certainly. I'll be glad to help you. The home is a well-designed colonial, in excellent condition, located in the Bradley School District. Where do you live?

During your phone conversations, switch back and forth from asking questions to giving information. That way the prospect will be satisfied that you're answering the questions. And you'll have the satisfaction of finding out what you need to know.

If you start too early in the call and you sense the prospect tightening up, go back to giving information. Then try again in half a minute.

Turning Renters into Buyers

By now, you should have a handle on how to transform a negative into a positive. But there's one other important area to discuss before we move on. That's how to turn a renter into a buyer.

Everyone you know who rents is a potential client. In time, if you keep up the relationship, they will become clients. After all, why should they be lining the landlord's pockets when they could be filling their own?

For anyone paying rent, owning a home is worth considering. For personal reasons, some may prefer to keep renting. But down the road, almost all of them will be looking to buy.

A number of states offer special financing to first-time home buyers. That's something you should know about. It could make a big difference when you're outlining the wonderful advantages of ownership.

The potential market among renters is so great, some agents manage to convert four out of every five calls for rental properties into buyers. That's right — four out of every five! Know your tax laws. Find out about special programs for new home buyers. Then you can be among the top converters, too.

To give you some ideas on how to handle calls about rental properties, here's a sample script (more are in Chapter 15):

> *One of the most serious thoughts that life provokes is the reflection that we can never tell, at the time, whether a word, a look, a touch, an occurrence of any kind, is trivial or important.*
>
> —Anonymous

Agent: Good morning, Turner Realty. May I help you?

Prospect: Yes. We're looking for a three-bedroom house to rent. Do you have anything available?

Agent: I wish I could say yes. Maybe I can help you anyway. How much rent did you want to pay?

Prospect: About $800 a month.

Agent: Well, that's reasonable. How many are in your family?

Prospect: My husband and I have two children.

Agent: In addition to the three bedrooms, were you looking for anything special in a home? Perhaps a big yard or a family room?

Prospect: I'd love a fenced yard so the children would have a safe place to play. My husband says he wants a garage; but if I had to, I could talk him out of it. As for a family room, that would be nice. But a big living room is just as good.

Agent: There is a three-bedroom home that seems to fit your requirements. It's in an excellent neighborhood. The backyard is totally fenced in. And with a small down payment, the home could be yours for about $900 a month. When you figure what you'll save on taxes, that's actually less than what you'd pay in rent. I could show you the home this afternoon. Is four o'clock all right, or would you prefer six o'clock?

Prospect: Well, we really weren't interested in buying.

Agent: I can understand that. Owning a home is a big commitment. But if you're willing to pay $800 a month in rent, it's something you should consider. By owning a home, you'd save thousands of dollars every year. May I ask if you've ever owned a home?

Prospect: No, we've moved around too much.

Agent: What if I show you the house we were talking about? It's vacant, so we won't be disturbing anyone. Then we can sit down and talk about ways you might be able to swing it. Is tonight

> " It takes sun and rain to make a rainbow.
> —Anonymous "

	convenient for you, or would you prefer tomorrow morning?
Prospect:	Well, tonight's okay. If we make it six o'clock, then my husband can join us.
Agent:	Wonderful. My name is Roberta Robinson. And yours is . . .?
Prospect:	Carolyn Davidson.
Agent:	Nice to meet you, Mrs. Davidson. Now where shall I pick you up?
Prospect:	We live at 313 N. Elm Street here in town.
Agent:	313 N. Elm Street. Great. I'll be there at six o'clock. I look forward to seeing you.
Prospect:	Thank you. See you soon. Good-bye.
Agent:	Good-bye, Mrs. Davidson.
Prospect:	CLICK (prospect hangs up first).
Agent:	CLICK (agent hangs up last).

Taking Notes

One advantage to farming by phone is your ability to take notes. In face-to-face meetings, you don't want to disrupt eye contact — jotting down their every word would make anyone nervous. But over the phone, no one ever even knows.

For effective note taking, you need to develop a system where you focus not on what you're writing, but on what the person is saying. Shorthand, of course, is the perfect solution. But few of us have the time to learn it. So we come up with personal scribbling systems.

For prospects who call in, you might want to create a special set of files. A sample file would include:

Potential Buyer File

Date_____ Ad reference_____

Property called about_____

Name_____

Address_____

City/state/zip_____

Phone(Home)_____ Work)_____

Jobs (M)_____ (F)_____

Family size_____ Currently owns___ Rents___

Desired area_____ House type_____

Price range_____VA?____ FHA?_____

Special features wanted _____

_____

_____

Comments_____

_____

_____

Contacts:

Date   Notes

_____

_____

_____

Having a form like this available while answering incoming calls will help you take better notes.

Keep forms like this handy while working the floor. Chances are that you'll be able to fill in the date and ad called about right off the top. The name and address will probably have to wait until later in the call.

If you're fortunate enough to run into a real conversationalist, take lots of notes.

Also keep a list of your contacts. Mark the date, purpose of call, and outcome. If you arrange to follow up, go back to the file and report on what happened. With this information, you'll be able to keep track of when and how often you touch base with a potential buyer.

Initially don't worry about taking too many notes. Instead worry about taking too few. Within a few weeks, you'll be able to pare down your note taking so it won't seem as cumbersome.

Remember to write down the name as soon as the person gives it to you. Keep referring to it throughout the call. It's especially good to use the name just before making a point that deserves special emphasis. That way, the prospect will pay more attention.

When working on the phone, it's a good idea to keep nearby several different colored pencils or pens. Take down your basic information in regular pencil. Then use the colored pens to highlight anything you want to think about or follow up later.

PRACTICE EXERCISE SIXTEEN

1. Start answering your phones — at home and the office — on the third or fourth ring.
    Get in the habit — it's a good one.
2. The next time you handle an incoming call, make a point of asking the caller at least five questions.
    Don't just give the information the caller wants — find out why they want it.
3. Write three possible responses to each of the three most common incoming callers' objections.
4. Call a competitor's office and inquire about a listing.
    Don't identify yourself.
    What techniques do they use to find out who you are?

CHAPTER 17

Telephone Technology

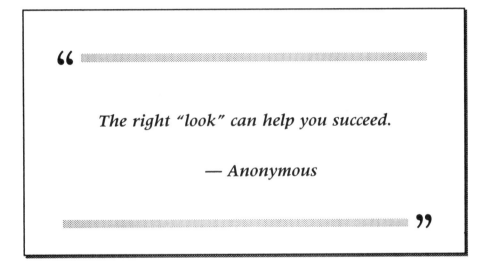

The right "look" can help you succeed.

— Anonymous

You feel comfortable now that you can overcome objections on your farming calls. You are also confident you can turn that incoming caller into a client. So, what's left?

With the amount of telephone technology available today, there are still a few ideas to cover. What do you do when you reach an answering machine? Do you leave a message or not? On that subject, do you need an answering machine (or voice mail) for yourself? What type of information do you leave on your machine's greeting? Should you get a cellular phone? A pager? Or both?

These may seem like simply questions, but many people do not know the answers. Or they do not use this technology to it's full benefit.

Leaving Messages

On this subject, you'll find recommendations on both sides of the fence. Some sales pros say it's okay to leave messages. Others suggest calling back later so you can talk to prospects directly. If you want to leave a message, make it assertive and positive.

For example, if you're calling the neighbors of a home you just listed, your message might go something like this:

If you leave a message, make it a clever one. But avoid the dramatics.

> *"This is Jeffrey Donaldson with Thompson Realty. I'm helping Ken Simmons down the block find a buyer for his home and I wanted to talk to you about it. My number is 555-6587. That's 555-6587. I'd appreciate it if you would call me back sometime this afternoon. Thank you."*

If you can, throw in a little teaser. Make the person wonder, "What do they want to talk to me about?" Try something like,

> *"This is Jeffrey Donaldson with Thompson Realty. Your neighbor, Ken Simmons, asked me to call you. Could you please get back to me this afternoon? My number is 555-6587. That's 555-6587. Thank you."*

Super-aggressive real estate professionals tend to leave messages like, "It's critical that Mr. Gephart call me back immediately."

Our advice? Avoid that approach. If they do call back, they're in for a big letdown when it turns out that what you want is relatively minor.

Think how much better it is to say something like this:

> *"Mention to Mr. Gephart that if possible, I'd really like to talk to him today."*

If he doesn't call back, call again. If he's still not available, check for the best time to try again. At this stage, the message taker is likely to be sympathetic and helpful.

If a child or someone who you don't feel will get the message straight answers the phone, ask what time the person you want to talk to will be home. Then call back.

If the prospect has an answering machine, leave a teaser message with a mild sense of urgency. If the prospect doesn't return the message, keep trying. You'll find them at home eventually. Nine callbacks are not unusual.

If you do run into someone who's hard to catch, calling around 9 a.m. is a good idea. Especially on Saturdays, when hardly anyone stirs outside before 10 a.m.

Taking Messages

Trying to find people who can take good messages is a problem that plagues almost every office in this country. That's especially true for real estate agents, who often don't have full-time receptionists.

Here's a simple rule: **If you want people to take good messages for you, take good messages for them.**

Some experts recommend writing down all kinds of extraneous facts. But when it gets right down to it, all you need to write is the time the person called, their name, and telephone number. In most cases, detailed messages *aren't* necessary.

But even getting the name and number straight can be a problem. It helps to have brightly colored message forms. That makes it a lot easier when you're searching for a message through a desk piled high with paper.

When you take a message for someone else, always double-check the caller's name and number. If you have questions about the spelling, ask.

If you take messages for others, take good ones. Then you can expect them to return the favor.

Often in real estate, friends tell other friends about us and give them our numbers. If they call and the message-taker transposes two digits, forget it. They'll think we just didn't bother to call back. And we'll have no idea how to find the right number. That's why taking good messages in a real estate office is so important.

If you want to see how your messages are handled when you're out of the office, call yourself. See if the person answering is courteous and warm and if they repeat the number and name to verify them. If he or she doesn't, mention it when you're back in the office.

Taking good messages is something most of us never bother to think about — until someone brings it to our attention.

If you're on the floor and someone calls for an agent who's with a client, generally the best thing to do is take a message. Then, as soon as the agent is free, they can return the call.

That avoids using the hold button or making the caller wait while you check to see if the agent wants to take the call.

A final but crucial point: If your handwriting is hard to read, take the time to print phone messages. It will save you tons of aggravation and ill feelings from other agents in your office.

TELEPHONE TIP:
Check your office's message manners.

At the busiest time of the day, call your office and ask for yourself. See if the person taking the message verifies the name and number and is warm and pleasant.

Answering Machines

Answering machines cost anywhere from $30 to $300, depending on the number of bells and whistles they have. On almost every model, you can select how many rings you want before the machine picks up the call. Since only a few offer three rings, go with four.

It's best to have a machine that lets your messages go as long as the caller wants. My first answering machine wound up cutting off about one out of every five calls, and people got very annoyed.

Usually your greeting is limited to about 20 seconds, after which the machine automatically puts on a tone. Then the caller knows to begin the message.

Almost essential these days is remote control. When you're calling in for your messages, as the greeting plays, you signal the machine with a special code (generally one of the buttons on a touch-tone phone) that identifies you.

After the machine plays back the messages, you again hit buttons and the machine sets itself up for more calls.

Answering machines and voice mail can be an agent's best friend. You'll never come home wondering how many people have been trying to reach you.

As for choosing a phone answering machine, it's really up to you. My experience has shown, however, that you get what you pay for. And since they may mean the difference between getting a message or not, you might as well get a good one. Leading consumer magazines recommend either digital or dual cassette models. But don't pour out a lot of money for features you'll never use.

Voice Mail

Basic voice messaging systems will answer your phone when you're away from it or on another call, let callers record messages, and allow you to retrieve them at any time. Basically, their functions are identical to answering machines.

The down side of voice mail is the frustration that many callers feel because they can't speak with a real person. This, however, can be overcome with a "dial zero" option that immediately sends the caller to a receptionist.

If you work in a large office, you may also have audiotex. With audiotex, callers can access information not only about specific properties but about all the properties in a given area or specific price range, new listings, or upcoming open houses, for example.

Jeanne Fawbush, an office manager for a realty company in Nashville, Tennessee, reported, "In nine months, we had 25,000 calls. Our inquiries and activity increased, and even though we have no specific proof, we feel that audiotex has had an impact on our 30% increase in sales."

In a more simplified audiotex, you also can have callers dial a number to hear a recorded description of a specific listing.

When selecting a system, be careful. If callers are given more than three or four options, they'll probably hang up. Make sure callers always have the option of reaching a real person.

Your Answering Machine or Voice Mail Greeting

Here are some tips on effective use of your answering machine or voice mail system.

First, in the greeting, identify yourself and give some information about where you are and when you'll return. Avoid the generic, "I'm not available right now." Try something like,

> *"I'm showing property this afternoon. I'll be back around 6 p.m. I'll also be in tomorrow morning from 9 to 12. In the meantime, I'll be checking in so leave your name, number and message and I'll get back to you."*

Change your greeting often. It doesn't take much time and callers will perceive you as on top of your communication network.

Listen to your greeting and critique it. Check to see if you spoke too slowly or too quickly. See what feelings the tone of voice conveys. Do you sound professional? Confident? Intelligent?

Good Greeting

"Hi, this is Tom Smith. It's Tuesday and I'm checking properties all afternoon. I'll be back around 6 p.m. I'll also be in the office tomorrow from 9 to 11. Please leave your name and number and the best time to reach you. I'll call back as soon as I can."

Having a detailed greeting will often prompt callers to leave more detailed — and usually better — messages.

Not-so-Good Greeting

"Hi, this is Tom Smith. I'm not here right now. At the sound of the tone, please leave your name and number and I'll get back to you as soon as I can."

Check in for messages every few hours and always return calls promptly. If you go on vacation, say so. Tell callers whom they can contact if they need to reach you immediately.

Cellular Phones

Being able to make calls from your car — or wherever — can keep up your business's momentum. You can be driving through a neighborhood with a prospective buyer — see a house they like — and call immediately to set up an appointment. If you're lucky, you can go right in.

Hand-held cellular phones consist of the dialing unit, battery, aerial and transceiver. They can weigh as little as 12 ounces and some models are small enough to fit into your pocket.

The drawbacks to portables is that they need to be recharged often (talk time averages about 90 minutes) and the unit produces less power than car-mounted phones or transportables, so it's harder to get a good connection. We recommend, however, getting a hand-held cellular with a cigarette lighter adapter for power so you don't drain the battery when in the car.

With cellular phones, you can get all the bells and whistles — call waiting, call forwarding, voice mail, and conference calling. While these aren't very expensive, monthly service charges are. Plans in the Los Angeles area start around $36 a month, with a minimum of a one year commitment and hefty penalties for withdrawing before then. Users are charged for both incoming and outgoing calls.

Most real estate agents spend around $150 to $600 a month. Group rates, however, can save $100 a month or more.

Pagers

To keep costs down, many agents with cellular phones use pagers to screen their calls and keep their phone use to a minimum. Pagers run from less than $10 a month to $25, depending on the area.

Pagers come in three general types: standard pocket models which beep when you have a message; digital models which display only the caller's phone number; and alphanumeric models which give the number and a brief message.

You can also get pagers which vibrate rather than beep — which can interrupt business.

Your Business Card

On your business card, put your office number, direct number (if different from your office number), and pager number. Some agents also have a separate voice mail number. Most agents also include their home numbers on the card, although some now leave that off and rely on pager numbers to alert them to calls. Because of the cost, many agents leave their cellular phone number off the business card.

PRACTICE EXERCISE SEVENTEEN

1. Listen to the greeting on your answering machine or voice mail.
    Analyze the voice tone and quality.
    For two days, change the greeting to make it more specific.
    See what reactions you get.
2. Write three messages to leave on answering machines or voice mail.
    How successfully do they whet the prospect's appetite for your next call?
3. Call two clients. Leave a "teaser" message with one.
    With the other, leave an informational message.
    Which seems to work best?

CHAPTER 18

Keeping in Touch by Phone

> *Success is one percent inspiration and ninety-nine perspiration.*
>
> — Benjamin Franklin

There's probably no better way to keep in touch with your prospects and clients than by telephone. In about 10 seconds, you can dial a number. In another two or three seconds, they can be on the line. Then you can take as much or as little time as you need. The telephone is a wonderfully flexible instrument, suitable for all kinds of purposes. Sometimes that simply means letting someone know, "I'm here if you need me."

Making a Commitment to Your Clients

Never forget a client and never let a client forget you. Let that be your secret to success.

Sales experts say that getting one new client costs 20 times more than holding onto an old one. Your clients trust you. They know you'll do a good job and they like you.

But all those good feelings after a successful transaction slowly peter out — if you close the sale and forget about your client.

Once you've got a client, keep up the relationship. From the beginning, stay on top of things. A client should never have to call you to find out what's happening.

Working with Sellers

Don't make your clients guess at what you're doing. Keep your buyers and sellers informed by calling them once a week.

If you're representing sellers, keep them abreast of details. Let them know when an appraisal is scheduled, a photographer will show up, or the house will appear in the Multiple Listing Book. Do them the courtesy of double-checking the wording for classified ads. Pass on the comments of prospective buyers. Make a point of calling at least once a week.

If there's a problem, don't hesitate to let your clients know. They can probably help you work it out.

It's up to you to keep the sellers aware of all of the work you're doing to earn your commission. To them, the sum probably seems exorbitant. If so, that's your fault. They don't realize all that you're doing for them. And they never will, unless you tell them — not directly, of course. Tell them indirectly by keeping them informed of every step you take to move along the process.

Working with Buyers

When you're representing buyers, stick to the once-a-week rule, too. Make a point of calling them.

Realize that finding a home is a major task. They probably think about it several dozen times a day. Maybe one day they have a new thought about what they want. Maybe they'd like to try a different neighborhood. Be there when they need you.

You should call every buyer as soon as the listings come out. If there's something they might like, schedule a showing right away. If nothing seems right for them, call them anyway. Let them know you're on your toes.

Calls like this are good for discussing a buyer's options. Many people don't realize that they can get a lot more house for their money if they're willing to have a rental unit in back. Or you could raise the question of whether they'd like a lease-option. Or maybe they would like to look at lots. The possibilities are endless. Make your clients aware of them.

Making Yourself Available

Tell clients — buyers or sellers — to call you any time. Give them your home and work numbers. Explain that if you're not home, the answering machine or voice mail will take their message and you'll get back to them as soon as possible. This is an offer not many people make. But it can do wonders for cementing relationships.

Many of this country's wealthiest men and women made their mark not by grabbing for the dollar, but by doing what they loved. Wealth was almost secondary. Learn from their example. Put people and their needs first. Then you'll find your needs met, too.

Through simple gestures, you can show your clients how important they are to you. Do things like return their calls promptly. Or leave word when you leave the office as to what time you'll be back.

Always make it easy for clients to reach you. Make sure you have enough phone lines or a call waiting system so no caller ever gets a busy signal.

With all the telephone options available, there's no longer any excuse for not answering promptly.

If you treat your clients well, your farm directory will start growing almost on its own. People will begin referring their friends, relatives, and neighbors to you. And remember, you have a much greater chance of closing a sale from a referral than from a cold farming call.

Don't think of a sale as the finale to your relationship with a client — instead think of it as beginning a new stage in your relationship.

Thank You Calls

Thank you calls can go a long way towards building a long-standing relationship with a client. They also are useful for heading off "buyer's remorse." Especially when there's a handsome, expensive home involved. It's only natural that two or three weeks after moving in, your client may begin to have second thoughts.

"

*Be yourself, and be the
person you hope to be.*
—Robert Louis Stevenson

"

That's the time to call. Have a friendly conversation and maybe stop by. Congratulate your client on the wisdom of selecting that property. Ask if your client has any questions. Find out if everything works the way it should.

Agents often forget that they may know more about a neighborhood than the people who live there. People are always curious about where they live and who their neighbors are. A follow-up visit gives you the perfect opportunity to talk about the neighborhood.

Six-Month Checkup

If you don't want to call out of the blue every year or so, how often should you call a client?

About every six months. That's enough time so you won't become a pest, but it won't seem like the calls are an afterthought either.

TELEPHONE TIP:

The calls don't have to be long. Just long enough so you can make sure everything is okay at the house. If it isn't, maybe you can suggest a repair service or contractor or plumber. If they've just added on or remodeled, why not drop by? See if they'd like to know how much more their house is worth.

Keep in touch with your clients. Call them every six months.

If they're in an affluent area, after six months you may want to suggest they consider buying commercial or rental properties. When you ask, be sure to have a few in mind.

Or maybe they know someone else who's in the market to buy or sell a home. Someone they might never have suggested if you didn't bring it up.

Here's a short checklist for keeping in touch with clients:

- Are they still happy in the home?
- Is everything working all right?
- Anything new in the family?
- Would they be interested in any commercial or rental properties?
- Do they know anyone else who's thinking of buying or selling their home?

Keep the conversation flowing naturally, so your call doesn't seem forced or contrived. Ask about the family and how everyone is doing (you should have notes to coach you). Show genuine concern. Ask about how work is going. If you've really gotten to know your clients the way you should, you won't have to worry about running out of things to say (see sample "Keep in Touch" script in Chapter 15).

About four years down the road, start dropping hints about the availability of some newer or bigger houses in the neighborhood. If there's a spark of interest, turn it into a fire. If the embers are cool, leave it be. They'll want to move eventually and you'll be there when they do.

Follow Up Pays Off

The greatest downfall of most real estate professionals is their failure to follow up. They close the deal, take the check, and they're off to another client. But most successful agents don't work that way. They can't. Because they know that past clients are their bread and butter.

When you represent people finding or selling a home, you learn things about them. You meet their family. You see how they live. You discover the things they like to have around them.

Maybe someone is a bird lover who wants a lot of trees in the backyard. Or a computer buff who needs enough space for a home office. Or maybe they plan to have a large family down the road, so they're looking at four-bedroom homes.

For each client, be on the lookout for items of special interest. If you run across an article about stamp collecting and you have a client with that passion, slip the article into the mail with a brief note and your card. Even if they've already seen the article, they'll appreciate the thought.

Always read the local section of the paper. If there's a wedding in the family, send a card. If there's a new baby, send a card. If there's a death, send your condolences.

Make a point of finding out your clients' birthdays and send special cards. Holiday cards are a must. Thanksgiving, Easter, and St. Patrick's Day cards are optional (see our other book, *How To Farm Successfully — By Mail*).

Keep your relationships warm and personal. One day, you'll be surprised at how many friends you've made over the years. And at the business they send your way.

> *Success is not how high and fast you reach the top, but how high and fast you bounce back after you hit the bottom.*
> —Anonymous

Final Points

Like an old record, we keep playing the same song: **Take care of your clients and they'll take care of you.**

Taking care of a client means keeping up the relationship. Don't close the deal and cut off the client. Stay in touch.

Keeping in touch starts right from the beginning of your relationship. No client should ever have to wonder what you're doing for them. It's your job to let them know. That means calling at least once a week. And it doesn't matter if it's a buyer or a seller. Otherwise, how will they know how hard you're working for them?

When a sale goes through, call and say "thank you." If you call two or three weeks after the sale is final, you could head off a bad case of buyer's remorse.

Six months later, start phoning on a regular basis. Don't make a pest out of yourself. Twice a year is fine. Just see how things are going or if there's anything new. Maybe they'd be interested in investing in some property. Or do they know someone who's thinking of buying or selling a home?

In addition to your calls, send cards. Always send them during the holidays. But if you spot a wedding announcement or death notice or some other news about them, let them know you're thinking of them with a card.

If you happen to come across an article a client might be interested in, pass it along. They'll appreciate the thought.

The bottom line is: *Be there for your clients.* Make them feel free to call you at home or at work anytime they need to. Not many will take you up on the offer, but you'll create a lot of goodwill.

> *Accept and welcome change — it will always be there.*

PRACTICE EXERCISE EIGHTEEN

1. Make a list of five past clients.
   For each, write down how many times you've contacted them in the past year.
   How many times have they contacted you?
2. Write out a holiday card.
   Think of exactly what greeting you'd like to use.
   Do you have a computerized mailing list of clients ready?
3. Pick five current clients — both buyers and sellers.
   How many times have you contacted each one in the past week?
4. Analyze how available you are to your clients.
   How often do you pick up messages?
   On the average, how long does it take for you to return a call?
5. Call a past client to "keep in touch."
   Ask the questions listed in the "Six Month Checkup" section.
   What kind of response do you get?

CHAPTER 19

You Can Do It!

> *Be persistent and thorough. Those who take short-cuts often get short-changed.*
>
> *— Anonymous*

Now the rubber meets the road. All the prep time in the world — the studying, script writing, and planning — are only tools. With a little work, you can become more disciplined, more assertive, and more compassionate. But deciding to succeed — making that commitment — is entirely up to you.

This book can't give you the will to succeed. It can help. But the depth of your commitment is your decision. Strength of will is admirable. It can give you the ability to persist long after others have dropped away.

Law of Averages

Depending on how you look at it, the law of averages can work for or against you in farming.

If you take a negative approach and focus on the nine rejections for every 10 calls, it's tough.

But you can look on the bright side and recognize that only one "yes" means a lot. And it doesn't take very many "yes"s to produce a steady stream of income.

> *You can do everything right and sometimes it still doesn't work.*

You also can take comfort in the fact that if you make enough calls, you're sure to get more "yes" s. You have to. The laws of mathematics say so. But you can't stop at the first trace of discouragement. Put that aside and let the numbers work for you.

Expect to succeed and you will.

How You Feel About Yourself Makes a Difference

Obviously we can't control every circumstance in our lives. But we can decide how we're going to respond to our circumstances.

For example, when the initial shock and disappointment of a job loss wears off, you can regard the loss simply as freeing you for a better opportunity. Or you can heap tons of blame on yourself and tell yourself you're not good for anything.

> *Take care of yourself. Keep your life balanced — at work and away from work.*

In real estate, you put yourself on the line every day. You're dependent on other people's acceptance or rejection. If you can't look past the rejection, you'll have a tough time maintaining a positive self-image. You'll be on an emotional roller-coaster that will diminish your effectiveness. Your strength and confidence must come from within. Look inside for the resources that will enable you to deal with rejection and don't depend on external circumstances.

A good way to start developing strong inner confidence is by concentrating on who you want to be — not on what you want to have.

Aim at cultivating certain character traits. This is something you can control. Think about traits such as honesty, integrity, self-discipline, hard work, and kindness.

Like what you do and be relaxed about it. When you talk real estate, your voice should light up with enthusiasm and interest. Set realistic goals for yourself and keep revising them upward. Know your limitations, especially at the beginning of your farming efforts. Make allowances for them.

It also helps to cultivate a certain sense of indifference. One day you might be in the pits. The next day you might be on top of the world. Level yourself out. During the slump, know that a good time is just around the corner. During the good times, prepare for a month when business slackens.

Take each day as it comes. Be grateful for what it gives you. When obstacles bar your way, view them as challenges or learning opportunities. Don't let them pull you down. In *A New Attitude,* Marian Thomas recommends these 10 steps to a positive attitude:

- Keep your life balanced.
- Don't give up.
- Make the most of the situation.
- Engage in positive self-talk.
- Visualize success.
- Attack problems head-on.
- Look for the bright side.
- Keep a sense of humor.
- Make work fun.
- Accentuate the positives.

Almost all of us want to succeed. We're willing to work long and hard. But then we run into something like rejection.

Fear of rejection holds back more people than you'd ever guess. But anyone can overcome those fears — if they're willing to face, accept, and confront them.

There are no pat answers on how to develop the inner resistance that enables you to overcome rejection. For each of us, the answer is different. But one way to start finding your answer is by making a commitment to work your farm with all the energy and enthusiasm you can. Then, when you run into a string of "no"s, tell yourself you

> *If it doesn't absorb you, if it isn't any fun, don't do it.*
> —D.H. Lawrence

> *Celebrate every success — no matter how small.*

> *The interesting thing is that there are so few important decisions. You don't have to go in the "right" direction. You don't have to enter the "right" business. What you have to do is to have made a decision as to what you're going to do and then you just have to figure out how to succeed at it.*
> —M. Kenneth Oshman

**TEN STEPS TO A
POSITIVE ATTITUDE***

** adapted from Marian
Thomas (1991). A New
Attitude. Shawnee Mission,
KS: National Press
Publications.
Used with permission.*

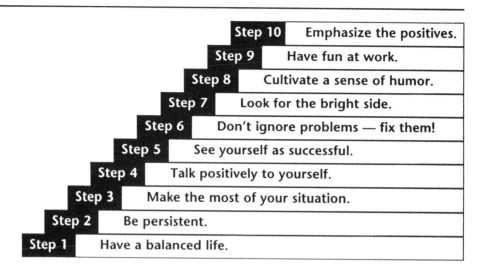

Step 10	Emphasize the positives.
Step 9	Have fun at work.
Step 8	Cultivate a sense of humor.
Step 7	Look for the bright side.
Step 6	Don't ignore problems — fix them!
Step 5	See yourself as successful.
Step 4	Talk positively to yourself.
Step 3	Make the most of your situation.
Step 2	Be persistent.
Step 1	Have a balanced life.

won't let them defeat you. Think about why you're getting them. Speculate on what you could do better. Change your language, your offer, your premium. Keep chugging away at meeting your goal.

By taking control of your own life, you can be the person you want to be. And when you are, you'll find you already have the things you want and need.

Keep a Positive Outlook

Face it. Real estate is one of the most competitive games in town. If you can't discount your prices, what do you have to offer that's unique?

For starters — you. What you're selling isn't only a house or a service, it's you — the you that comes across in every letter, on every phone call, and in every personal visit.

You are different from any other agent in town. That can be a tremendous asset.

If people are going to trust you to help them make the biggest financial decision of their lives, they've got to like you. So do your best to have a winning personality.

Many years ago, Norman Vincent Peale handed out a few tips in *The Power of Positive Thinking.*

Here's our updated version:

1. Remember people's names. Using a name is a sign that an individual is important to you.

2. Make it easy for people to be with you. Be a comfortable person who puts others at ease.

3. Have a relaxed attitude toward life, taking the hard knocks in stride.

4. Make yourself an interesting person to talk to. Read the latest magazines, keep up with the local news, and know a little about a lot of things.

5. Encourage others. Be a positive and uplifting force in others' lives. Weed the "little negatives" out of your thinking and your speech.

6. Keep your focus on others, not on yourself. Don't spend all your time trying to impress people with how great you are. Instead be naturally humble.

7. Clear your mind of anger, jealousy, and envy. When misunderstandings happen, straighten them out right away. Don't harbor negative emotions.

8. If there's a rough edge to your personality, smooth it over.

9. Genuinely like every person you meet. If you do, they can't help liking you back.

Don't Sell — Help People Buy

It's an old, old saying, but we never *sell* real estate. We only *help* our clients *buy* it. This means we attract and develop prospects' interest by phrasing our offers in terms that demonstrate how they personally will benefit. The fact that you want a sale won't induce anybody to buy real estate. But the fact that a prospect wants and needs a particular house or service, well . . .

Maybe a prospect needs a fast escrow. Or personal attention. Or detailed explanations. Whatever it is, make your offer desirable from the prospect's point of view.

During prospecting calls, focus on what you can do for them.

A prospect might ask,

"Could you also handle the escrow?"

You can respond,

"What I can do is work closely with the escrow company. I can call every day and keep track of every piece of paper. Believe me, I would never just turn over the paperwork to a company. I know how important it is for you to be in a new home as soon as possible."

> There are only three types of people: those who make things happen, those who watch things happen, and those who say "What happened?"
>
> —*Anonymous*

This example brings up a key point. An important part of your job is making prospects feel you understand them.

I remember visiting scores of agents when looking for a home. They kept showing me pictures of tract houses, the last thing in the world I wanted. They neither heard nor understood me.

If you want to find the right house for a person, work at understanding them. Pick up on the idiosyncrasies of your prospects' personalities. Don't project your own likes, dislikes, and values onto them. Everyone is different and everyone's taste is unique.

Sometimes, even when clients have doubts, they'll go ahead with buying a home because you're so sure it's right for them. And they believe you understand them.

It is hard for some people to make decisions. At times, we have to help them along. But we should only do it when we're confident that it's really what they want and need.

It helps to use words like "we" instead of "I." And to talk in the present tense instead of the past. Make people feel involved and important. Give them individualized attention.

And remember, people don't like to buy or pay or sell. They like to own.

Nine Ways to Kill a Farm Call

Just as a refresher, let's go over some of the absolute no-no's for your farming calls. Remember your calls are supposed to be warm and personal. Their goal is to build a relationship between you and your prospect. Nothing will kill a budding relationship faster than if you do one of the following:

Keep learning. Always look for new and better ways to do things.

1. Interrupt a prospect or finish their sentences.
2. Try to educate your prospect.
3. Force your own feelings, prejudices, and opinions onto your prospect.
4. Miss the feelings behind a prospect's words.
5. Misinterpret what a prospect is saying.
6. Overly flatter a prospect.
7. Sound rushed or impatient.
8. Have a complicated offer, making it hard for the prospect to understand.
9. Lie or exaggerate.

How to Become a Farming Superstar

Assume you've resolved to farm your field diligently. You've got your system set up. The first calls have been better than you expected. You're gung ho for three months, but then you hit a slump. What happened?

In this business, there are ups and downs. But there's also the personal factor. Often someone who's polishing up their skills follows through for awhile, but then gets tired. They hit a hump that they can't seem to get over.

Here the top-notch professionals will dig in their heels, grit their teeth, and declare, "Nothing is going to stop me. I'm going to make a success of this if it's the last thing I do!"

Less-determined agents will blame the slump on a lack of leads or a slow season or financial conditions. They'd never dream of pinning the blame on themselves.

Everyone has slow times. When you fall into one, check your attitude. Are you still as enthusiastic as ever? Does conviction still radiate in every word of your farming calls? Or has a note of boredom set in? Are you getting tired of the uphill struggle?

If you are, pull yourself out of it. Remember the vigor with which you first attacked farming. Recapture it.

At times like these, often the hardest part is admitting to ourselves that we're the ones with the problem, not our uninterested prospects.

> *The difference between a successful career and a mediocre one sometimes consists of leaving about four or five things a day unsaid.*
>
> *—Anonymous*

If we're not enthusiastic about what we're doing, how can we possibly expect them to be? So stay out of a slump by watching your own attitude. Guard and nurture your enthusiasm. If you see it slipping away, do something to pump it back up.

You know, there is a smart way to approach farming — a way that will save you time, money, and grief. It involves keeping records and evaluating yourself on a regular basis.

After a few months, when you see where you're most effective, channel your energies into that area. Build on what you're best at. Put all these principles to work in a personal way. Find out what brings you the best results. But do it intelligently. Don't just cut out things you don't like to do. Recognize that there are certain basics essential to success.

Ask yourself these questions:

> "
>
> *You must have long-range goals to keep you from being frustrated by short-term failures.*
>
> *—Charles C. Noble*
>
> "

1. Am I familiar with every listing my office is handling? Do I know which listings are similar?

2. Do I check new listings as soon as they come out every week?

3. Do I make a point of driving through my farm once a week?

4. Do I have a set schedule every month for farming calls?

5. Do I set aside time every week to call clients and see if they're still happy in their homes?

6. Do I make a habit of asking for referrals?

7. If I say I'm going to call someone back, do I do it as soon as I can?

8. If I promise to send out some information, is it in the mail that day? Do I call a day or two later to see if they have any questions?

9. Do I have records so I can keep track of my performance? Do I evaluate myself at the end of every day, month, and year?

Do all of the above and you will be well on your way to successful farming. Ignore any of them, and watch out.

Final Thoughts

Don't expect miracles overnight. Just as with agricultural farming, real estate farming takes time. Moreover, whether you farm by phone, by mail, or in person, successful farming is a series of small steps which make the big ones possible.

Thousands of real estate professionals nationwide have proved the success of farming — and you can, too. Good luck!

References

Real Estate Selling

Berger, Warren. *Specializing: An outlet for Bigger Profits?*, Real Estate Today®, October 1993. Reprinted by permission of the National Association of Realtors®. Copyright 1993. All rights reserved.

Bleasdale, Julie A. *Think Globally, Sell Locally*, Real Estate Today®, June 1992. Reprinted by permission of the National Association of Realtors®. Copyright 1992. All rights reserved.

Real Estate Farming

Blood, Ernie & Torrence, Bernie. (1991). *The Pocket Prospecting Guide for Real Estate Professionals.* Canton, OH: Carmel Publishing Group.

Huckfeldt, Klaus D. (1983). *Seeding Right Through Impact Farming.* Palm Springs, CA: Real Estate Edition.

Caughman, Joyce L. (1994). *Real Estate Prospecting: Strategies for Farming Your Markets* (2nd Edition). Real Estate Education Company.

Thompson, P.J. (1989). *Real Estate Farming: Campaign For Success* (2nd Edition). Kricket Publications.

Telemarketing

Bleasdale, Julie A. *Give Your Cold Calling Skills a Workout.* Real Estate Today®. March 1994. Reprinted by permission of the National Association of Realtors®. Copyright 1994. All rights reserved.

Dugger, Jim. (1991). *Listen Up: Hear What's Really Being Said.* Shawnee Mission, KS: National Press Publications.

Gamble, Teri & Gamble, Michael (1992). *Sales Scripts that Sell!* New York: AMACOM.

Goodman, Gary S. (1987). *You can Sell Anything by Telephone!* New York: Simon & Schuster.

Maciuba-Koppel, Darlene. (1992). *Telemarketer's Handbook.* New York: Sterling Publishing.

Mahfood, Phillip E. (1993). *Teleselling: High Performance Business to Business Phone Selling Techniques.* Chicago: Probus Publishing.

Morey, Doc. (1994). *Techniques of Effective Telephone Communication* (2nd Edition). Shawnee Mission, KS: National Press Publications.

Morgen, Sharon Drew. (1993). *Sales on the Line: Meeting the Business Demands of the 90's Through Phone Partnering.* Portland, OR: Metamorphous Press.

Richardson, Linda. (1992). *Selling By Phone: How to reach and sell to customers.* New York: McGraw Hill.

Shahiroff, Martin D. & Shook, Robert L. (1990). *Successful Telephone Selling in the 90's.* New York: Harper Perennial.

Sobczak, Art. (1991). *99 Ways To Sell More By Phone.* Omaha, NE: Business By Phone.

Advertising/Selling

Caples, John. (1974). *Tested Advertising Methods* (4th Edition). Englewood Cliffs, NJ: Prentice-Hall.

Estes, Sherrill Y. (1993). *Sell Like A Pro: A Buyer-Friendly Approach to Sales and Success.* New York: Berkeley.

Iacocca, Lee. (1984). *Iacocca.* New York: Bantam Doubleday Dell Publishing Group. Used with permission.

Levinson, Jay Conrad. (1993). *Guerilla Marketing: Secrets For Making Big Profits From Your Small Business.* Boston: Houghton Mifflin.

Stone, Bob. (1987). *Successful Advertising Methods.* Lincolnwood, IL: Crain Books.

Ziglar, Zig. (1984). *Zig Ziglar's Secrets of Closing the Sale.* Berkley Books.

Self-Improvement

LeMon, Cal. (1990). *Assertivenuess: Get What You Want Without Being Pushy.* Shawnee Mission, KS: National Press Publications.

Peale, Norman Vincent. (1956). *Power of Positive Thinking.* Englewood Cliffs, NJ: Prentice Hall.

Thomas, Marian. (1991). *A New Attitude.* Shawnee Mission, KS: National Press Publications. Used with permission.

Quotes

Fast Forward . . ., Quotable Quotes. The Real Estate Professional. July/August 1994.

Ray, Michael & Myers, Rochelle. (1986). *Creativity in Business.* New York: Doudleday.

Zera, Richard S. (1992). *1001 Quips & Quotes for Business Speeches.* New York: Sterling Publishing Company.

Appendix A – Farm Worksheet

Sizing Up Your Farm

Prospective Farm #1

Your Annual Commission Goal $ _____

1. **Average Gross Comm. Percentage**
   - #___Co-Op Listings   x___%   = _____
   - #___Solo Listings   x___%   = _____
   Sum_____   Total%   = _____
   Divide Total % by # of listings   + _____
   Average Gross Commission % = _____%
2. **Average Sales Price**
   - Add up all sales prices for farm area and divide by the # of homes sold= $ _____
3. **Average Gross Comm. Dollars**
   - Multiply Avg. Sale Price (#2) _____ by Avg. Gross Comm. % (#1)   x _____
   Avg. Gross Comm. Dollars $ _____
4. **Number of Listings Needed**
   - Divide Annual Comm. Goal _____ by Avg. Comm. Dollars (#3)   ÷ _____
   Number of Listings Needed   = _____
5. **Annual Turnover Rate**
   - Divide number of sales for year _____ by total number of homes in prospective farm (or MLS) area ÷ _____
   Annual Turnover Rate   _____%
6. **Farm Size if You Got 100% of Listings**
   - Divide Number of Listing (#4) _____ by Ann. Turnover Rate (#5) ÷ _____
   Farm Size at 100% of Listings = _____
7. **Farm Penetration**
   - Est. percentage of homes in the farm on which you'll get the listing = _____%
8. **Final Size of Farm Needed for Goal**
   - Divide Farm Size at 100% (#6) _____ by Farm Penetration (#7) ÷ _____
   Actual Size of Farm Needed   = _____

Prospective Farm #2

Your Annual Commission Goal $ _____

1. **Average Gross Comm. Percentage**
   - #___Co-Op Listings   x___%   = _____
   - #___Solo Listings   x___%   = _____
   Sum_____   Total%   = _____
   Divide Total % by # of listings   + _____
   Average Gross Commission % = _____%
2. **Average Sales Price**
   - Add up all sales prices for farm area and divide by the # of homes sold= $ _____
3. **Average Gross Comm. Dollars**
   - Multiply Avg. Sale Price (#2) _____ by Avg. Gross Comm. % (#1)   x _____
   Avg. Gross Comm. Dollars $ _____
4. **Number of Listings Needed**
   - Divide Annual Comm. Goal _____ by Avg. Comm. Dollars (#3)   ÷ _____
   Number of Listings Needed   = _____
5. **Annual Turnover Rate**
   - Divide number of sales for year _____ by total number of homes in prospective farm (or MLS) area ÷ _____
   Annual Turnover Rate   _____%
6. **Farm Size if You Got 100% of Listings**
   - Divide Number of Listing (#4) _____ by Ann. Turnover Rate (#5) ÷ _____
   Farm Size at 100% of Listings = _____
7. **Farm Penetration**
   - Est. percentage of homes in the farm on which you'll get the listing = _____%
8. **Final Size of Farm Needed for Goal**
   - Divide Farm Size at 100% (#6) _____ by Farm Penetration (#7) ÷ _____
   Actual Size of Farm Needed   = _____

This form is designed to help you determine the size of your farm or to compare a couple of prospective farms.

Appendix B – Recommended Reading

Art Sobczak's Telephone Selling Report. Omaha, NE.

Ausich, Austin, Ann. (March 1994). *Give Your Cold-Calling Skills A Workout.* Real Estate Today®, pp. 17-20.

Bacon, Mark S. (1994). *Do-It Yourself Direct Marketing.* New York: John Wiley & Sons.

Blood, Ernie & Torrence, Bernie. (1991). *The Pocket Prospecting Guide for Real Estate Professionals.* Canton, OH: Carmel Publishing Company.

Caughman, Joyce L. (1994). *Real Estate Prospecting: Strategies for Farming Your Markets* (2nd Edition). Real Estate Education Company.

Cohen, Jeffrey. (April 1993). *Out of the Office? Yes! Out of Touch? No!* Real Estate Today®, pp. 57-60.

Dugger, Jim. (1991). *Listen Up: Hear What's Really Being Said.* Shawnee Mission, KS: National Press Publications.

Gamble, Teri & Gamble, Michael. (1992). *Sales Scripts That Sell!* New York: AMACOM.

Goodman, Gary S. (1987). *You can Sell Anything by Telephone!* New York: Simon & Schuster.

Jermain, Paul C. (October 1992). *Will Voice Mail Deliver For You?* Real Estate Today®, pp. 43-47.

LeMon, Cal. (1990). *Assertivenuess: Get What You Want Without Being Pushy.* Shawnee Mission, KS: National Press Publications.

Levinson, Jay Conrad. (1993). *Guerilla Marketing: Secrets For Making Big Profits From Your Small Business.* Boston: Houghton Mifflin.

Maciuba-Koppel, Darlene. (1992). *Telemarketer's Handbook.* New York: Sterling Publishing.

Mahfood, Phillip E. (1993). *Teleselling: High Performance Business to Business Phone Selling Techniques.* Chicago: Probus Publishing.

Morey, Doc. (1994). *Techniques of Effective Telephone Communication* (2nd Edition). Shawnee Mission, KS: National Press Publications.

Morgen, Sharon Drew. (1993*). Sales on the Line: Meeting the Business Demands of the 90's Through Phone Partnering.* Portland, OR: Metamorphous Press.

Richardson, Linda. (1992). *Selling By Phone: How to reach and sell to customers.* New York: McGraw Hill.

Shahiroff, Martin D. & Shook, Robert L. (1990). *Successful Telephone Selling in the 90's.* New York: Harper Perennial.

Sobczak, Art. (1991). *99 Ways To Sell More By Phone.* Omaha, NE: Business By Phone.

Stone, Bob. (1987). *Successful Advertising Methods.* Lincolnwood, IL: Crain Books.

Thomas, Marian. (1991). *A New Attitude.* Shawnee Mission, KS: National Press Publications.

Index